Contemporary Political Ideologies

Contemporary Political Ideologies

Movements and Regimes

ROY C. MACRIDIS

Brandeis University

Winthrop Publishers, Inc.
Cambridge, Massachusetts

Library of Congress Cataloging in Publication Data

Macridis, Roy C
   Contemporary political ideologies.

   Includes bibliographies and index.
   1. Political science—History. 2. Comparative
government. I. Title.
JA81.M316   320.5   79-21464
ISBN 0-87626-164-0

Cover design by Susan Marsh

© 1980 by Winthrop Publishers, Inc.
17 Dunster Street, Cambridge, Massachusetts 02138

Printed in the United States of America

10   9   8   7   6   5   4   3   2

To the memory of my late son, Peter

Contents

Part Three THE TOTALITARIAN RIGHT

Part Four IDEOLOGIES IN FLUX: OLD AND NEW

Preface

This book is in a sense an acknowledgment of the vitality of political ideologies and the need to know them and understand them better. Without ideology we are almost without a conscience, without law and order, without an anchor and a port. But also, without ideology we can have no vision of the other worlds we want to sail to. Ideologies fashion our motivations, our attitudes and the political regimes under which we live. They shape our values.

A number of colleagues have helped me at various stages of the writing of this book. Professors David Schmitt of Northeastern University and Professor Fred von der Mehden of Rice University read the manuscript twice and made valuable suggestions with regard to emphasis, organization and substance. I am deeply indebted to both, and as they can see I followed their suggestions in a great number of instances. Professor George J. Graham, Jr. of Vanderbilt University went through the first draft, and his many careful comments and observations helped me clarify my presentation and correct quite a few errors. Professor Robert McHenry of Montgomery College read the sections on democracy and communism and his vigorous reactions, even if positive, made me realize how easy it is to appear "ideological" in discussing political ideologies. I have tried to avoid it. Marc Posner, a graduate student in Politics at Brandeis, checked a number of references, supplied many others and helped me with the bibliographical and biographical material and sketches. Needless to say, I am responsible for all mistakes and interpretative statements.

Some authors and their books were of particular value to me and they should be singled out. Bogdan B. Denitch's *The Legitimization of Revolution: The Yugoslav Case* (New Haven, Conn.: Yale U.P., 1976) is excellent. K. Dietrich Bracher's *The German Dictatorship* (New York: Praeger, 1970) is, to my best knowledge, the most thoughtful and sober account of the Hitler movement and Nazi regime. I found Edward R. Tannenbaum's *The Fascist Experience* (New York: Basic Books, 1972) very helpful, and the same is true for Herman Finer's *Mussolini's Italy* (New York: Henry Holt, 1935), which, though written in the late 1930s retains a remarkable freshness. James R. Townsend's *Politics in China* (Boston: Little, Brown, 1974) sets high standards of analysis and interpretation. If these authors find that I have followed some of their observations even when I fail, inadvertently, to cite them, I hope they will accept this acknowledgment of my thankful appreciation.

Barbara Nagy, Geraldyn Spaulding and Zina Goldman—all ladies who keep Brandeis going—typed various versions of the manuscript and they have my warmest thanks. Acknowledgments and thanks go also to my wife for her great help with the early stages of the book.

Last but not least, my friend James Murray III, President of Winthrop Publishers, has been, as in the past, a constant source of encouragement and support.

This book is dedicated to my late son, Peter, who turned out to have been the only "ideologue" in the family. He drowned in the Columbia River on March 11, 1978, while trying to realize a youthful dream with his friend, Tim Black—crossing the United States from West to East by canoe.

Waltham, Mass.   Roy C. Macridis
February 1, 1979

*One person with a belief is a social power equal
to ninety-nine who have only interests.*
JOHN STUART MILL Representative Government

1

Political Ideologies: Introduction

> *Every . . . state is a species of association, and . . . all associations are instituted for the purpose of attaining some good. . . . We may therefore hold . . . that the particular association which is the most sovereign of all, and includes all the rest (the state) will pursue this aim most and will thus be directed to the most sovereign of all goods.*
>
> ARISTOTLE Politics

All of us, whether we know it or not, have an ideology, including even those who claim openly that they do not. All of us believe in certain things. All of us value something—property, friends, the law, freedom or authority. All of us have prejudices, even those who claim to be free of them. We all look at the world in one way or another—we have "ideas" about it—and we try to make sense out of what is going on in it. Also, we are all attracted to those with similar values and ideas, who like the same things we do, have prejudices similar to ours, and who, in general, look upon the world in the same way we do. In fact, we talk of "like-minded" people, and individuals who share certain beliefs tend to congregate —in clubs, churches, political parties and movements, various associations, and so on. Lastly, no matter how independent we claim to be, we all are influenced by ideas: we are sensitive, in varying degrees and ways, to "ideological" appeals—to our honor, patriotism, family, religion, pocketbook, race or class—and we can all be manipulated and aroused. We are creators and creatures of ideas—

1

of ideologies—and through them we manipulate others or are ourselves manipulated.

Ideologies are very much a part of our lives; they are not dead and they are not on the decline anywhere, as some authors have argued. The chances are that they will be with us for a long time to come.

> Ah, but a man's reach should exceed his grasp,
> Or what's a Heaven for?

wrote Browning in 1885. Almost a century later a strong upsurge in ideological and utopian movements made powerful governments totter as many sought their own vision of heaven and earth. "Be rational; think of the impossible" was one of the slogans of the intellectuals and the students in the late 1960s.

Not only are ideologies surviving; their all-embracing importance is again being recognized. "Neo-Marxists" agree now that a drastic revolutionary overhaul of the society, if there is to be one, must be above all a moral and intellectual revolution: a revolution in the *ideology* of society. It must create its own "counter-consciousness," its own "counter-culture"—a new set of beliefs and values and a new style of life that will eat, like a worm, into the core of prevailing orthodoxy. Only with its ideological core gone can the old society be changed and replaced. The socialization of the means of production, economic planning, communism, the abolition of income inequalities—none of them have a chance of success until and unless the ideas people have about society and about their relations with each other change.

What Is an Ideology?

The term "ideology" has a number of meanings and connotations.

1. One meaning is that of "deception," "distortion," or "falseness." It conveys the notion of subjectivism as opposed to objectivity; of relativism as opposed to permanence. When we say that a person is too ideological, we mean that he or she may well be prejudiced, thoughtless, volatile. We suspect ideological political parties for the same reason, and tend to prefer pragmatic parties, because we feel they deal better with the real world.

2. Ideology also conveys the notion of a *dream*, of an impossible and unrealizable quest. An ideological person is one who is constantly dreaming of other and better worlds: world government, perfect equality, abundance for all, elimination of force and abolition of war. All ideologies have something of this quality, but those having it in an exaggerated form are called *utopias*, a word derived from the Greek for "nowhere." If we give this particular meaning to the term we are implying that an "ideologue" is either naive or dangerous or a little bit

crazy, ignoring Shakespeare's pithy remark that dreams are the stuff that life is made of!

3. Ideology means also what may be called the *consciousness of a society* at any given moment; the values and beliefs and attitudes that hold it together; the image that individuals hold in common about their society. This term conveys a holistic meaning: the same ideology covers all who live in a particular society. But ideology may relate also to the complex of ideas and values and beliefs that bind only a certain group or a given number of individuals. In this case, we can hardly talk of one ideology in the society. Many ideologies coexist and very often are in conflict. In one and the same society there may be many particular ideologies mobilizing different groups and individuals for different purposes. Sometimes there can be no reconciliation among them—the ideologies will not compromise.

4. Ideologies often correspond to *social criticism*. Many beliefs have yielded to it, to be replaced by others. Criticism confronts existing beliefs and attempts through argument and persuasion to challenge and change them. Does the sun turn around the earth? Is the earth flat? Do germs exist? It was only through demonstration and persuasion that these questions were finally answered. Critical and rational examination of social and political beliefs has played also an important role in the development of some ideologies and the rejection of others. Institutions like slavery, property, hereditary monarchy, bureaucratic centralization, and many others have been critically challenged and accordingly abandoned, or qualified.

5. Ideology also provides *a set of concepts* through which people view the world and learn about it. People receive messages from the world outside and have to put these messages into some kind of order— into concepts. These concepts, and ultimately the knowledge we derive, will depend on ideology. People may also reject messages because of their ideology. A mystic is blind to the world outside; for a scientist it is a constant source of wonder to be studied and explained. For some the condition of the poor calls for study and concern; for others it is a bore—their situation is attributed to innate laziness. These may be extremes. More frequent are the cases of interpretation or evaluation, where the same event is seen from a different viewpoint, from a different ideological perspective. The assassination of a political leader is applauded by some and regretted by others. Any Soviet move anywhere in the world is an indication of the communist expansionist conspiracy for some; for others it is an inevitable reaction to American provocation!

6. While ideas may pulsate within our individual minds, ideologies are directly addressed and directly related to the outside world. They involve or at least affect *many minds*—they become a "group mind." Ideologies are a call for *concerted action*. They make people act, work, organize. Look at the way the issue of abortion has stirred

up various groups, mobilizing even individuals who have no personal interest in the matter. It touches upon profound beliefs that are of primary importance to a citizen's values. To invade them one way or another is to invade someone's personality and life. Thus, ideologies become the mainspring of political action.

7. Finally, ideology often becomes, under certain circumstances, a powerful instrument of manipulation. Usually in times of social distress and anxiety, or when society seems divided into warring groups and when frustration warps our lives, simple propositions and promises on how to straighten the evils that beset us fall upon receptive ears and minds. The demagogue, the leader, the self-professed savior is lurking somewhere in all societies in such times to spread his or her message and to manipulate those who seem to have nowhere else to turn.

To summarize then: an ideology consists of a set of ideas and beliefs through which we perceive the outside world and *act upon our information*. It is a medium through which we try to learn and comprehend the world; but it also generates emotions which hold people together. Finally, ideologies are action-oriented. That is, they consist of ideas shared by many people who act in unison or who are influenced to act in unison in order to accomplish posited ends.

Philosophy, Theory and Ideology

A distinction should be made between philosophy or theory on the one hand, and ideology on the other. "Philosophy" means literally love of wisdom—the detached and often solitary contemplation and search for truth. In the strictest meaning of the term, "theory" is the formulation of propositions that causally link variables to account for or explain a phenomenon. Such linkages should be, again in the strict sense, empirically verifiable. But this is so primarily in the natural sciences; in social sciences it is very difficult to come up with empirical verifications.

Take, for instance, the various theories of human nature—from which many ideologies stem. It is very hard to "prove" that man is either good or wicked. A theory, however, must at least have a logical coherence. It must consist of propositions which fit together so that logically the one supports the other. A theory, let us say, that posits the inherent goodness of individuals and postulates that tyranny is the best form of government in order to curb those individuals' base instincts is not convincing. It would be equally difficult to reconcile theories of racial or religious supremacy with equality. However, even when there is logical coherence among the various propositions, the demonstration of the validity of a theory in the social sciences through actual verification is virtually impossible.

What separates theory or philosophy from ideology is that while

PLATO (C. 427–347 B.C.)

Greek philosopher, a disciple of Socrates, and the founder of philosophic idealism, according to which ideas exist in themselves and by themselves, forming a perfect and harmonious universe. As a political philosopher Plato developed in *The Republic* an ideal state with a strict class structure ruled by philosopher-kings who divested themselves of property and family ties in order to rule for the common good. Plato's description of a more practical state can be found in his *Laws.*

the first two involve contemplation, organization of ideas and whenever possible demonstration, ideology incites people to action. It shapes beliefs that move people into action. Men and women organize *to impose* certain philosophies or theories and to realize them in a practical way. Ideology thus involves action and collective effort. Even when they originate (as they often do) in philosophy or theory, ideologies are inevitably highly simplified, and even distorted, versions of the original doctrines. It is always interesting to know the philosophy or the theory from which an ideology originates. But it is far more important to understand ideology as a distinct and separate entity to be studied in terms of its own logic and dynamics rather than in terms of the theory from which it stems, or the closeness of resemblance to it.

It is extremely difficult to understand when and under what circumstances a theory or a philosophy becomes transformed into an ideology—that is, into an action-oriented movement. Important theories and philosophic doctrines remain unnoticed and untouched for generations, only to be "discovered." History may be compared to a freezer where ideas and theories are stored to be used at a later time. Different works of Plato, for example, have been at different times the origin of different ideological movements. Similarly, while a powerful ideological movement developed from the major works of Karl Marx, it is his early works today—the early Marx or the young Marx—that have been adapted to suit some contemporary movements and tastes. It is very difficult, therefore, to state with any certainty whether it is philosophy and theory that create ideologies and ideological movements or whether it is a social need which finds convenient the appropriate philosophy or theory. There is a dialectic between ideas as such and social needs, and both are needed in order to have an ideology. Heartfelt demands arising from the social body may fail for the lack of ideas; and ideas may go begging for a long time for the lack of relevance to social needs.

The Functions of Ideology

An ideology, then, is a set of ideas held by a number of people; it spells out what is valued and what is not; what must be maintained and what must be changed; it shapes accordingly the attitudes of those who share it. An ideology, to repeat the point, does not have to be rational. Even more, ideologies are generally immune to empirical argument or evidence. The Nazis built their movement on the assumption that the Aryan race was supreme. It became a belief. To have had it "disproven" would in no way have affected the emotional fervor of Hitler's movement. In contrast to philosophy and theory then, which are concerned with knowledge and understanding, ideologies relate to social and political behavior and action. Ideology, all ideologies, perform many distinct social functions:

Solidarity and Mobilization

A common sharing of ideas integrates individuals into a group, a party or a movement. Ideas, commonly held, define the things that are acceptable and the tasks to be accomplished, and exclude others. Ideologies play the same role that totems and taboos play in primitive tribes by defining what is common to the members and what is alien. The Soviet communist ideology, for instance, unifies those who adhere to it by branding the outside world of capitalism as the enemy. All ideologies perform this function of unifying, integrating and giving a sense of identity to those who share it, but with varying degrees of success. All political movements and all political parties provide a sense of common purpose and common action. Nationalism, for instance, as an ideology has provided the unifying and integrating force that has made it possible for nation-states to emerge and retain their positions. The greater the integration sought and the stronger the solidarity to be maintained, the greater also the emphasis on unifying symbolisms.

Organization

An organization exists when people perform different roles and functions to accomplish a given end. The end is a common goal commonly perceived by the participants. The same is true for the means required to realize it. It is the task of ideology to provide this common perception of goals and of the related means to accomplish them. This is true of a golf club, of the Salvation Army and of the Democratic Party, as well as of communists and even anarchists. The ideology imbues the members with a common purpose and encourages them to perform the designated tasks.

Expression

Ideology provides a vehicle to express our wants, our interests and hopes, and even our personal drives and anxieties. Some have argued that the primary function of an ideology is to rationalize and protect material interests or to provide for a powerful medium for their fulfillment. Thus, liberal democracy has been viewed as the rationalization of the interests of the rich and the relatively well-to-do, while revolutionary Marxism is an instrument for the satisfaction of the demands of the propertyless, the workers and the poor.

But it is not only interest that spawns an ideology. Emotional drives and personality traits are expressed through different ideologies. It has been argued, for instance, that there is a distinct "authoritarian personality" which finds expression and fulfillment through being subject to rank and authority. In this manner, any ideology can provide a form of expression, and usually brings like-minded people together. The Anti-vivisection League, environmentalists, anti- and pro-abortionists, proponents or opponents of the Equal Rights Amendment, as well as democrats, communists and fascists, all may give vent to their personality, interests and emotions through their particular ideology.

Manipulation

Ideologies move people to action, as we have pointed out, but to what kind of action, and for what purpose, depends very much on certain factors and considerations which we shall discuss later on. Manipulation of ideas is a special case. It often involves the conscious and deliberate formulation of propositions which will incite people to action for ends that are perceived clearly only by those who are in power. They may promise peace in order to make war, freedom in order to establish an authoritarian system, socialism in order to consolidate the position and privileges of the property holders.

Manipulation is very close to propaganda and there is virtually no political system that does not practice both, sometimes in good faith and sometimes in bad. Ideological manipulation marshals support for undetermined ends, controlled only by the leadership.

Communication

A coherent body of ideology shared by a given number of people makes communication among them much easier. It provides a common, highly simplified special language, like shorthand. Words have special meaning—"the Reds," "the bleeding-heart liberals," "the pigs," "the Establishment," "fat cats," "the power elite," "the chosen people," "communist conspiracy." These are terms easily understood by those who belong to a given group, and help others to place them within a given ideological family. They are of course very crude terms, and ideologies usually provide more sophisticated ones. "The last stage of capitalism," "neo-colonialism," "avant-garde of the working-class," "democratic centralism," "democratic pluralism," "human rights," "gradual change" are commonly understood by those who use them in their own respective political group or party and can help the outsider again to identify the ideological family to which the speaker belongs. Ideologies simplify communication and make common effort easier for all those who accept them.

Affect

Finally, another important function of all ideologies is to provide emotional attachment. People are proud of their ideas and proud of each other and all those who share them. They belong to the group that espouses them just as some belong to their families. They relate to it, and help each other in a common search of realization. A person who has an ideology that is shared within a group of people is likely to be happy and secure, basking in the togetherness of the common endeavor. Identifying with it, he or she is never alone.

The overall functions of ideology which we have outlined indicate also the purposes for which they can be used and are in fact used by political or other leadership groups—to mobilize, consolidate, criticize or elicit support for or against a policy, a government, or even a political regime.

Types of Political Ideologies

Political ideologies address themselves to values: the quality of life, the distribution of goods and services, freedom and equality. If there were agreement on each and all there would be one single ideology shared by all. But there is no agreement within any society nor, needless to say, among the various political societies of the world. People hold different views; nations project different values and beliefs.

It is precisely here that we see the role of political ideologies: they mobilize men and women into action in favor of one point of view or another, and in favor of one movement or party or another. Their aim is invariably either the preservation of a given point of view or the overhaul of the existing state of things, including the political system itself. The British squire who defended his privilege and his property; the workers who formed trade unions or parties to defend their interests; the American conservatives—all have had a common set of ideas which united them into a common posture. The same is true for the small terrorist bands who seize planes. They want to destroy what they despise most—the complacency of an orderly society interested in material satisfaction.

We may divide political ideologies into three broad but distinct categories:

1. Those that defend and rationalize the existing economic, social and political order at any given time in any given society. We may call them *status quo* ideologies. Another term would be *conservative*, but this might be misleading since quite a few *status quo* ideologies are not always considered to be conservative.

2. Ideologies that advocate far-reaching changes in the existing social, economic and political order. We may call them *radical* or *revolutionary* ideologies.

3. In between there is, of course, a large gray area favoring gradual changes. We may call these the *reformist* ideologies.

One way to state the difference between *status quo, reformist* and *revolutionary* ideologies is to think of maps and map-making. Someone who diligently learns to read a map and to travel by following given routes and signals may be considered to represent a status quo mentality or ideology: he or she simply follows the rules and the signs and is guided by them. On the other hand, a person who attempts to trace his or her own route and to change the signals, but not the destination, is a reformist. There is an agreement that the means must change, not the end. But a revolutionary changes both the map and the destination.

This classification is only a formal one. Ideologies shift and change in content, but also in the particular functions and roles they perform. A revolutionary ideology, for instance, may become transformed into one of status quo when it succeeds in imposing its own values and beliefs. Similarly, the same viewpoint may be a status quo ideology, protecting the existing order of things in a given place at a given time, and a revolutionary one in a different place or at a different time. Soviet communism is in the Soviet Union a status quo political ideology, while in other countries communism is considered to be a revolutionary one. While workers in the nineteenth century were rising in the name of socialism against Western European liberalism which had become a status quo ideology, liberalism was very much a revolutionary ideology in the eyes of many in Central Europe and in Russia.

Major Political Ideologies:
Criteria of Choice

If we look at the spread of contemporary political ideological movements we have a rich choice of subjects: liberalism, capitalism, democratic socialism, socialism, communism, consociationalism, corporatism, Eurocommunism, anarchism, Gaullism, Stalinism and post-Stalinism, communalism, self-determination in industry, Titoism, Maoism, welfarism, to say nothing of variations that come from the Third World under various labels. Which ones shall we discuss, and why? We obviously need some criteria to help, and I suggest four: comprehensiveness; pervasiveness; extensiveness; intensiveness.

Comprehensiveness: By comprehensiveness I have in mind the overall scope of an ideology, but also its internal logic and structure. Is it complete? Does it spell clearly a set of goals, and the means to bring them about? Do its various propositions about social, economic and political life hang together? Is there an organization—a movement or a party—to promote the means of action envisaged? Are the goals varied and many, or do we rather have a single overriding goal?

Pervasiveness: Pervasiveness refers to the length of time during which an ideology has been "operative." Some ideologies may show decline over a period of time only to reappear. Others have been operative over a long period, despite variations and qualifications. Whatever the case, the basic test is the length of time during which an ideology has been shared by people, has affected their lives and shaped their actions.

Extensiveness: This refers simply to a crude numerical test. How many people have shared a common ideology and how many people presently share it? One can draw a crude "ideological map" simply showing the number of people sharing by and large common political ideologies. The larger the "population space" of a given ideology the greater its extensiveness. How many people are influenced today by

ARISTOTLE (384–322 B.C.)

Greek philosopher, disciple of Plato. His works covered the widest possible range of topics, with emphasis on scientific inquiry—the formulation of laws and theories that called for empirical observation and verification. He wrote, among other works, essays on *Logic, Physics, Metaphysics, Ethics,* and *Rhetoric.* His political works include the *Politics* and *The Constitution of Athens.*

In his *Politics* Aristotle developed the theory of the second best state, the *polity,* a semi-republican form of government in which all classes of society are given political roles so as to prevent domination of any one. Law played an important role in limiting the government and in this sense many consider Aristotle to have been the first to develop a theory of constitutionalism.

communism? By liberalism? Socialism? Anarchism? An estimate of numbers will answer the question of extensiveness.

Intensiveness: Finally, by intensiveness I mean the degree and the intensity of the appeal of an ideology—irrespective of whether it satisfies any of the other three criteria. Does it evoke a spirit of total loyalty and action? "Interest is sluggish," wrote John Stuart Mill. Ideas are not. They are like weapons that in the hands even of a small minority may have a far greater impact on society than widely shared interests. Intensiveness implies emotional commitment, total loyalty, unequivocal determination to act even at the risk of one's life. It was this kind of intensiveness that Lenin managed to impart to his Bolsheviks, the Communist Party.

Ideally we should choose among various ideologies only those that satisfy *all* the criteria here set forth—comprehensiveness, pervasiveness, extensiveness, and intensiveness. However, this would fail to do justice to some ideologies that have played or are playing an important role in political life, even though they may satisfy only one or two of these criteria, and I intend to take such movements into account.

For each ideology to be discussed, I shall begin by examining the basic theoretical formulations to which it owes a major debt, and describe its transformation into a political movement and, in some cases, into a political regime. We should never lose sight of the fact that we are dealing with ideas that become political movements and lead people to political action; that their "influence" can be assessed in terms of the strength of the movements and parties through which ideas become readied and armed for a struggle for supremacy. Ideologies are not disembodied entities; they are not abstractions. They exist because men and women share them and adopt them as part of their own lives. Ideologies are weapons when men and women make them so; but they are also havens that produce companionship, cooperation and fulfillment.

One last remark is in order. If there are so many ideologies and if all of us share different ideologies to help us "know" the outside world and prompt us to act in one way or another, which one of them is "correct"? If all ideologies provide us with different views of the world, how do we know what the world is really like? This is the nagging question throughout the book—the question of the *validity* of a given ideology. For it is true that since we look at the world through an ideology we may be gazing at a splintered mirror, trying to see our face and that of our society in it. When it comes to the political ideologies with which we are concerned here there is really no authoritative test to produce definitive proof of validity. We can only present the various ideologies in terms of their internal logic, their coherence, and their relevance to the outside world.

This book does not ask, therefore, which ideologies are "true" and which are "false," even if it criticizes and passes judgment on them. Rather, our approach will be expository: Where does an ideology come from? What does it posit? What does it purport to achieve? What have been its accomplishments?

Bibliography

Aristotle. *Politics*. Translated by Ernest Barker. New York: Oxford U.P., 1962.

Aron, Raymond, *The Opium of the Intellectuals*. New York: Norton, 1962.

Bell, Daniel. *The End of Ideology*. Rev. ed. New York: Free Press, 1965.

Bluhm, William T. *Ideologies and Attitudes: Modern Political Culture*. Englewood Cliffs, N.J.: Prentice-Hall, 1974.

Brown, L. B. *Ideology*. New York: Penguin, 1973.

Grimes, Alan, and Horowitz, Robert (eds.). *Modern Political Ideologies*. New York: Oxford U.P., 1959.

Lerner, Max. *Ideas Are Weapons: The History and Uses of Ideas*. New York: Viking, 1939.

Lichtheim, George. *The Concept of Ideology and Other Essays*. New York: Random House, 1967.

Mannheim, Karl. *Ideology and Utopia*. New York: Harcourt, Brace and World, 1955.

Oakeshott, Michael. *The Social and Political Doctrines of Contemporary Europe*. New York: Cambridge U.P., 1942.

Plamenatz, John. *Ideology*. New York: Praeger, 1970.

Wolin, Sheldon. *Politics and Vision*. Boston: Little, Brown, 1960.

part one

DEMOCRACY: MANY ROOTS AND FAMILIES

Our constitution is called a democracy because power is in the hands not of the few but of the many.
THUCYDIDES   Funeral Oration Of Pericles

Democracy literally means "the government of the people." It comes
from the Greek word *demos*, people, and *kratos*, government or power.
The concept developed first in the small Greek city-states, and the
Athenian democracy (roughly between 450 B.C. and 350 B.C.) is what we
always go back to as the principal early example. Pericles, the great
Athenian statesman, speaking in 431 B.C. defined it in the following
terms:

> Our constitution is named a democracy, because it is in the
> hands not of the few but of the many. But our laws secure
> equal justice for all in their private disputes and our public
> opinion welcomes and honors talent in every branch of
> achievement . . . on grounds of excellence alone. . . . Our cit-
> izens attend both to public and private duties and do not allow
> absorption in their various affairs to interfere with their knowl-
> edge of the city's. . . . We decide or debate, carefully and in
> person all matters of policy, holding . . . that acts are fore-
> doomed to failure when undertaken undiscussed.[1]

In this classic formulation Pericles identifies the following characteristics of a democracy:

1. Government by the people with the full and direct participation of
   the people.
2. Equality before the law.
3. Pluralism—that is, respect for all talents, pursuits and viewpoints.
4. Respect for a separate and private (as opposed to public) domain
   for fulfillment and expression of an individual's personality.

Participation, equality before the law, pluralism and individualism for
everyone (except for women and also the many slaves): these were the
cornerstones of early democracy, before it disappeared from Greece
and the then known world after a brief and unsuccessful revival in
Rome.

Contemporary Democracy: Major Phases

Contemporary democratic thought goes back to the sixteenth century
and earlier. It has many roots—feudal practices and institutions, theories about natural law and natural rights, religious wars and the demand for toleration, the assertion of property rights and freedom to
pursue individual economic ventures, the notion of limitations upon

---

1. Thucydides. *The History of the Peloponnesian War.* Edited and translated by Sir
Richard Livingstone. Oxford U.P., "The World's Classics," 1951, pp. 111–13.

political authority—these are only some of them. The basic landmark is provided by the English philosopher John Locke, who, writing in the latter part of the seventeenth century, developed in some detail four of the cardinal concepts of democracy: equality, individual freedom, government based upon consent of the governed, and limitations upon the State. Locke's theories led to the development of representative and parliamentary government.

The second historical landmark in the emergence of liberal democracy are the works of Adam Smith, especially his *Wealth of Nations* (1776), and of a new school of radical philosophers known as the utilitarians, who developed in detail the theory of "economic man" driven by the twin desire to satisfy pleasure and to avoid pain. In line with Adam Smith, they constructed theoretically a limited State which would allow individuals freedom to pursue their own interests. The utilitarians became the exponents of economic liberalism and individualism between 1790 and 1850.

Throughout the nineteenth century Locke's theory of consent and representative government were broadened, but economic liberalism and economic individualism came constantly under scrutiny and criticism. The works of the French philosopher Jean Jacques Rousseau, especially his *Social Contract* (1762), were used to broaden the theory of participation so as to include everybody. The role of the State was reassessed in favor of more intervention in economic and social matters for the better protection of the poor, the unemployed, the old, the young, and other disadvantaged groups. For the first time the notion of a *Positive State*—one that acts to provide social services and to guarantee rights—appears.

Finally, beginning in the twentieth century, and extending well into our days, socialists and a growing number of democrats have begun to broaden the notion of a Positive State. They ask for sweeping reforms of the economic system so that the State assumes the obligation of providing an ever-increasing number of services. This is the Welfare State.

Socialists question economic individualism and wish to replace it with a system in which productive resources are owned and managed by the State itself. The economy is to be run by the State, no longer for the purpose of profit, but to further social and community needs. Many of the socialist parties today are committed to this, and they represent a synthesis which combines democratic political and individual rights with massive state intervention in the economy and socialization of major units of production.

In discussing democracy as an ideology, we are dealing with a very rich and comprehensive body of thought and action, one that has undergone shifts and changes in the last three centuries and has produced a great variety of political movements. We shall look at the liberal phase of democracy first, and then its growing welfarist, socialist or collectivist orientation.

2

Liberal
Democracy

Laissez-faire, laissez-passer

The individual—his experiences and his interests—is the basic concept associated with the origin and growth of liberalism and of liberal societies. Knowledge and truth are derived from the judgment of the individual, which in turn is formed by the associations his or her senses make of the outside world, from experience. There is no established truth, nor any transcendental values. Individual experience becomes the supreme value in itself, and the joining of many individual experiences in deliberation the best possible way for a community to make decisions.

Liberalism is a pure and simple individualistic ethic. In its earliest phase, individualism is cast in terms of natural rights—freedom and equality. It is steeped in moral and religious thought, but already the first signs of a psychology that considers material interests and their satisfaction to be important in the motivation of the individual appear. In its second phase it is based on a psychological theory according to which the realization of interest is the major force that motivates individuals.

Interest in turn is related to satisfaction of pleasure. Liberalism is anchored on this simple proposition: men and women strive to maximize pleasure and to minimize pain. But it is not up to the collectivity to impose it; it is not up to a philosopher or a political party to determine it. On the contrary, it is up to individuals to pursue it and in so doing fulfill themselves. Knowledge that stems from experience and education will presumably set limits beyond which pleasure-maximization will not be pushed.

The propositions of early liberalism were directed against eighteenth century absolutism and the many feudal practices that lingered on. Absolutism, supported by a landed aristocracy, stifled human activity while maintaining the feudal privileges of the nobility at a time when the growth (even if ever so gradual) of manufacturing and commerce had begun to open up new vistas of individual effort, exploration, wealth and change. Yet nations were divided internally into many jurisdictions with different laws, different standards, different tariffs, different regulations, different weights and measures, all of which impeded communication, trade and individual freedoms. The famous expression *laissez-faire, laissez-passer* was the battle-cry of the burghers, the tradesmen, the money-lenders, the small manufacturers. "Let us do; let us pass" was the motto of the new middle classes. This liberalism was a challenge to the existing order, for laissez-faire capitalism, as we still call it, was the ideology that expressed the interests of the middle class—against absolutism, and especially against political and economic constraints.

Liberals proclaimed individualism and individual freedoms—especially freedom of movement and trade; they borrowed from the past to develop what gradually became a comprehensive theory of individual rights to challenge and to limit absolute political power; they appealed to and represented the rising new classes and the new forms of wealth which began to appear in Western Europe. They also received the support of the peasants (against the landed aristocracy) and the workingmen (who became attracted by the promise of freedoms and equality). As a political ideology, liberalism appealed, therefore, to large sectors of the society, while being opposed by the monarchy, the landed aristocracy, and also the Church.

The Three Cores of Liberalism

There are three elements within liberalism. One is *moral*, the second *political* and the third *economic*. The moral core contains an affirmation of basic values and rights attributable to the "nature" of a human being—freedom, dignity, and life—subordinating everything else to their implementation. The political core includes primarily political rights—the right to vote, to participate, to decide what kind of government to elect and what kind of policies to follow. It is associated with representative democracy. The economic core has to do with economic and property rights. It is still referred to as "economic individualism," or the "free enterprise system," or "capitalism"—the rights and freedoms of individuals to produce and to consume, to enter into contractual relations, to buy and sell through a market economy, to satisfy their wants in their own way and to dispose of their own property and labor as they decide. Its cornerstones have been private property and a market economy, free from State controls and regulations.

The Moral Core

Long before Christianity the notion had developed that the individual human being has innate qualities and potentialities commanding of the highest respect. With a spark of divine will or reason, each and every individual should be protected and respected and given freedom to seek fulfillment.

The Stoics and the Epicureans put individuals—their freedom, their detachment, their personal life—above all considerations of social utility or political expediency. Early Christians went a step further— all individuals are the children of God; we are all brothers and sisters; our duty is to God above all; salvation is the ultimate fulfillment. Temporal powers cannot impinge on this, but even if they did (in order, for example, to collect taxes or to maintain order) there were still many things that belonged *only* to God.

A number of inferences stem from this notion of the moral and rational nature of the individual. Many of them have been institutionalized in the practice of liberalism and continue to be essential to it. The United States' recent proclamations supporting human rights is in reality one of the oldest battle cries of liberalism.

PERSONAL LIBERTY

Personal liberty consists of all those rights guaranteeing the individual protection against government. It is the requirement that men and women live under a known law with known procedures. Locke wrote: "Freedom is . . . to have a standing rule to live by, common to everyone of that society and made by the legislative power erected in it."[1] Such a law protects all and restrains the rulers. It corresponds to individual "freedoms"—freedom to think, talk, worship. No policeman will enter one's home at night without due authority; no individual, even the poorest or lowest, will be thrown into a dungeon without a chance to hear the charges and argue before a judge; nobody will have to discover one Sunday morning that his or her church is closed, or that their son or daughter has disappeared, and so forth. To American students such freedoms appear self-evident and naturally due. Unfortunately this is not quite so, for in fact, they exist, even today, in but a small number of countries.

1. Locke. *Second Treatise on Civil Government.* Chapter 4.

While personal liberties in general define a set of protections, civil liberties indicate the free and positive channels and areas of human activity and participation. They are, in the liberal ideology and practice, equally valued. Basic to the liberal faith is the concept of freedom of thought. The only way to define this positively is to state it as the right of individuals to think their own thoughts and learn in their own ways from experience, with nobody impeding the process. Freedom of thought is closely associated with freedom of expression, freedom of speech, freedom to write and freedom to publish and disseminate one's thoughts, freedom to discuss things with others, freedom to associate with others in the peaceful expression of ideas. We find these freedoms enshrined in the First Amendment of the United States Constitution, and also in many solemn documents in British and European political history—the Bill of Rights, the Petition of Rights, the Declaration of the Rights of Man, etc.

The achievement and implementation of full civil liberties in the societies of Western Europe and the United States took time. Until the middle, and often until the end, of the nineteenth century people were excluded from political participation for religious and other reasons. Censoring of books, pamphlets and the press was a common practice for long after Milton wrote his famous pamphlet against censorship, *The Areopagitica*, in 1644. Freedom of the press had a particularly shaky existence until the end of the nineteenth century, and freedom of association—to form clubs, groups of like-minded people, political parties, trade-unions, and religious sects—was hedged and qualified until almost the same time.

What is more, at no time could civil liberties be taken for granted. There were and still are constant exceptions and setbacks. There is always an inclination on the part of certain groups to deny to others what they do not like, and there is a pervasive suspicion on the part of political authorities of non-conformist and dissenting groups.

SOCIAL LIBERTY

Freedom of thought and expression, protections against government in the form of personal and civil rights, have little value if the individuals are not given a proper recognition so that they can work and live in accordance with their talents and capabilities. Social liberty corresponds to what we call today opportunities for advancement or social mobility. It is the right of all individuals, irrespective of race and creed and irrespective of the position of their parents, to be given every opportunity to attain a position in society commensurate with their capabilities. Personal liberties may become an empty or purely formal prescription if political or social practices impose or allow for disabilities or discrimination. There is little hope in the life of a Mexican peon, or a black, or the poor generally, if they know that they and their children will always remain tied down to the same occupation, status, education and income. Only when equal opportunities are seen to be provided for all can all forms of discrimination be said to have been abolished.

Emphasis upon legal rights characterized the liberal movement at its early stages. Material rights, as part of the broader discussion of economic rights, became the major preoccupation of liberalism in the twentieth century.

The Economic Core

As already pointed out, liberalism was the ideology of the middle classes rising to replace the old landed aristocracy. Their purpose was to liberate individual economic activity, to establish large trading areas that corresponded to the nation-state and if possible the world, and to do away with all obstacles to the transportation and the trading of goods. It was their aim to reorganize the economy, introduce new methods (the market) and to invest capital in factories and machines.

Economic liberties, and in general the economic core of liberalism, assumed just as great an importance, if not greater, than what we have called the moral core. The right to property, the right of inheritance, the right to accumulate wealth and capital, freedom to produce, sell and buy—all contractual freedoms—became an essential part of the new social order. Emphasis was put on the voluntary character of the relations between various economic actors, whether the employer, the worker, the lender, the producer or the consumer. Freedom of contract was more valued than freedom of speech. The pattern of social life, according to which people were born and belonged in certain social categories and groups, was shattered, and the individuals became free to shape their own situation by voluntary acts and contractual relations with others. One great British historian, Sir Henry Maine, claimed precisely that the essence of liberalism lay in this transition from "status" (fixed group relations) to "contract" (individual self-determination).

The meeting point of various individual wills, where contractual relations were made, is the market. Here the individual—the famous "economic man"—propelled by self-interest, buys and sells, hires laborers, borrows or loans money, invests in joint-stock companies or maritime ventures, and finds employment. The market reflects the supply and demand for goods, and this in turn determines their prices. The market is the best thermometer to register economic activity, for demand obviously pushes prices up, and hence incites production until the demand is met and prices begin to level off. Since the market does not sanction the incompetent and the inefficient, goods produced that do not meet a demand or are not widely desirable fall in price, until the producer is driven out of business, to be replaced by a shrewder one.

Thousands of individual entrepreneurs face not only millions of consumers, who compare quality and prices, but also each other. If a given product sells well and fast, other manufacturers will produce it, increasing the supply and thus bringing prices down. The system is supposed to be both sensitive to consumer demand as well as entirely open, allowing for entry of new competitors and the exit of unsuccessful ones. Prices faithfully register the volume of demand and supply adjusted to it.

It is a system that at least in theory favors the consumer: prices cannot be fixed, the volume of production cannot be controlled, competition makes monopolies or cartels impossible. But the advantages for the producers are also great: they can take advantage of the same law of supply and demand in hiring or dismissing workers, in settling on the wages to be paid, the price of raw materials but also the prices of new products. It is a system that provides the best mechanism for production and the satisfaction of wants, and its classic formulation was provided by Adam Smith.

ADAM SMITH AND "THE WEALTH OF NATIONS"

The bible of liberal economic theory was, and still remains, Adam Smith's *The Wealth of Nations*. Smith's purpose was to open the channels of free individual economic effort and to defend the free market economy as the best instrument for the growth of wealth, individual, national and world-wide. Each person, he assumes, is the best judge of his or her actions and interests. If people are allowed a free hand to pursue these interests they will do so, and by so doing will improve the wealth of the society and the nation as a whole. What counts above all is to give free rein to individual action and to limit the role of the State to the simple maintenance of order and defense.

Adam Smith rose against every conceivable state intervention in commerce, agriculture and manufacturing. He was against tariffs, trade associations and combinations, labor unions and state regulations, but also against monopolies and almost any form of public enterprise. He favored free contractual relations. The State had to keep its hands and agents off.

Though Adam Smith spoke of the "Divine hand of Providence" bringing order and wealth out of the myriads of individual wills and interests that compete with each other in trying to satisfy their respective interests, his faith was not in divine providence. Rather he believed that a social and economic harmony would result from the free competition and interplay of economic interests and forces. In his words, natural order would be promoted in every country by the natural inclinations of the individuals if political institutions had never thwarted those natural inclinations. If all systems of restraint were completely taken away, the system of natural liberty would establish itself. Or as one of Smith's followers put the matter even more succinctly:

> As soon as a need becomes the object of public service the individual loses part of his freedom, becomes less progressive and less man. He becomes prone to moral inertia which spreads out to all citizens.[2]

JEREMY BENTHAM AND UTILITARIANISM

But the real father of philosophic and political liberalism was Jeremy Bentham. His philosophy, followed also by James Mill and John Stuart Mill, is known as *utilitarianism*, from the term utility. Its basic elements can be summarized as follows:

1. Every object has a utility—that is, every object can satisfy a want.
2. Utility, as the attribute of an object, is subjective. It is what we like or do not like. It is amenable only to some crude quantifiable criteria that relate to the duration, the intensity, and the proximity of the pleasure that a given object can provide. There are no qualitative criteria that can be established by anybody but the user. For some a poem has a greater "utility" than a hot dog. For others the hot dog comes first. The market ultimately registers utility as it reflects the volume of goods in demand.
3. The purpose of our lives is to satisfy pleasure (that is, to use goods that have utility for each one of us) and to avoid pain. This is the *hedonistic* or the *felicific calculus* that applies not just in economic life but also in any other aspect of an individual's existence.

In order to work, this utilitarian model must be allowed to operate freely. If every man and woman were free to maximize pleasure and avoid pain, "the greatest happiness for the greatest number" would result. More people would be happy than unhappy!

The concept of utility and the utilitarian ethic is not restricted to the economy. It applies to everything. Social institutions, artistic works, education, philosophy—they all must meet the test of utility and provide pleasure, in varying degrees, to some, or conversely result in pain if they are absent. *Utility* as a criterion of social, political and economic life replaces moral and natural *rights*.

Bentham had no great respect for abstract moral rights, yet in a peculiar way he defends, *in terms of utility*, many of the freedoms and rights that were defended previously, in terms of a natural law, or which stemmed from what we have called the moral core of liberalism. Bentham defended freedoms on the basis of their utility. It is more pleasurable for instance (or less painful) for a greater number of people in a system to freely express their ideas, worship God in their chosen

2. Cited by Harold Laski in *The Rise of European Liberalism*, p. 203.

ADAM SMITH (1723–1790)

Social philosopher and political economist best known for his major work, *An Inquiry into the Nature and Causes of the Wealth of Nations* (1776), in which he developed his theories of economic liberalism, competition and free trade. His major plea was to release human activity from all State administrative and economic controls, allowing the individuals to seek individual profit and the satisfaction of wants. Adam Smith claimed that there were fundamental economic laws, such as the law of supply and demand, that provided for the self-regulation of the economy. He is the father of economic liberalism.

way, and to read what they please. Conversely, it would be painful if there were censorship and lack of freedom of expression and worship.

Thus millions of individuals armed with small calculators, so to speak, constantly sift the pleasurable in a given society from the painful, maximizing the first and minimizing the second. The calculations are always directly related to self-interest, but they are not necessarily simple. The individual will have to balance a number of requirements—

for example, the immediate utility an object may have compared to the far greater utility it may represent in five or ten years; the possibility of suffering deprivation and even pain *now* in order to enjoy pleasure later on; the pain that may be suffered in order to derive pleasure from protecting loved ones; the intensity of a given pleasure as opposed to its duration; and finally, overall considerations of peace and tranquility at home and national defense against outside enemies. They too represent a utility, no matter what the immediate pain of providing for them may be.

These considerations show that while self-interest and the pleasure-maximizing calculations are the motivating force for all of us, a point comes when considerations other than their pure and simple realization enter into the equation of social, political and economic life. Self-interest gives place to *enlightened* self-interest.

JOHN STUART MILL AND ENLIGHTENED SELF-INTEREST

Enlightened self-interest becomes an important criterion to guide the individual. For instance, someone who foregoes an immediate pleasure in order to derive a greater one later on shows enlightenment. Accepting a lesser pleasure in order to maintain a *fairly* pleasurable existence, rather than insisting on the maximum pleasure possible and in the process risking the loss of everything, is also enlightenment. The same criteria apply to groups of people or to classes of people. If they act in terms of enlightened self-interest, they may consider concessions to other social groups or classes rather than risk in the loss of all they have.

John Stuart Mill came to grips with this problem by redefining utility. He introduces qualitative standards and establishes a hierarchy of pleasures on the basis of criteria that are *not* subjective. Some pleasures are better than others because of their intrinsic quality, and not because of the particular pleasure they give to an individual. A poem has more utility than a hot dog!

There is, therefore, a necessary gradation in the utility of different goods. Some have a higher value even if they give pleasure to only few; others may in the long run prove to be painful even if they give pleasure to many. What then? Shall we introduce a dictator or a philosopher-king who will impose his hierarchy of pleasures upon society and make it produce goods and services that correspond to it? Or should we expect individuals to make the right choice?

The question is not speculative. It is right before us. Driving a car is pleasurable, but by depleting our energy resources American drivers weaken the country to the point where it may be unable to defend many of the values that are equally pleasurable to us—our freedoms, for instance. A comprehensive scheme of public transportation would be preferable to private ownership of cars. But how can the people be led to make the right decision?

The utilitarians, and particularly John Stuart Mill, put their hopes

JEREMY BENTHAM (1748–1831)

Founder of the utilitarian school, according to which plea-sure-maximizing, pain-avoiding (the so-called *felicific calculus*) is the source of human motivation. His various works, such as *Fragment on Government* and *Defense of Usury,* and most particularly his *Introduction to the Principles of Morals and Legislation,* expounded the theories of individualism and eco-nomic freedom. Benthamite liberals were extremely influential through the nineteenth century in England in pushing for ad-ministrative, criminal law, taxation and economic reforms.

in education, and in the wisdom and self-restraint of the middle classes. It was the obligation of the State to establish education, and it was the function of education to en*light*en self-interest in terms of collective, group, social and national interests and considerations. Education would transform an essentially hedonistic society into a body of civic-minded citizens—that in the last analysis would choose public transportation.

The Political Core

Four basic principles make up the political core of liberalism: individual consent; representation and representative government; constitutionalism; and popular sovereignty.

INDIVIDUAL CONSENT

As we have already noted, "status" had been giving place to "contract." Contractual theories became the basis of political authority. Men and women simply consent to bind themselves in a political system and to accept its decisions. The Mayflower compact of 1629, when the Pilgrims wrote a "constitution," is the best illustration.

It was John Locke who developed the theory of consent in detail. Men and women, he pointed out, live in the state of nature with certain natural rights: life, liberty and property. At a given time they discover that it is difficult to safeguard these rights without a common authority committed to them and to their protection. So they agree to set up a civil society—that is, to set up a common legislature, a common judge and a common executive. The first will interpret and safeguard the natural rights, the second will adjudicate conflicts about these rights, and the third will provide for their enforcement. The contract is made by all individuals and those who do not agree are not bound by it. They can leave! *The source of political authority and the powers of the State over those who stay is their consent.* The purpose of the State is the better preservation of the natural rights of life, liberty and property.

REPRESENTATION

But who can make decisions within this system? According to Locke it is the legislature, elected by the people (at the time, to be sure, on a very limited franchise). However, the legislature must accept certain restraints, all of them implicit or explicit in the original contract setting up the political system. It cannot deprive individuals of their natural rights, cannot abolish their freedom, do away with their lives or take away their property. The political authority—the legislature—in other words, is restrained by the very nature of the compact which originally established it.

Locke's idea of representative government then is based on the notion that political authority derives from people. But moral, civil and economic or property individual rights cannot be transgressed. The majority and its elected representatives can make all and any decisions. But the original contract and the good sense of the people who made it, as well as of their representatives, restrain it from violating the people's natural rights. Thus the British tradition established parlia-

JOHN STUART MILL (1806–1873)

English philosopher, who had studied under the strict tutelage of his father, a foremost utilitarian, James Mill. John Stuart Mill considerably modified utilitarian thought to abandon the simple pleasure-maximizing, pain-avoiding formula, and to seek qualitative criteria to evaluate human behavior and motivation. In his essay *On Liberty* he developed the theory of moral (as opposed simply to economic) individualism, and linked it to requirements of education and enlightenment. While arguing against state intervention he was forced to introduce collective and social considerations and thus had to allow, contrary to what he seemed to profess, for state intervention. Many consider Mill, because of this, to be one of the precursors of socialism. He is known, however, primarily for *On Liberty,* in which he appears a strong advocate of individualism.

mentary sovereignty and majority rule, rather than the checks and balances and judicial review that have been the case in the United States.

It should be noted, however, that while Locke gave to the legislature the right to make decisions without any limitations, his theory of representation and representative government applied only to a small number—those who held property. They represented the middle classes and the landed aristocracy. It was only much later, when the franchise was expanded to most citizens, and ultimately to all, that the problem of how to limit the majority—who might decide to take away the property of the few—assumed particular importance.

Theories of representation and representative government also stemmed directly from utilitarian premises that led ultimately to the "one man, one vote" principle. At first the utilitarians attacked the vested interests—aristocracy, landowners, the Church and the well-to-do—and discarded the notion that these groups more than others had a special stake in the country and hence had a special right to represent the community and govern it. Mill argued that the best individual protection was to allow each and all to select their representatives. "Human beings," he pointed out, "are only secure from evil at the hands of others in proportion to their ability to protect themselves,"[3] and he considered representation was the best protection.

However, John Stuart Mill did not quite accept the notion of the supremacy of the representatives—the legislature—and with it the right of the majority to govern. He and many other liberals feared that if the mass of people were given the right to vote, to elect their own representatives, and if decisions in the representative assembly were to be made by majority vote, then the many (the poor) would use their numerical strength to take care of *their* interests at the expense of the middle classes and all others. There were, therefore, a number of direct and indirect restraints. One was the proposition that representative government could function well only when the educational level of the voters had improved. Citizens should learn to think of the "general prosperity and the general good" rather than of their own immediate interest; in other words, the system could work well only when people as a whole acted according to their enlightened interest. Mill wrote:

> The positive evils and dangers of representative government can be reduced to two: general ignorance and incapacity, and the danger of its being under the influence of interests not identical with the general welfare of the community.[4]

He mentioned specifically the "body of unskilled laborers" who were ignorant and likely to act at the expense of the general welfare.

Mill had also an aversion to the development of large national political parties which could mobilize the vote and capture a majority

3. J.S. Mill. "Considerations on Representative Government" in *Utilitarianism*. Chapter 3, page 43.
4. Ibid., chapter 6, page 86.

JOHN LOCKE (1632–1704)

English philosopher generally considered as one of the founders of empiricism. His principle works include *Essay Concerning Human Understanding* (1690), *Thoughts on Education* (1693), *Letters on Toleration* (1689–92). As a political philosopher Locke developed in his *Two Treatises on Government* the "contract" theory of the State, according to which the State is the custodian of natural rights and is founded upon the consent of the governed in order to protect these rights—specifically, the rights of life, liberty, and property. It led to the elaboration of institutions of a limited State and a limited government.

through the organization and discipline of its members. He was, more-over, not against property and age qualifications. He favored these at least for the candidates for election, who in this way would come from the middle classes and would have the proper level of maturity and moderation. He also favored giving a great weight—more votes—to people with education. Finally, he was in favor of a second chamber, the House of Lords, representing "personal merit" and acting as a "moral center of resistance" against the decisions of a popularly elected assembly—that is, against the majority.

Despite their insistence on representation and elections the liberals hedged and hemmed the power of the legislature and the right of the majority to decide. They did not have enough confidence in the people. Yet, notwithstanding their fears of the poor, the ignorant and "the many," the utilitarian premises led gradually to universal suffrage. Representation and representative government gradually spread, and with it majoritarianism, the right for the majority to form a government and make decisions for all, gained legitimacy.

CONSTITUTIONALISM

The notion of restraints on political authority as proposed by Locke influenced the framers of the United States Constitution. They feared arbitrary and absolute power so much that they rejected a concentration of power in the hands of any one body, even the legislature, and even the majority of the people. While stressing the idea of natural rights, of individual freedoms and the derivation of authority from the people, they wanted to find a way to make it impossible for any single organ of government to become truly sovereign and overwhelm the others. Their emphasis was more on how to restrain political power even when it was based on the will of the people than on how to make it effective.

The answer was a written Constitution which limits power, sets explicit restraints (including the ten amendments) on the national gov-ernment and on the individual states, and which institutionalizes the separation of powers in such a manner that one power checks another. At no time would it be possible for one branch—executive, legislative or judicial—to overwhelm and subordinate the others. Having accepted the idea of fully representative government through periodic elections, the founders of the American Constitution put heavy restraints upon it.

This is essentially what we mean by constitutionalism. Constitu-tionalism provides solid guarantees for the individual by explicitly limiting government; it also provides procedures ruling how the func-tions of government are to be carried out. In many cases it establishes a watchdog, in the form of a judicial body, to safeguard the Constitution and all the restraints written into it. In addition it provides procedures through which the responsibility of the governors to the governed, through periodic elections, is maintained. The government is both *lim-ited* and *responsible*. But the idea of limitations is far more important than that of popular sovereignty. The United States Constitution established a republic, not a democracy.

POPULAR SOVEREIGNTY

It was Jean Jacques Rousseau who set up the model of a popular democracy before the French Revolution of 1789. He, too, found the source of political authority in the people. They were sovereign, and their sovereignty was "inalienable, infallible and indestructible."[5] In contrast to those who favored representation and representative government, Rousseau believed in direct government by the people. There were to be no restraints on the popular will. He called it "the general will" and claimed that under certain conditions it was always right: representation would only distort it. In the last analysis, he argued, nobody could really represent anybody else. Something like town meetings in small communities would be the only appropriate instruments for the expression of the general will.

Rousseau's affirmation of the absolute power of the general will that many interpreted to be the will of the people had revolutionary implications. It pitted an extreme doctrine of popular sovereignty against absolutism—current in France and many other continental countries in the eighteenth century. But it also antagonized liberals, who believed in representative government with restraints and were particularly reluctant to see all the people participate directly or indirectly in decisions.

Consent, representation, popular sovereignty leading to majority rule and constitutional restraints upon the state and its government (even upon a majority) obviously emphasize different forms of liberal thought and put the accent on different values. They inevitably lead to different political institutions. Emphasis upon constitutional restraints and the protection of individual and minority rights—economic rights at first—led to the type of liberalism, still very much in evidence in the United States, which restricts the majority and allows the judiciary to act as the supreme umpire. Emphasis, on the other hand, upon the Rousseauian idea of popular sovereignty leads to unrestricted majority rule, either directly by the people or by their representatives. In between these two extremes liberals and liberal institutions attempted, not always successfully, to find a solution that reconciles the idea of majoritarianism with the notion of restraints. Limitation upon representative assemblies, various voting qualifications, a bicameral legislature in which one chamber is not directly elected by the people but represents wealth or birth or some other attribute of "moderation," the veto of the monarch or a president—these were the devices most often used to deny a numerical majority the power to make decisions.

5. Rousseau. *The Social Contract.* Book 2.

Throughout the nineteenth century the main stresses within the political core of liberalism lay in the conflict between those who, in line with Locke and some of the utilitarians, advocated restraints upon the legislature and the majority, and those who, in line with Rousseau's theory of popular sovereignty, pressed for uninhibited majority rule.

The State and the Individual

Liberalism was an anti-State philosophy and remains one in the sense that, all other things being more or less equal, it values the individual and his initiative more than the State and its intervention. Nowhere has this position been better set forth than in John Stuart Mill's essay *On Liberty*, published in 1859. To approach it, let us set forth two models, the totalitarian and the liberal. According to the first, the individual and the civil society (i.e., the family, economic organizations, school and universities, etc.) are controlled by the State. It is the State, therefore, which shapes the social institutions on the basis of a predetermined scheme of values. The State exacts conformity and obedience.

The liberal model presents an entirely different order of things. Individuals and their social institutions are separate from the State. Strictly speaking, they constitute two different spheres of life and action. But when the two spheres do intersect, the intersection should cover only a limited and recognized area. Spontaneity, creativity, experimentation and the search for truth are within the domain of individuals and their social institutions. It is at best and at most the function of the State to maintain order, to see that nobody in his or her relations with others uses force, to protect civil liberties and personal freedom, but also to maintain the economic freedom of the individual. In other words, the role of the State is to protect the individual.

On Liberty summarizes this by asserting:

1. That every restraint imposed by the State is bad.
2. That even if the individual cannot do certain things well, the State should not do them for fear that it might undermine the individual's independence and initiative.
3. That any increase in the powers of the State is automatically bad and prejudicial to individual freedoms: it decreases individual freedom.

Thus Mill views the State on the one hand and society and the individual on the other in a mechanical and antithetical kind of relationship. The increase of the powers of the state necessarily involves the decrease of powers of individuals. While it is highly desirable to strengthen the power of the individual correspondingly, people must be extremely vigilant not to allow an increase in the power of the State.

The most crucial problem for liberal thought has been the iden-

JEAN JACQUES ROUSSEAU (1712–1778)

THE BETTMANN ARCHIVE

French philosopher who, in contrast to the rationalism of the French eighteenth century philosophers (the Encyclopedists), stressed the role of sentiments and emotions, thus becoming the precursor of many nineteenth century romantics. He wrote widely on a number of subjects, but his two most important works are on education *(Emile)* and on politics *(The Social Contract).* In the latter he argued for the sovereignty of the people, claiming that the "general will" emanating from them is absolute and infallible. It was the combination of this theory of general will and his emphasis on feeling and emotion that led him to glorify nationalism as an all embracing myth that creates unity and solidarity among a people. The best exposition of his theory of nationalism can be found in his *Considerations on the Government of Poland,* written in 1770.

tification of where exactly the lines separating the State on the one hand, and society and individuals on the other, intersect. One might develop an elastic concept, allowing a fairly wide area within the intersecting lines, in which the State can intervene (numbers 2 and 3 in figure 1). Or, in line with the thinking of early liberals, one might allow for the minimum area of intersection in which the State can intervene (number 1 in figure 1). Here the intersection would encompass only order and protection. In this latter case, the State becomes something like a policeman or a night watchman, making sure that the factory does not burn down and no thieves break in, and otherwise allowing full autonomy within the factory, or the university, or the home, or the school. The smaller the area included within the intersecting lines of figure 1 the closer we are to laissez-faire liberalism: the larger the area the more we move in the direction of the Positive State or the Welfare State, perhaps even getting close to socialism.

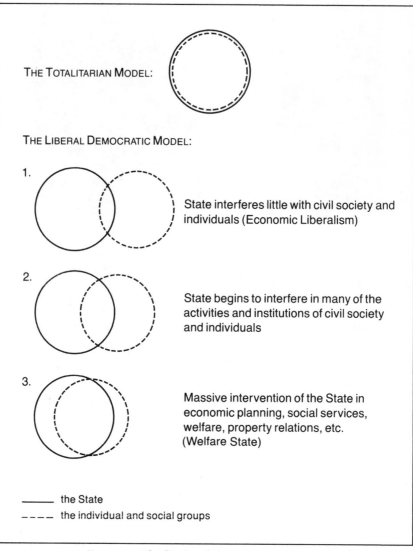

FIGURE 1   *The limits of State intervention.*

Different periods in the history of liberalism tell us where the lines have been drawn. War, for example, makes for State intervention. But this was considered to be an exception, since there is an understanding that with the passing of the national emergency the situation would revert to the original liberal model. John Stuart Mill provided us with a criterion in terms of which we can draw the lines. For Mill, all individual acts that concern the individual—*self-regarding acts*, as he called them—are acts that cannot be controlled or regulated by the State. Acts, however, that concern and affect others—*other-regarding acts*—can and should come under the control and regulation of the State. Thus the area within our intersecting circles should include the other-regarding acts.

But "concern" provides no clean standard. Is smoking self-regarding or other-regarding? Is the use of drugs self-regarding or other-regarding? What about alcoholism? What about pornographic literature? Violence on television? The manufacture of drugs? The administration and the high cost of hospitals? The additives put in our foods? Ownership and use of private cars? Nuclear energy? This is just the first set of questions that comes to mind.

The second set of questions is more complex, and relates to exactly *when* the State should bring into its purview other-regarding acts (if we have managed to define exactly what they are). Can it do so only after an act *is shown* to affect others, or can it control it because it *might* affect others? The first would provide a very strict and limiting criterion. the State could regulate the manufacturing of drugs only when it is shown that they have caused cancer. The second interpretation, however, provides a very generous criterion whereby the State can intervene. It would do so every time there is some doubt about the consequences certain drugs can have upon individuals. Drugs that *might* cause cancer should be taken off the market. Whenever certain acts *might* affect others, they should be regulated and controlled.

Mill did not have to answer these questions explicitly, because of the way he defined self-regarding and other-regarding acts. *All individual acts, he claimed, are self-regarding except those that cause harm to others. The criterion in terms of which other-regarding acts are defined is that of harm. Only if harm is done can the State intervene.* Commerce, production, consumption are self-regarding.[6] The State should not intervene. But so, of course, are freedom of thought and expression and freedom of association. The State should not intervene here, either. So, in the last analysis, the individual has the right to get drunk and to use drugs. However, your actions become other-regarding, and hence invite State intervention, when they cause harm to others.

---

6. J.S. Mill. "Of the Limits of the Authority of Society over the Individual" in *Utilitarianism*. Chapter 4.

You can stay in your attic drinking beer as long as you want. You are free to indulge in this self-regarding act. But when you open the window and start throwing the empty cans out you endanger passers-by, and the act becomes other-regarding.

However, the moment we give a more relaxed definition of what is other-regarding, and introduce the concept of *affect* or *influence* rather than *harm*, then we move in the opposite direction to favor State intervention and regulation. The policeman may try to save you from too much beer, even if you have not harmed anybody!

Achievements: The Expansion of Liberalism

If we take a fairly thick brush and paint onto the canvas of the nineteenth century all the liberal achievements in the realm of economic rights, civil liberties and political rights, the picture that emerges is breathtaking. The liberals and the liberal movements and parties changed the economic, social and political structure of Europe, and drastically modified the international community as well. Some of the major achievements are listed here.

Slavery was outlawed. In the United States it continued until the Civil War, but the importation of slaves after 1808 had been declared illegal. In England, the slave trade was banned in 1807 and slavery was abolished in the British Empire in 1833. France followed in 1848; the Netherlands in 1869; Argentina in 1853; Portugal in 1858; Brazil in 1888. Serfdom was abolished in Russia in 1861.

Gradually *religious disabilities* against holding political or other offices were abandoned virtually everywhere. Catholics, Protestants, Jews, Quakers and other nonconformist religious minorities were allowed full participation by the end of the nineteenth century.

After bitter controversies, *toleration* was granted and the Church and State were separated in many countries. Religious affiliations and worship became a personal right.

Freedom of press, speech and association were granted. By the end of the nineteenth century, at least in Western Europe, Britain and its dominions and the United States, rare were the cases where people could not express their views or were penalized for the views they did express, no matter how heretical or subversive.

The State began to provide *education* and to require children to attend school up to the age of ten, twelve or fourteen.

The vote was gradually extended to all males, first, and to women only after World War One. There was virtually universal suffrage in England by 1884; in France in 1848; in Italy by the end of the century; in Russia in 1905 (but not for long); and in Germany and the Scandinavian countries in varying degrees by the end of the century. In the United States male universal suffrage (limited to whites) was established in the 1820s. Property qualifications for voters and candidates were eliminated, but some other qualifications—literacy, age, or residence—remained. All in all the prediction of Lord Macaulay that "universal suffrage is utterly incompatible with the existence of civilization" proved quite wrong!

Nothing illustrates the force of liberalism better than the reforms undertaken in France after the revolution of 1830. The second chamber was changed from a hereditary one to one in which members sat for life; the electorate was broadened by lowering the age qualifications to twenty-five instead of thirty; property qualifications were reduced from three hundred francs to two hundred. Candidates for office were to be thirty years old instead of forty, censorship was abolished, extraordinary tribunals were eliminated, schools were set up in every commune by the State and the control of the Church over them was put to an end. These reforms were modest; indeed, they stopped far short of what democrats wanted to accomplish. But they were moving in the direction of democracy. It took, for example, just eighteen years (after another revolution) before universal suffrage was introduced to France, in 1848.

Similarly, the liberal Reform Act of 1832 in England provided for a property qualification of ten pounds a year, thus excluding the poor and the workers from voting, but allowing the middle classes to do so. The act increased the electorate to about 750,000 out of a total population of about 13.5 million. Further extension in 1867 and 1884 followed, bringing the workers into the political system.

Constitutions, constitution-making and constitutionalism were everywhere in the air. Even where a constitution had only symbolic character it still echoed the aspiration of citizens to limit government and to establish the rules that made the holders of power responsible to the people or their representatives.

In Russia a movement for a constitution which would limit the powers of the Tsar emerged in 1824; in Greece liberal constitutions were promulgated in 1827 and again in 1843; in Germany a liberal constitution was prepared by a convention that met in Frankfurt in 1848; in France liberal constitutions were promulgated (after the failure of the ones established during the French Revolution) in 1830, and again in 1848 and 1871. In Spain, Portugal, Italy and in many Latin American republics, constitutional documents came into force by the end of the nineteenth century and often earlier. Even Poland, the Austro-Hungarian Empire and the Turkish Empire experienced liberal reforms that were embodied in constitutional documents or charters.

These reforms were not granted easily; occasionally they were granted only to be withdrawn. Frequently liberal political movements were repressed, but the overall impact was the same, broadening and safeguarding civil liberties, and extending political participation to an ever-growing number of people in every political system. Above all, they imposed responsibility and restraints, no matter how fragile and temporary, upon the holders of political power. This in itself helped to erode the claims of absolutism.

Representative government became increasingly accepted throughout Europe and in the English-speaking countries. With the exception of Russia (with a notable interval between 1905 and 1914), there was hardly a political system in the nineteenth century which did not introduce representative assemblies and did not give them some (often considerable) power over decisions. In many cases, the assembly was given the power to censure the government and force it out of office. Representative assemblies participated in the formulation of laws and decided on taxation and expenditures. Within limits (and sometimes without any restriction) debate was free and representatives were not liable for their words and actions in the legislature.

As the suffrage expanded to new groups, *political parties* began to emerge, seeking the vote in order to govern on the basis of pledges they offered to the electorate. They became transmission belts between the people and the government, making the latter increasingly responsive to popular demands and aspirations and helping translate demands and wants into policy and action. Parties emerged, at first in the United States where male universal suffrage was introduced as early as 1824, with platforms, leadership, organization and ideological loyalties. In England they gradually evolved from factions and cliques, manipulated and controlled by the King and the landed gentry, into national organizations representing the new towns and the middle classes. The Liberals and Conservatives, the two large parties, established national headquarters, designated candidates, prepared their platforms, solicited membership and vied for office against each other after the middle of the nineteenth century. The Conservatives followed the logic of liberalism and enacted legislation enfranchising new groups by lowering property qualifications. Their leader, Disraeli, spoke of the union between "the cottage and the throne," an expression that symbolized the reconciliation of the aristocracy with the principles of democracy and the needs of the common man.

In France the nobility continued to influence the vote and political parties were many, badly organized, regional rather than national, and without clear-cut platforms. Until 1880 their differences were about the political regime, some favoring the Republic, others a return to the Monarchy and still others aspiring to Bonapartism. It was only by the very end of the nineteenth century that the socialists became unified into one party; the centrist groups—republican, anticlerical and liberal—formed the Radical-Socialist party.

In Germany the powerful Social Democratic Party had the best organization and the largest membership, and became revisionist and reformist rather than a revolutionary party. It was opposed by the Center Catholic Party (liberal but appealing to Catholic groups), the Liberals (a middle-class party) and the Conservatives.

Almost everywhere the development of political parties strengthened the liberal-democratic principles and institutions. It allowed the people to opt directly for candidates and policies, and brought the governments that emerged from elections closer to their control.

Liberalism had, of course, a profound impact on *economic life*. Freedom of movement (a simple right in our eyes) became for the first time a reality. A journeyman, a merchant, a manufacturer, a farmer could move not only their produce and goods but themselves without any prior restraint and prior permission. They could dispose of their property and do as they pleased with it. Individuals became free to change professions just as easily as they could change their domiciles: they could enter into partnership or agree to provide their services on the basis of mutually binding agreements.

Not only their home but also their property became a "castle" against intervention, regulation and confiscations by an arbitrary ruler. There was (though not everywhere) a *trend against all forms of tariffs* and all indirect restrictions on the movement of goods—first, against internal tariffs that allowed cities, municipalities or regional authorities to tax goods at the point of their entry or exit. But even more, a great movement got under way, spearheaded by British industrial and trading groups, to reduce, even to do away with, all external tariffs that taxed goods coming into or moving out of a state. It favored world-wide free trade. As one of Adam Smith's disciples wrote in 1846:

> There is no human event that has happened in the world more calculated to promote the enduring interests of humanity than the establishment of the principle of free trade.[7]

Despite their aversion to state intervention in social and economic matters, liberals were forced to consider *limited interventions*. Poor laws were introduced to keep the destitute from starvation. As unemployment assumed menacing proportions in the 1840s, public workshops were established in France and at one time they employed as many as a quarter-million people. Child labor legislation gradually began to prohibit the employment of children under certain ages, and required them to go to school. A ten-hour working day was decreed in England in 1846. Factory laws began to provide for the safety of workers. They were to receive compensation for accidents caused in their work. By the end of the century many of these measures had been expanded to provide added protection, including the first steps in the direction of health insurance.

In the name of liberalism a vast movement in favor of *national self-determination* and national independence spread all over Europe. It culminated in the Wilsonian principles of self-determination. Throughout the nineteenth century dynasties disintegrated and new

---

7. Cited by Donald Read in *Cobden and Bright*. London, St. Martin's Press, 1968, p. 65.

nations came into being. Greece (1827), Norway (1830) and Belgium (1830) became independent. A Polish liberal national uprising in favor of independence took place in 1831. Italy became a unified national state in 1870 and Germany followed in 1871. The Ottoman Empire, encompassing the Balkans, Turkey and the Middle East, cracked wide open, allowing for the emergence of a number of independent states, some late in the nineteenth century and the beginning of the twentieth. Bulgaria, Rumania, part of Yugoslavia and Albania became new national states. The same is the case with the Austro-Hungarian Empire from which came Hungary, Serbia and ultimately Czechoslovakia. Powerful liberal independence movements manifested themselves within the Tsarist Empire. Most of these new states undertook, in the name of liberalism, constitutional reforms providing for individual rights, election and popular participation and restraints upon the government.

Conclusion

In overall terms, nineteenth century liberalism shows a remarkable record in bringing forth and institutionalizing civil rights, political rights, and economic freedoms. It was equally potent in causing a profound reconsideration of the position of the aristocracy, the Church and many unreconstructed traditionalists. But the century was also remarkable for the growth and the unprecedented development of technology and production. This, despite the many miseries that continued to afflict the workers, gave credence to some of the assertions of Adam Smith and the utilitarians. Economies grew; world population began a rapid climb; water and rail communications were established, bringing people closer together in their national community but also in the world; cities developed fast and many old ones were literally torn apart and rebuilt; currency in gold or paper money and new banking practices facilitated exchange while savings were channeled into new investments. Nations mushroomed in the name of self-determination.

At the end of the century a new factor was injected into the liberal philosophy. This was social justice, seen as the need to support individuals in one form or another when their self-reliance and initiative could no longer provide them with protection, or when the market did not show the flexibility or the sensitivity it was supposed to show in satisfying basic wants. A new spirit of mutual aid, cooperation and service began to develop. It became stronger with the coming of the twentieth century, to which we now turn.

Bibliography

Black, Eugene (ed.). *Victorians: Culture and Society*. New York: Harper and Row, 1973.

————. *Posture of Europe, 1815–1940*. Homewood, Ill.: The Dorsey Press, 1964.

Briggs, Asa. *The Age of Improvement*. London: Longmans, 1959.

Clark, G. Kitson. *An Expanding Society: Britain 1830–1900*. New York: Cambridge U.P., 1967.

"Declaration of the Rights of Man and of the Citizen," in Paul H. Beik. *The French Revolution*. New York, Harper and Row: 1970.

Dicey, A. V. *Lectures on the Relationship Between Law and Public Opinion in England During the 19th Century*. New York: Macmillan, 1952.

Friedman, Milton. *Capitalism and Freedom*. Chicago: University of Chicago Press, 1963.

Hamilton, Alexander; Madison, James; and Jay, John. *The Federalist Papers*. New York: New American Library, 1961.

Hartz, Louis. *The Liberal Tradition in America*. New York: Harcourt, Brace and World, 1962.

Hayek, Friedrich A. *The Road to Serfdom*. Chicago: University of Chicago Press, 1944.

Hobhouse, L. T. *Liberalism*. New York: Oxford U.P., 1964.

Jefferson, Thomas. *Drafts of the Declaration of Independence*. Washington, D.C.: Acropolis, 1963.

Laski, Harold J. *The Rise of European Liberalism*. Atlantic Highlands, N.J.: Humanities Press, 1962.

Locke, John. *Two Treatises on Government*. Edited by Peter Laslett. New York: New American Library, 1965.

MacPherson, C.B. *The Political Theory of Possessive Individualism*. New York: Oxford U.P., 1962.

McIlwain, Charles H. *Constitutionalism: Ancient and Modern*. Ithaca, N.Y.: Cornell U.P., 1958.

Mill, John Stuart. *Consideration on Representative Government*. New York: Bobbs-Merrill, Library of Liberal Arts, 1958.

————. *On Liberty*. 1956.

————. *Utilitarianism*. 1957.

Palmer, R.R. *The Age of the Democratic Revolution*. 2 volumes. Princeton, N.J.: Princeton U.P., 1959.

Palmer, R.R. and Colton, Joel. *A History of the Modern World Since 1815*. New York: Knopf, 1971.

Pinson, K.S. *Modern Germany, Its History and Civilization*. 2nd ed. New York: Macmillan, 1966.

Rugiero, E. *The History of European Liberalism*. Boston: Beacon Press, 1959.

Rousseau, Jean Jacques. *The Social Contract and Discourse on Inequality*. New York: Washington Square Press, 1967.

Smith, Adam. *The Wealth of Nations: Representative Selections*. New York: Bobbs-Merrill, 1961.

Tawney, R.H. *Religion and the Rise of Capitalism*. New York: New American Library, 1954.

Thomson, David. *Europe since 1815*. 2nd rev. ed. New York: Knopf, 1957.

———. *France: Empire and Republic, 1850–1940*. New York: Walker and Co., 1968.

———. *Democracy in France Since 1870*. 4th ed. New York: Oxford U.P., 1964.

Weber, Max. *The Protestant Ethic and the Spirit of Capitalism*. New York: Charles Scribner's Sons, 1958.

3

Democracy and Socialism

But man in society not only lives his individual life: he also modifies the form of social institutions in the direction indicated by reason—in such a manner . . . that will render them more efficient for securing freedom . . .

SYDNEY OLIVER The Fabian Essays in Socialism

Using the three basic cores of the liberal democratic ideology as a guide, it is relatively easy to map out its evolution and to assess its present position.

The year 1848 represents the watershed of European liberalism. From it powerful and divergent currents began to flow. From Paris to Palermo, from Frankfurt and London to Budapest, Vienna and Madrid, the poor, the workers and the peasants, who had left the countryside for the urban centers, rose to take power away from the propertied classes in the name of *radical democracy* and *socialism*. Writing in the same year, John Stuart Mill commented on the industrial and technological achievements of the period but pointed out that they had improved the living standard of the middle classes only. "They have not as yet," he added, "begun to effect those great changes in human destiny, which it is their nature and in their futurity to accomplish."[1]

The middle classes found themselves wavering. Some sided with radical democrats and the socialists and joined forces with them in an

1. Cited by Asa Briggs. *The Age of Improvement.* London: Longmans, 1959, p. 303.

45

alliance that could not last. Others backed conservative groups—the nobility, the Church, the landowners—which had resisted liberalism.

Radical Democrats

Radical democrats accepted the moral core of liberalism and its civil rights, individual freedoms, freedom of press, religion and association (though they insisted on the secularization of many of the functions that the Church provided, for instance education, and favored outright expropriation of its landed domains). They also supported the political core but interpreted it in Rousseauian terms: all political power should come directly from the people and a majority could make all decisions directly or through sovereign representative assemblies. They were against all voting qualifications and against any restraints on the exercise of popular will. They also began to express fundamental reservations about the economic core.

Radical Democrats in England and France

A strong radical democratic movement developed in England roughly between 1830 and 1850. This was *Chartism*, a movement of middle class reformers with working class support. Their program (the Charter) seemed to be primarily political, calling for universal manhood franchise, equal electorate districts, "one man, one vote," annual parliaments, elimination of all property qualifications and the secret ballot. The leaders, Feargus O'Connor, Francis Place and William Lovett, attempted time after time to pressure Parliament into passing legislation in accordance with Charter, but without success.

But in addition to political reform, there was also among the Chartists a group urging social and economic reform. Sometimes they came close to the socialist ideas that were circulating in England and the Continent at the time. They demanded the regulation of hours of work and wages, and for social benefits for the workers.

> Eight hours to work; eight hours to play
> Eight hours to sleep; eight bob [shillings] a day

was one among many Chartist slogans. Some of the Chartist leaders openly advocated socialist measures:

> It is the duty of the Government to appropriate its present surplus revenue, and the proceeds of national and public property, to the purchasing of lands, and the location thereon of the unemployed poor. . . .

> The gradual resumption by the State . . . of its ancient, undoubted, inalienable domain, and sole proprietorship over all

the lands, mines, tributaries, fisheries, &c., of the United Kingdom and our Colonies; for the same to be held by the State,
as trustee in perpetuity, for the entire people . . .

It is the recognized duty of the State to support all those of its
subjects, who, from incapacity or misfortune, are unable to
procure their own subsistence.[2]

In France during the same period, radical democracy took a more
extreme form. Louis Blanqui, one of the early social reformers, moved
very close to revolutionary socialism and led a number of armed uprisings against the governmental authorities. Louis Blanc, another social reformer, came closer to the Chartist position. Political reforms he
believed were essential, but it was the duty of the State to safeguard
the "right to work". He urged the government to set up national workshops to employ workers and he believed that such workshops would
compete successfully with privately-owned firms. As time went on,
radical democracy in France moved increasingly in the direction of
economic and social reforms, especially after 1848, when universal
manhood suffrage, one of the major demands, was adopted. It raised
the electorate overnight from a quarter million to nine million voters!
    Thus many radical democrats parted company with liberals on the
definition of the economic core. They questioned the laissez faire model
of capitalism as it had been portrayed by Adam Smith. They were in
favor of using the State in order to correct some of the evils and the
uncertainties of the market. But they went beyond the mere search for
corrective measures. They emphasized the importance of social and
collective goals that could be best implemented by collective (i.e., State)
action. They favored extensive State regulation not simply through
legislation but through direct action and performance. Not just laws
regulating child labor, but inspection and enforcement was demanded;
not only poor laws providing for relief, but the actual operation of State
workshops to provide employment to the poor. They demanded that
the provision of social services be implemented directly by the public
authorities.
    Most radical democrats, however, did not advocate socialism.
Their position was that the State should act and intervene where major
social services and needs were involved without reaching out to ex-
propriate property or to directly take over economic activities such as
production and trade. They favored wide regulations and occasional
direct controls, but not the socialization of the means of production.
    Thus, if we situate the radical democrats in terms of our basic cores
of liberalism, we shall find them strong on the political core (leaning
all the way to majoritarianism and popular sovereignty), strong on the
moral core, but faithful to only a few of the basic principles defined

2. Cited in G.D.H. Cole and A.W. Filson. *Working Class Movements: Selected Documents.*
N.Y.: St. Martin's Press, 1965, p. 79.

as the economic core of early liberalism. In 1869 the French politician Jules Gambetta summed-up the *political* program of radical democrats everywhere in his Belleville Manifesto, but intimated at the same time the need for economic reform:

> . . . I think that there is no other sovereign but the people and that universal suffrage, the instrument of this sovereignty, has no value and basis unless it be radically free.

> . . . the most radical application of universal suffrage; . . . individual liberty to be . . . protected by law; . . . trial by jury for every kind of political offense; complete freedom of the Press; . . . freedom of meeting . . . with liberty to discuss all religious, philosophical, political, and social affairs . . . complete freedom of association . . . separation of church and state; free, compulsory, secular primary education; . . . suppression of standing armies; . . . abolition of privileges and monopolies.[3]

Liberal and Radical Democrats: Reconciliation

With the exception of a few who remained attached to the economic philosophy of Adam Smith, in general most liberals and what we have called radical democrats came gradually to terms. Liberals accepted the full logic of democracy. The franchise has been extended to cover all citizens, male and female, above eighteen, nineteen, or twenty-one. All of the many qualifications for voting based on literacy, age, residence, income, etc., have been eliminated. Restraints upon representative assemblies have been virtually lifted except in cases where the chief executive is also elected directly by the people. In all existing constitutional monarchies the monarch has become a mere figurehead.

The people were mobilized in large mass parties and these parties in many countries exercise a controlling influence over their representatives. In some instances provisions for referenda give the people an additional measure of direct democracy. Popular democracy and majority rule expressed through direct elections for or against the members and candidates of large national political parties has been accepted by all liberals and democrats to be the major source of policymaking. At the same time, the moral core of liberalism in the form of individual and minority rights has been reaffirmed.

There has been also a similar reconciliation between radical democrats and liberals with regard to economic matters. Liberal, but also many other parties, even when they call themselves conservative, have found themselves increasingly in agreement. State intervention to sup-

3. Cited in David Thomson. *Democracy in France Since 1870.* 5th ed. N.Y.: Oxford U.P., 1969, pp. 315–16.

port economic activities, in the form of price and other controls is considered necessary; State intervention through direct or indirect means to stimulate economic activity is again deemed desirable; State regulation of a growing number of economic activities is viewed as indispensable; State direct involvement in providing for unemployment assistance and State indirect and direct action to provide for employment is now taken for granted in most democracies. Thus the functions of the State are viewed not only as supportive or regulatory. They have actually become complementary to the private sector.

The Socialist Impulse

Socialism as a philosophy of life and as a scheme for the organization of society is as old as (perhaps older than) democracy or any other form of social, economic or political organization. Some consider it, in fact, to have been prevalent among primitive societies where land, it has been suggested, was collectively owned.

Socialism represents also an ethic diametrically opposed to that of private ownership and private profit, and the inequalities that these systems may lead to. It is an ethic of an egalitarian and free society, from which the words "mine" and "yours" have been eliminated.

Utopian Socialism

Utopian socialists, beginning with Thomas More (1478–1535), through Francis Bacon (1561–1621) and Tommaso Campanella (1568–1639) down to some of the most important French and British utopian socialists of the nineteenth century, shared a set of common ideas.

1. An aversion to private property and the exploitation of the poor by those who owned the wealth, whether landed, commercial, or later, industrial. "Property is theft" was the curt aphorism of the French socialist Proudhon. The Romantic poet Shelley voiced early nineteenth century socialist beliefs:

The seed ye sow, another reaps,
The wealth ye find, another keeps,
The robes ye weave, another wears,
The arms ye forge, another bears.

2. A passionate commitment to collectivism—the common ownership of wealth. This was partly based on notions about primitive communism, but partly on ideas of mutual cooperation and social solidarity. Thus socialism was seen as the way to extirpate strife, antagonisms and selfishness. Utopian socialists shared the nostalgic vision of the Roman poet Virgil about bygone happy ages:

No fences parted fields, nor marks nor bounds
Divided acres of litigious grounds,
But all was common.

In a famous passage, Rousseau expressed similar thoughts:

> The first man, who after enclosing a piece of ground, took it
> into his head to say, *this is mine*, and found people simple
> enough to believe him, was the real founder of civil society.
> How many crimes, how many wars, how many murders, how
> many misfortunes and horrors, would that man have saved
> the human species, who pulling up the stakes or filling up the
> ditches should have cried to his fellows: Beware of listening
> to this impostor; you are lost, if you forget that the fruits of
> the earth belong equally to us all, and the earth itself to
> nobody![4]

3. A passionate belief in what might be called "social collectivism," emphasizing the interdependence and solidarity of social life—
the "social nature" of men and women, as opposed to the individualistic or utilitarian ethic. Communitarianism was the supreme value;
individualism, competition and self-interest were detested.

4. There were many divergences among the early utopian socialists
on *how* to bring socialism about. Some believed in violence and revolution, but did not spell-out any details; others believed in persuasion
and example. For instance, the British socialist Robert Owen
(1771–1856) set up a model textile factory in East Lanark, Scotland,
where such features as the good working conditions and wages, and
the participation of the workers in some of the profits, were to become
a model to convince other businessmen that it was in their own interests
to follow the same pattern. Most utopian socialists, however, believed
in education. If men and women were properly educated they would
opt for socialism, and it was the task of the intellectuals to provide this
kind of education.

5. Many, especially among the French utopian socialists, were
what we would call today social engineers. Society would be controlled
and manipulated, so that under proper conditions and with the proper
social organization, human beings could attain perfection, both moral
and material.

6. Most of the utopian socialists were not democrats. They paid
lip-service to the moral core of liberalism but argued that liberal political and economic principles and practices could not bring it about.
A "new ideology" had to be imposed first, or inculcated through
education.

Utopian socialists never managed to form a party or even a political

4. Rousseau. *The Social Contract and Discourse on the Origins of Inequality.* Book 1.

movement. But their writings had a profound influence upon the development of socialist thought.

Democratic Socialism

We have already noted that by the end of the nineteenth century there developed a gradual reconciliation between the proponents of liberalism and the radical democrats, in the form of political democracy. A similar reconciliation was also beginning to take place, one that developed throughout the twentieth century, and accounts for what is generally called today democratic socialism.

Nineteenth century democrats endorsed popular sovereignty and majoritarianism while accepting the individual and civil rights that we have discussed as the moral core of liberalism. This set the tone for state intervention, to regulate the market, to correct malfunctioning and to provide social service. But socialism, as first propounded by Marx and some Utopian socialists, rejected the political core of liberalism. Thus, even if for a short period of time, socialism appeared to be directly opposed to basic democratic principles and practices.

However, revolutionary Marxism gave place by the end of the nineteenth century to "revisionism." In France, in Germany, especially in England, but also in Belgium, Holland, and the Scandinavian countries, socialist parties began to increasingly accept the logic and the techniques of democracy. Their goal was modified to bringing about social change through peaceful political means and established democratic procedures, and they became attached to the moral core of liberalism, its stress on individual and civil rights. Socialists began to consider these ideals as ends in themselves rather than as means to be used for the conquest of power. They became increasingly attracted to electoral politics, especially when socialist candidates won appreciable numbers of votes at the polls. They began to see in democracy the proper instrument for change, substituting democratic process for revolution and force.

THE FABIANS

In England at this time a number of intellectuals were expounding upon socialism. Most important were the Fabians (who took their name from the Roman general Fabius, whose defensive "wait and see" tactics gradually weakened Hannibal's invading forces until they were defeated). The Fabians and the Fabian Society which they established in 1884 relied upon three forces: *time*, which meant that socialism would come about gradually; *education*, to persuade the elites and the people that socialism was a superior system, morally and economically, to capitalism; and *political action in the context of democratic and parliamentary institutions*. This meant the formation of a Socialist Party that would present its socialist doctrine to the people for their approval. There was not even a mention of the use of force, and nothing about a dictatorship: in fact, many of their socialist principles were inspired by the Bible. British socialism was steeped in moral, egalitarian and humanistic values, seeking human dignity and freedom in a society from which profit and selfishness had been removed.

The philosophic foundations of Fabian socialism were set forth in *The Fabian Essays*, published in 1889. Wrote George Bernard Shaw, one of the movement's leaders:

> It was in 1885, that the Fabian Society . . . set . . . two definite tasks; first to provide a parliamentary program for a Prime Minister converted to Socialism . . . and second, to make it as easy and matter-of-course for the ordinary respectable Englishman to be a Socialist . . .[5]

The Fabians favored socialization of the means of production, state controls, and broad welfare measures to bring about as much social equality as possible. They had no regard whatsoever for the economic core of liberalism, and advocated drastic overhaul of the economy, going way beyond the simple regulation of social legislation advocated by radical democrats (and increasingly acquiesced in by liberals). They favored the abolition of property and of the free enterprise system. Socialism was declared, however, to be an advanced form of individualism: "Socialism is merely individualism rationalised, organised, clothed, and in its right mind."[6]

At the beginning of this century, in 1901, the Fabians and the leaders of the major British trade unions formed the Labour Party, and by 1906 were running their own independent candidates for election. They won 323,195 votes and secured twenty-nine seats in the House of Commons. Socialism began to gain the respectability that the Fabians wanted to give it (see table 2.1).

In 1918, Fabian intellectuals provided a definitive platform for the Labour Party. The party declared the need for

> . . . the gradual building up of a new social order based, not on internecine conflict, inequality of riches, and dominion over subject classes, subject races, or a subject sex, but on the deliberately planned co-operation in production and distribution, the sympathetic approach to a healthy equality, the widest possible participation in power, both economic and political, and the general consciousness of consent which characterise a true democracy.[7]

5. Shaw (ed.). *The Fabian Essays in Socialism*. London: George Allen and Unwin, 1958, p. 33. (1st ed. 1889.)
6. Ibid., p. 99.
7. Cited in G.D.H. Cole. *A History of the Labour Party Since 1914*. London: Routledge and Kegan Paul, 1948, p. 65.

SIDNEY AND BEATRICE WEBB

Sidney Webb (1859–1947), an Englishman of petit bourgeois background, spent over ten years in the service of the Colonial Office. In 1885, the year he joined the bar, he joined also the Fabian Society, a group of British socialists dedicated to the education of the British people in socialist principles. In 1889, Webb, along with other notable Fabians such as George Bernard Shaw and Graham Wallas, issued *The Fabian Essays in Socialism,* a book which was to become a classic of non-Marxist socialist thought. In 1887 Sidney Webb was married to Beatrice Potter (1858–1943), a woman of similar views. Both were actively concerned with social issues, and were active in the formation of the British Labour Party. Sidney drafted its manifesto—*Labour and the New Social Order*—which served as the party's platform in the elections of 1918, 1922, and 1924.

TABLE 2.1   *The rise of the Labour Party vote*

General Election	Seats Contested	Members Returned	Labour Vote
1900	15	2	62,698
1906	50	29	323,195
1910 (Jan.)	78	40	505,690
1910 (Dec.)	56	42	370,802
1918	361	57	2,244,945
1922	414	142	4,236,733
1923	427	191	4,348,379
1924	514	151	5,487,620
...	...	...	...
1945	640	393	11,632,891

Socialism was explicitly and proudly endorsed by the Labour Party, in order

> to secure for the producers by hand or by brain the full fruits of their industry, and the most equitable distribution thereof that may be possible, *upon the basis of the common ownership of the means of production* and the best obtainable system of popular administration and control of each industry and service.[8] (Emphasis added.)

EUROPEAN REVISIONISM

In Western Europe it was revolutionary Marxism that remained the dominant intellectual force and inspiration of working class socialist movements. But in the latter part of the nineteenth century democratic socialism (in the name of "revisionism") began to gain the upper hand.

Revisionism became a distinct ideological movement, based on the works of Eduard Bernstein, a German socialist who produced the most comprehensive criticism of Marx and Marxism. He pointed out that:

1. The liberal capitalist system was not about to collapse, as Marx had anticipated.

2. The number of capitalists and property-owners was increasing absolutely rather than decreasing, as Marxist theory stipulated it would. Thanks to the corporations and the stock exchange, a greater number of people began to "own" property in the form of stocks.

3. The capitalistic economy was generating an ever-increasing number of jobs as production became more specialized. The middle classes were in fact growing in number and changing in character. They no longer consisted only of people who owned property, as in the past, but of new salaried personnel: technicians, engineers, white-collar workers, service personnel, civil servants, liberal professions, teachers, and so on. Thus, instead of a pyramid with a huge base and sharp apex, the changing class structure under liberal capitalism was beginning to resemble a stepped pyramid in which blocks of decreasing width were superimposed upon each other.

According to Bernstein, class structure could be schematized, as shown to the left of figure 2, as a stepped pyramid made up of many intermediate layers. This was contrary to Marx's view, (right), which represents society as a smooth-sided pyramid, with the capitalist class at the apex.

4. As societies democratized, allowing for equal and universal franchise, associational freedoms and the formation of political parties, strong working class parties would be able to assume political power against the capitalist class and use the State as an instrument for their own protection and to secure a better allocation of goods and services. This would be accomplished through legislation and nationalizations.

8. Ibid., p. 72.

EDUARD BERNSTEIN (1850–1932)

Eduard Bernstein was born on January 6, 1850 in Berlin. Forced to flee to Switzerland by German anti-socialist laws in 1878, he edited the official newspaper of the German Social Democratic Party in Zurich. He moved to London in 1888 where he worked with Friedrich Engels. Bernstein was the founder of "revisionism," which held that Marx's prediction concerning the eventual breakdown of capitalism due to internal contradictions was incorrect, and that neither the pauperization of the working class nor the triumph of the monopolies over democratic political systems were taking place. He rejected the idea of a class dictatorship, and became an advocate of reform rather than revolution, and of gradual incremental change taking place in a democratic context. Bernstein's views on socialism and social change became the basis for democratic socialism.

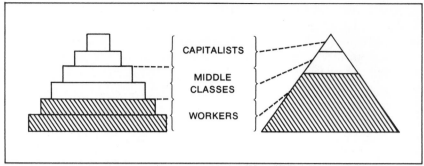

FIGURE 2 *Bernstein's schematization of society (left) compared to Marx's (right).*

Bernstein felt that Marx had underestimated seriously the capabilities of the democratic state to intervene in favor of the workers and the underprivileged.

In the light of these observations, Bernstein concluded that *Evolutionary Socialism* (the title of his book, published in 1899—ten years after *The Fabian Essays*) and not revolutionary socialism was to gain ascendancy. It was step-by-step and stage-by-stage development of socialism that would gradually replace capitalism. Bernstein's influence was profound. Revisionism was gradually adopted by the socialist parties, and revolutionary socialism and its tactics abandoned. Socialism became synonymous with *democratic socialism*. It accepted parliamentary government and elections, and emphasized almost exclusively political activity within the framework of bourgeois legality and democracy. It signified the abandonment of revolutionary class struggle.

The workers were to devote themselves to improving their working conditions, their pension benefits and their wages within the capitalistic economy, and to see to it that a larger share of the national wealth went to them and their families. The trade unions, and democratic political action were to become the instruments for the realization of such tasks.

The socialist movements and parties in Europe began to move, therefore, close to the position of the British Labour Party. They, too, accepted the logic of democracy and began to rely more and more on elections, votes and the conquest of political power through elections. In so doing they endorsed fully both the moral and the political cores of liberalism, but remained hostile to private property and the market economy, promising to socialize the means of production when they achieved full power. But, as with the British Labour Party, their approach became gradualistic, even eclectic, and pragmatic. Socialists on the continent and the Labour Party in England began to propose only specific and selective measures, dealing primarily with the major industries. Small shopkeepers, manufacturers, farmers, and also many large industrial firms and groups would be allowed to operate on their own.

What revisionism accomplished was to mobilize a strong percentage of the workers in favor of democratic change, and to convince them (not always completely) that they could promote and defend their interests within the democratic political institutions. Socialism as such remained the ultimate end, and strong socialist parties, supported by the vote of the workers, were expected to press for or undertake comprehensive measures for the welfare and well-being of the workers. Even if socialist parties did not gain a majority, they could still carry great weight within representative assemblies and could influence governments directly to adopt measures favoring the working class. Broad educational reforms, health, accident and unemployment insurances, retirement benefits, paid holidays, the reduction of the hours of work, paid vacations, collective bargaining, retirement pensions, welfare measures for the poor and the incapacitated, public works, reform in tax policies favoring low income groups and progressively increasing taxes on middle and higher incomes—those were essential and beneficial measures to ameliorate the conditions of the workers within the broad framework of both capitalism and democracy. The dismantling of capitalism, in the form of widespread nationalizations, could wait, or be selectively undertaken under propitious political and economic circumstances.

The Great Synthesis: Democratic Socialism

This was the general posture ultimately assumed by European socialist parties (and the Socialist Party of the United States) at the end of World War One. Socialist parties have been advocating ever since the cause of socialism in a democratic setting with full respect for democratic institutions. In so doing they have been extending further the pact between liberals and radical democrats into what in effect has become a liberal-radical and democratic-socialist synthesis or, better, *democratic socialism*.

The concept of the triple core of liberalism will again help us identify the consensus that has evolved over the last fifty years. Democrats *and* socialists now accept fully *both* the moral core and the political core. In fact, the political and moral cores have expanded. Freedoms have been maintained and extended—for workers, the underprivileged and minorities. It is not only political parties but (even more so) the various interest groups and associations which make their demands known and participate in policymaking.

Differences continue to exist when it comes to the economic core but they are no longer sharp or irreconcilable. In many cases agreement on the content of policies to be pursued by far overshadows ideological or policy differences. Reconsideration by democrats of the validity and the efficacy of laissez faire economics, but equally significant, second thoughts on the part of socialists on the efficacy and wisdom of nationalizations and state controls, have helped bridge and reconcile differences.

A consensus position has been very much in evidence. While democrats, socialists and sometimes even self-styled conservative groups have fully endorsed and broadened individual and civil rights, they have shown also a growing convergence with regard to the economy. Already before World War Two the Conservative Party in Britain had established direct State control and operation over broadcasting; they had brought under State control the London Transport system and the management of the Port of London.

In the 1945 post-war election Labour gained for the first time a clear majority. The first Labour government nationalized the railroads, the coal mines, electricity, gas and the production of steel and iron, together with long-haul busing. A Welfare State was created: a comprehensive scheme of health insurance at virtually no cost was introduced and has remained operative ever since; there were new and special measures for paid vacations, child care, expanded retirement benefits and the right to work. To pay for it all, taxes on inheritance and the graduated income tax, initiated already before World War One, rose steeply. When the Conservative Party came to power six years later, in 1951, and formed a new government, they only denationalized steel and iron production. The rest of the socialist structural reforms together with the Welfare State remained virtually intact.

The Labourites eventually became skeptical of the efficacy of nationalizations. They realized that it was not a cure for all economic problems. Indeed, they began to observe rigidities and inefficiencies in nationalized industries not unlike the ones they had criticized in the past in large capitalist firms. The Labour Party went through a period of soul-searching. Should they abandon their programmatic commitment to the "common ownership of the means of production"— in other words, to nationalization? Though they decided not to, the very fact that the question had been posed indicated the profound waverings of socialists on what used to be their ideological gospel.

In *Germany*, the socialists, the Social Democratic Party, went further. They *did* abandon their commitment to socialism at the Congress of Godesberg in 1957. If an enterprise performs well, so much the better. If it does not, only then might State intervention and nationalization be warranted. This admission that the free market economy could operate well and efficiently would have sent shudders down the spines of the nineteenth century German social democrats. However, their successors concentrated their efforts on social measures—on wages, participation of workers in management and the proceeds of firms, longer vacations, better medical and educational benefits, supports against unemployment, broader and better retirement coverage. The efficiency of the West German economy after World War Two, without nationalizations, surprised most everybody.

The German socialists also collaborated closely with the Christian Democratic Party and the Free Democratic Party—the Liberals—and have been the governing party in Germany for almost ten years. The collaboration between German parties typifies "consensus politics," a fundamental agreement not only on individual and civil liberties, not only on the political institutions and practices of democracy, but also on major economic policies. It is an excellent illustration of the liberal-radical democratic-socialist synthesis.

With the liberation of *France* in 1944 from German occupation and control, the traditional distinction between the left (represented by socialists, Marxist communists and radical socialists) and the right (represented by an assortment of parties which came together in support of General De Gaulle) became blurred. It was the Gaullist government, nominally right-wing, which proceeded with some of the important structural reforms of the French economy. It consolidated the nationalization of the railways initiated by centrist and liberal parties more than forty years before, and undertook the nationalization of the Renault automobile factory, gas, electricity, the coal mines, and some of the banks. In the meantime, the state was rapidly extending its control over the economy. De Gaulle introduced economic planning to promote some key economic activities. The French economy was, and remains, a flexible one based on a mixture of indirect controls and incentives. A national health insurance scheme was adopted, special allowances for families with more than one child were provided, paid vacations were extended, retirement benefits and supports for widows and orphans were improved. Socialists participated in most governments between 1946 and 1958, and for all practical purposes were indistinguishable from the other political parties, except of course the communists.

In *Italy,* massive nationalizations were also undertaken after World War Two, with the full cooperation and often under the initiative of the Christian Democrats—again considered to be a center-right party. In *Holland, Norway* and *Denmark* the same sweeping measures for a Welfare State were introduced under the auspices of both socialist and democratic parties.

But the country in which the fullest and most comprehensive support is given to the individual is Sweden. There is hardly a social need from the cradle to the grave that is not fully covered by various associations and public authorities. Every citizen is fully insured against every evil that haunted the days of the Industrial Revolution and the nineteenth century. The socialists are mainly responsible for this legislation since they have been in power for a long period of time. The Liberals, however, who came to power in 1976, have not shown any inclination to dismantle or even to tamper with the system. There is a consensus, and this consensus is strengthened by the attachment of all parties to the fundamental moral and political principles of liberal-democratic socialism. There is also a genuine participatory movement since most of the welfare legislation is administered by cooperative arrangements and private property is held by association and groups of citizens.

Today, in many democracies an appreciable part of the industrial production is in the hands of the State. The State also controls indirectly a substantial part of economic activity—investment, income, exports, imports, economic growth, prices, etc. In other words, many democracies have moved increasingly in the direction of socialism.

The U.S.A.: Is There a Synthesis?

As for the United States, major social and economic reforms were undertaken by the Democrats under Roosevelt's New Deal in the 1930s. There were no nationalizations and no direct public ownership and operation except for the Tennessee Valley Authority (TVA), a public corporation to provide for electricity in the southeastern region of the country. But massive federally supported public works programs gave employment to millions. The federal government began to regulate credit; it provided low interest loans to homeowners and small businessmen; it established controls on the production of agricultural commodities; it regulated hours of work for the first time and set minimum wages; it promoted collective bargaining and introduced a comprehensive social security system which was to be broadened with the passing of time, to provide for unemployment and retirement benefits. Many of the federal controls were indirect but welfare measures provide also for direct supports to those in need. For the first time virtually all aspects of an individual's life came within the purview of federal jurisdiction.

Most of these measures were expanded with the passage of time while civil rights legislation, affirmative action laws and federal legislation on voters' registration provided fuller participation of all minority groups in the political process and insured them against any discrimination in employment and education. Massive aid to education through direct supports, grants-in-aid, federal scholarships and interest-free or low interest loans, provided for an unprecedented expansion in educational facilities and opportunities. Some $125 billion out of a total budget of $540 billion are alloted today to the Department of Health, Education and Welfare. About $200 billion every year go out to help and support individuals.

Democrats and Republicans differ only in details about the overall trend and direction of welfare and State controls. Better and broader medical supports, health care for the aged, higher welfare payments for mothers with children, and increased social security benefits have been enacted or expanded by both Republicans and Democratic administrations.

Yet the United States has not reached, and may well never reach, the democratic-socialist synthesis we have discussed. First of all, the

American Socialist Party has been attracting only very small support from workers and voters. Secondly, economic liberalism was extremely successful until the Great Depression of 1929, and witnessed a spectacular revival in providing for economic growth, higher wages and a better standard of living for American families since World War Two. A strong body of American "liberals" therefore remained opposed to many of the policies of Roosevelt's New Deal. In fact, liberalism split into two groups. The first espoused and continues to espouse State controls and regulation, social legislation and welfare measures. The second group stood fast to the fundamental tenets of nineteenth century economic liberalism. It still relies on the efficiency and sufficiency of the market economy to provide goods and values, as we shall see in chapter 4.

Conclusion

Where do we stand today? Early liberalism stressed personal rights and civil rights—the moral core. This was retained by democracy, which also expanded the political core of liberalism by institutionalizing majoritarianism, organizing political parties, doing away with all

The Great Depression of 1929 heralded to many, even within the U.S.A., the decline of capitalism. A typical picture of the unemployed in the 1930s, in one of what became known as the "Hoovervilles" a shanty town for the unemployed. (Photo by Lewis Hines, from the International Museum of Photography at George Eastman House)

voter qualifications and minimizing restraints upon the power of the representative assemblies. It also urged the regulation and control of economic life. Socialism maintained respect for individual and civil rights (the moral core), accepted the political core and introduced squarely the question of comprehensive economic controls and welfare measures while favoring collectivization of the means of production, gradually and selectively, but with many qualifications and hesitations over last two decades.

Liberals, democrats and socialists find themselves in agreement on most policy issues confronting modern democracies, or at least their disagreements appear to divide them less. There is an ideological convergence—indicating an attachment to the principles of democracy, and only secondary differences with regard to the running of the economy.

Democracy: Prospects and Crisis

Democracy, liberalism, radical democracy, democratic socialism—in successive waves through the nineteenth century and into the twentieth, these movements have shaped the "great synthesis." Its major feature is the reconciliation of individual and political rights and freedoms with massive State intervention in the economy—an intervention that in some countries has gone so far as socialization of some of the means of production. It is a synthesis that in varying degrees can be found in most contemporary democracies.

Today, looking at the map of the world, we find this new synthesis implanted in the whole of Western Europe, North America, Australia and New Zealand. It seems to have gained some roots in India and even more so in Japan. It has become "operational" for more (with India) than a billion people. Many of them have a standard of living that ranks among the highest, and live under conditions of "modernity." Indeed, if we were to exclude India, we can say that they represent the countries with the highest per capita income in the world.

It would be downright silly, however, to assume or to pretend that the synthesis we have outlined is complete, that it has been everywhere successful and that it has been widely accepted. Democracies face serious internal problems. Democratic systems and ideologies have not gained new recruits especially in the Third World nations where the label is often used but with a very different meaning. Finally, all contemporary democracies face some immediate and urgent challenges. There are many strains and stresses. Some people, in fact, talk of a crisis of democracy.[9]

9. M.J. Crozier, S.P. Huntington, and J. Watanuki. *The Crisis of Democracy*. New York U.P., 1975. I have summarized some of the arguments of the authors.

Everybody is familiar with the term "the revolution of rising expectations." It is common not only among poor nations which have gained
their independence recently and are underdeveloped, but also among
the peoples of the rich countries, in Western Europe and the United
States. The most characteristic manifestation of the "revolution" is that
people, all people, want *more* of *everything*—more wealth, a higher
standard of living, better education, greater security, better health care,
more participation in decision-making, more leisure and greater equality. The speed with which these expectations have escalated and have
converged has created serious problems.

The crisis of modern democratic regimes is primarily caused by
the disparity between ideology and institutional capabilities. Ideology
conjures up a world of plenty and immediate fulfillment. It shapes the
new moral imperatives of equality and of equal sharing in opportunities
and also of benefits. Institutions are slow to respond to the pressure.
As a result, democratic regimes are faced with the prospect of
instability.

It is simply difficult to meet all the rising demands, not only because resources are limited, but because structural and institutional
changes are needed in order to meet them. New services are required,
and new institutional mechanisms must be put in place. Even the most
open and responsive systems experience a time-lag between demands
being made and registered and new mechanisms developing to respond
to them—let alone satisfy them.

The intensity and number of demands from minorities, professional organizations, trade-unions, student groups, cultural associations, and so on, many couched in sharp ideological terms, threaten
to overwhelm the existing democratic institutions. This is a *revolutionary prospect*, for it is likely to cause upheavals in the institutional
framework of democratic societies. But it is also conceivable that democratic elites may have to resort to repressive measures in order to curb
demands and stifle the rising expectations. This is the *authoritarian
prospect*. There is of course the possibility that some democratic societies may "muddle through," adjusting their institutions to meet the
new demands, constantly experiencing temporary dislocations but capable of reforms.

The Crisis of Institutions

Representative institutions, either in parliamentary or presidential systems, face a double crisis: in performance and legitimacy. Gone are the
days when the radical democrats believed that universal manhood
suffrage and representative government would solve all social and
economic evils. Only a small number believes now that representative

assemblies really represent the people. Few think that out of the welter of interests represented in the representative assemblies a common purpose and common policies for society as a whole can evolve. There is a crisis of democratic representative institutions.

If the representative assemblies are no longer viewed as being truly representative, new institutions must be sought to safeguard the interests of the people at large. One such proposal is direct participation. This is the demand for direct participation in decision-making by all those who are affected. The corollary is decentralization of the decision-making mechanism; the virtual dismantling of the bureaucratic apparatus of the State into small and manageable units—the city, the locality, the particular administrative services, the neighborhood. Thus the citizen can participate and the recipients or beneficiaries of services may have a direct say and direct supervision of them. Questions about urban renewal or new housing construction should be decided by those living in the particular areas concerned, and welfare service should be decentralized in a manner to allow for the recipients' direct control and management. The accent is put on "community control," on "neighborhood city-halls," and direct democracy in the economy. Grass-roots politics, parochial and local "nationalisms" are beginning to develop. Small towns, localities, neighborhoods are beginning to claim precedence over national representative organs.

The Crisis of Authority

Institutional weakness, real or imaginary, seems to parallel a profound moral crisis—a crisis of the authority of the democratic State. It is translated into a widespread decline in the consensus democracies enjoyed in the past. Many of the traditional authority structures have weakened, for instance the Church, the family, the social elites, and more recently the trade-unions and fraternal associations. Similarly, highly valued organizations like the army or the university have declined in importance. None of them play the role they played in the past, serving to structure demands, to slow down the urge for immediate fulfillment and to inculcate respect for existing institutions. These agencies no longer play the role of intermediaries between the State and the public at large to sustain its authority and to secure agreement to its decisions. On the contrary, particularisms have begun to assert their primacy—special interests, particular ethnic groups, special localities, different religious bodies—they all assert their virtual autonomy. This further undermines consensus to a democratic policy and makes compliance with the decisions of the democratic State uncertain.

The Crisis of Legitimacy

These are the words of a noted sociologist:

Democracy, as the sorry history of Europe has shown, is a fragile system . . . [it may collapse] when political parties or social movements can successfully establish "private armies" whose resort to violence—street fighting, bombings, the break up of their opponent's meetings or simply intimidation—cannot be controlled by the elected authorities, and whose use of violence is justified or made legitimate by the respectable elements in society.[10]

Daniel Bell is of course referring here to the Nazi and fascist movements, and their counterparts in Central Europe that we shall discuss in chapter 9. But today both the legacy of guerrilla war and the growth of terrorism pose the same dangers for contemporary democracies.

Guerrilla warfare occurred widely after World War Two as the various colonies attempted to oust the colonial power. It took the form of both political organization and military confrontation. Small detachments with makeshift arms at first would begin to harass the colonial administration and the forces allied to it. At the same time a large network of political support was being built to support the guerrillas. Under a leadership and a party, the indigenous population was organized to give its total support to the fighting forces.

Guerrilla warfare and terrorism in advanced democracies, in the form of urban guerrillas such as Italy's Red Brigades, or Germany's Baader-Meinhoff group, have been responsible for the assassinations of top political leaders. Here and in other democratic societies, extremist groups advocating revolution, separatism or anarchism approximate the model of guerrilla warfare. A prerequisite to this activity is the organization of a group of faithful supporters who will support the terrorists, urban guerrillas and revolutionaries. How can democracy defend itself?

The most pressing danger is that democratic societies faced with dissent and acts of violence by terrorist organizations may seek counter-revolutionary policies which will force them to jettison democratic principles and practices. Repressive measures, serious qualifications of political and individual freedoms, special forms of control and police surveillance may be introduced, indeed *have* been introduced, in the name of counter-terrorism. Democracy remains fragile indeed, and never more so than when multiple and conflicting ideological movements begin to undermine the support it needs.

Democracy in the Third World

While a number of the moral assumptions of liberal democracy—individual freedom, human dignity, religious freedoms—have been en-

10. Daniel Bell (ed.). *The Radical Right.* N.Y.: Doubleday, 1963, p. 33.

dorsed in the abstract by many of the leaders of the new nations in Asia and Africa, political and economic freedoms (what we have called the political and the economic core) and also the democratic institutions themselves, were given new interpretations, so much so that democracy has come to mean something very different from what it has meant in Western Europe or the United States. Basic principles like pluralism, and basic institutions like representative government and the political parties, which allow for dissent and competition, have been rejected. Instead they have been superseded by the search for a "popular" or "communitarian" will, one that is often expressed by a single party or very often by a single leader. The terms "democracy" or "republic" are used even when in practice the system is a dictatorship—with powers concentrated in the hands of one leader or a military junta that claims to represent the community as a whole. "Democratic dictatorship," "guided democracy," "controlled democracy" are the expressions one finds frequently.[11]

Some of the reasons for this are historical. In almost all cases the emancipation of the colonies was the outcome of collective and communitarian effort. It called for complete mobilization and organization of the population. While the guerrillas had fought for independence, the population had to be organized; their hearts and minds had to be conquered. This called for a highly disciplined political party, and the development of total control with an ideological and political conformity. This was seen as the only way to sustain the fighting men and women. The population was, in Mao's expression to the guerrillas, what water is to fish. It sustained, sheltered and nourished them; it provided them with a built-in hiding place. In Algeria, in Vietnam, in some African colonies, efforts to build totalitarian control were made during the national liberation wars and the party developed into a State within a State, with its own schools, courts, tax collectors and administrative apparatus. It sought conformity, discipline and obedience to leadership.

It was this tight political organization and control that accounted above all for the ultimate victory of independence movements and the withdrawal of the colonial powers. But it carried its legacy after independence. The party remained a disciplined para-military force allowing no freedoms and competition. Its energy was now directed to other ends—national integration, economic development, the elimination of internal dissent and of "counter-revolutionary" forces, and the subjugation of traditional elites, whether religious, linguistic, tribal or economic, that might obstruct its efforts. Total effort led to "total" regimes, after liberation.

In institutional terms this meant that competition and political pluralisms could not be accepted and representative assemblies could

11. Paul E. Sigmund, Jr. *The Ideologies of the Developing Nations.* N.Y.: Praeger, 1964.

not be allowed to serve as the spokesmen of particular and competing interests. Instead they should speak for a whole and united community from which they derived their mandate. If they would not, then the leader would become the spokesman for the new nation.

The one-party system has been defended as truly democratic. "Does democracy necessarily imply several parties?" asked Jomo Kenyatta. "We say no," he answers. Political parties according to him are a reflection of classes and economic interests. But when no diversity exists or is permitted to exist in terms of interests and classes, then many parties are not needed. One is enough. Many political parties would divide the people, and give rise to rivalries that would disrupt national unity.

In the same vein, the leader of Guinea, President Sekou Touré, has spoken of a "democratic dictatorship." "If the dictatorship exercised by the government apparatus emanates directly from the whole people, this dictatorship is popular in nature and the state is a democratic state . . ."[12] The late leader of Egypt, Gamal Abdel Nasser, rejected a multiparty system. The latter would serve the interests of the colonial powers by dividing the Egyptian people. His answer was the National Unity Party, a mass popular organization representing all the people.

Virtually none of the new nations has accepted economic liberalism. Many of them claim to be "socialist." Socialism is distinguished, however, from Marxism and communism, and though there is widespread admiration for the Soviet system, none of the new states has fully endorsed its model of economic organization. Generally the control of the State is accepted for the key economic activities and for investment. There is a public sector controlled and manned by the State. But there is also a private sector, with a fairly wide margin of initiative in commerce, farming, and manufacturing. Socialism is described as "democratic" but some speak of "democratic collectivism."[13]

Socialism, almost everywhere in Africa (but in parts of Asia too) is defined in "humanistic" terms. The African intellectual, Leopold Senghor, suggests that African socialism should develop in the form of a synthesis that brings together the works of Marx, the utopian socialists, trade unionism, and democratic socialism. It represents a reaction against both "capitalistic and Communist imperialism."[14] In many of the new nations, but especially in Africa, religious beliefs continue to play a more important role than material and economic considerations. Even more important, religions and religious values make the acceptance of Marxism difficult.

Thus most of the new nations pay lip-service to democracy but reject dissent, political competition and pluralism and endorse the one-

12. Ibid., pp. 162–63.
13. For the early manifestations of African socialism, see William H. Friedland and Carl G. Rosberg, Jr., (eds.) African Socialism. Stanford, Ca.: Stanford University Press, 1964.
14. Sigmund, op. cit., p. 245.

party system or personal authoritarian leadership. They strive to consolidate the unity they have acquired, and wish to defend it against the outside interventions that internal divisions may invite.

Bibliography

Beer, Samuel H. *British Politics in the Collectivist Age.* New York: Vintage, 1969.

Bell, Daniel, and Kristol, Irving (eds.). *Capitalism Today.* New York: New American Library, 1971.

Bernstein, Eduard. *Evolutionary Socialism.* New York: Charles Scribner's Sons, 1961.

Buber, Martin. *Paths in Utopia.* Boston: Beacon Press, 1958.

Cole, G.D.H. *A History of Socialist Thought.* (6 volumes) London: Macmillan, 1953–60.

Colton, Joel. *Leon Blum: Humanist in Politics.* Cambridge, Ma.: M.I.T. Press, 1974.

Crossman, R.H.S. (ed.). *The New Fabian Essays.* New York: Praeger, 1952.

———. *The Politics of Socialism.* New York: Atheneum, 1965.

Crozier, M., et al. *The Crisis of Democracy.* New York: New York U.P., 1975.

Cyr, Arthur I. *Liberal Party Politics in Britain.* New Brunswick, N.J.: Transaction Books, 1977.

Dahl, Robert A. *Democracy in the United States.* 3rd ed. Chicago: Rand McNally, 1976.

Galbraith, John Kenneth. *American Capitalism: The Concept of Countervailing Power.* Rev. ed. Boston: Houghton Mifflin, 1956.

———. *The New Industrial State.* Boston: Houghton Mifflin, 1967.

Gay, Peter. *The Dilemma of Democratic Socialism.* New York: Columbia U.P., 1952.

Girvetz, H.K. *From Wealth to Welfare: The Evolution of Liberalism.* Stanford, Ca.: Stanford U.P., 1950.

Goldberg, Harvey. *The Life of Jean Jaurés.* Madison: University of Wisconsin Press, 1962.

Halévy, Elie. *The Growth of Philosophic Radicalism.* Boston: Beacon Press, 1955.

Hancock, Donald M., and Sjoberg, Gideon (eds.). *Politics in the Post-Welfare State.* New York: Columbia U.P., 1972.

Harrington, Michael. *Socialism.* N.Y.: Bantam Books, 1972.

Heilbroner, Robert L. *The Limits of American Capitalism.* New York: Harper and Row, 1967.

Joll, James. *The Second International, 1889–1914.* New York: Praeger, 1956.

Lowi, Theodore J. *The End of Liberalism*. New York: Norton, 1969.

Manuel, Frank. *The Prophets of Paris*. Cambridge, Ma.: Harvard U.P., 1960.

Mills, C. Wright. *The Power Elite*. New York: Oxford U.P., 1956.

Paterson, William E. and Campbell, Ian. *Social Democracy in Post-War Europe*. New York: St. Martin's Press, 1974.

Rawls, John. *A Theory of Justice*. Cambridge, Ma.: Harvard U.P., 1971.

Research Institute on International Change. *The Relevance of Liberalism*. Boulder, Co.: Westview Press, 1977.

Schlesinger, Arthur, Jr. *The Age of Roosevelt, vols. 1 and 2*. Boston: Houghton Mifflin, 1957.

Schumpeter, Joseph A. *Capitalism, Socialism and Democracy*. New York: Harper and Row, 1950.

Shaw, George Bernard (ed.). *The Fabian Essays in Socialism*.

4

Conservatism: England and the U.S.A.

The good citizen is a law-abiding traditionalist.
RUSSELL KIRK   What is Conservatism?

Conservatism is, perhaps, more a state of mind than a political ideology. In order to be conservative one must have something to conserve—property, status, power, a way of life. Conservatives are therefore likely to be those who have power or wealth or status, and who simply want to keep things the way they are. Also, a significant number of people, mostly among rural groups, those who live in small towns, the old and the uneducated, cannot imagine something different, or are afraid of change. They, too, want to keep their way of life the way it is.

But the conservative ideology has its own inherent logic, which can be formulated in terms of a number of general principles. The most significant is the aversion to rapid change, but conservatism remains fundamentally consistent with the tenets of democracy. In contrast to supporters of authoritarianism, conservatives accept representative institutions and universal suffrage and are particularly committed to individual rights and limitations upon government power through constitutionalism.

70

The best formulation of conservative ideology was given by Edmund Burke, in the latter part of the eighteenth century. The best implementation of it has been, through the nineteenth century and until today, that of the British Conservative Party.[1] Variants of the British model could be found in Germany under Bismarck, in France during the so-called Orleanist period (1830–1848) and some of its offshoots during the period of the Third French Republic (1871–1940) and in Gaullism. But almost nowhere on the Continent did an alliance of the aristocracy and the upper classes, the Church, the monarchy and the army lead to the posture of conservatism tied to constitutional democracy that prevailed in England.

European conservatives chose in many instances to reject constitutional democracy and representative government. In the U.S.A. there have been many variants of a conservative ideology, but the absence of a nobility, and the success of the egalitarian ethic and liberalism, account for the virtual absence of any genuine conservative movement or ideology which has had any impact.

Classic conservatism is characterized by certain basic propositions which relate to political authority, to a conception of society and the nature of the individual, and to the relationship between national economy and the State.

The Political Society

Society, according to early British conservative thought, is organic and hierarchical. Classes and social groups fit together in the same way as do the various organs of our bodies. One is indispensable to the others, nor can it function without them. Relations between them must be harmonious and balanced, and each group and each class performs the functions that are necessary to the others for the good health of the whole. Society is not like a machine, say a clock, in which the motions are eternally identical and where each part has no idea of what the other parts are doing. It is rather a combination of many parts, each one of which understands its role and perceives society as a whole. Unlike the machine, society knows it has a purpose; unlike a clock it grows and changes. "The whole," wrote Edmund Burke, ". . . is never old, middle-aged or young." It "moves on through . . . perpetual decay, fall, renovation and progression."[2]

1. An excellent discussion of the evolution of conservative ideology can be found in the relevant parts of Samuel H. Beer. *British Politics in the Collectivist Age.* N.Y.: Vintage, 1949.
2. Burke. *Reflections on the French Revolution.* p. 162.

Society thus consists of interdependent parts—and all the parts are equally conscious of the interdependence. Each one does its own work, but what it does makes sense only when the whole is understood and valued. Farmers grow crops; soldiers keep order and give protection; priests improve our minds and souls; the leaders govern and balance the various parts. The parts working together almost lose the sense of their separateness. Society is not a "mixture" of various roles, groups, qualities and activities. It is, as Aristotle said, much more of a "compound" in which the parts blend with each other to become something different from what they are individually. They become a society.

Different functions and roles inevitably suggest a hierarchical organization and social inequality. Some of society's roles are more important than others, and some people do more important things than others. This means that there must be a subordination of some individuals to others. Persons endowed by nature with certain qualities that others do not have should play the most important roles. Equality and freedom, as abstract propositions, are not acceptable to the conservative ideology. Rather it emphasizes *rights* and *liberties*. These derive not from rational principles or from natural law but from specific institutional and legal arrangements, and from history and tradition. They give to individuals and to groups specific benefits, protections and claims that are commensurate with their functions and roles. Nor is the idea of material equality for all seriously entertained. Material benefits should correspond to the talent shown and the work done. Men have equal rights but not equal things.

The "whole"—this society that consists of the harmonious interdependence of many parts—is formalized in the Constitution. This is not a written document, and in fact there is no way, according to conservative thinkers, a constitution can be set down. The Constitution is a set of customs, understandings, rules and especially traditions, that define political power and set limits upon its exercise. Power thus enshrined by habit, custom and tradition becomes authority—that is, it is accepted and respected. In this way it is the Constitution that binds the whole of the citizenry to its rulers and the rulers to the citizenry within the nation. But conservatives are not necessarily nationalists. To them the nation-state is a social and historical reality, the product of many centuries of common life and togetherness. But it is not a supreme moral value unless it has managed to embody justice and order. "To make us love our country, our country must be lovely" was the pithy comment of Burke.

Political Authority

In contrast to those who establish the foundations of political authority on contract and consent, conservatives find it in tradition, custom, and what they call inheritance and prescription. Society as a living whole

EDMUND BURKE (1729–1797)

The most eloquent expounder of British conservative ideology. Originally Burke appeared to be a liberal arguing not only against the prerogatives of the crown and in favor of parliament but also for the autonomy of the colonies in North America. These views were expressed in *Thoughts on the Causes of the Present Discontents* (1770). It was the French Revolution and its excesses that accounted for his masterpiece *Reflections on the French Revolution* (1790), in which he presented arguments favoring tradition and prescription and the sanctity of law and authority while cautioning against anything but the most gradual expansion of popular participation in affairs of the State.

is the result of natural evolution. The Constitution of England and its various parts—the monarchy, the House of Lords and the nobility, the House of Commons, individual rights, the judiciary—are an "entailed inheritance." One accepts it to live on it, but cannot waste it. In a famous passage Burke sees in the State something like a mystery: its parts and its majesty cannot be dissected, analyzed and put back together in the same or in a different way. *The State cannot be made.* He wrote:

The State ought ... to be looked upon with ... reverence.
... It is a partnership in all science; a partnership in all art;
a partnership in all perfection ... between those who are living, those who are dead and those who are to be born. ...
Each contract is but a clause in the great primeval contract of
eternal society, linking the lower with the higher natures, con-
necting the visible with the invisible world, according to a
fixed compact sanctioned by the inviolable oath which holds
all physical and all moral natures, each in their appointed
place.[3]

Conservatives therefore have no use for the "contract" theory of
the State propounded by the early liberals. The idea runs counter to
the organic theory of society and to the role history and tradition play
in the formation of a State. Burke insisted that even if there were a
contract it was shaped by history and tradition and once made "it
attaches upon every individual of that society, without any formal act
of his own." We are born into political society like our fathers and
forefathers; we do not make it.

Change

Given the emphasis on tradition, conservative thought is generally opposed to change unless it is gradual. Our "partnership with the dead"
should not be broken, for fear that this would undermine the living
and those still to be born. Modifications become necessary, but on
balance the past carries more weight than the present. As for the future,
there are many would-be reformers and social engineers, and conservatives distrust them. Innovation is suspect, and Burke claimed it was
prompted by "selfish temper and confined views." As a result the
conservatives fall back upon the existing and widely shared values that
have kept the society together. Religion is one of the most important;
so is common law; even prejudices. As Edmund Burke put it, "wise
prejudice," consecrated by long usage is "better than thoughts untried
and untested."
Religion, tradition, the common law, prejudice—they all give the
individual shelter and solace; they provide stability which in the last
analysis is a higher value than change, which moves us into unchart-
ered waters. All these things, together with the State and its organs,
must be strengthened with the proper pomp and ritual that appeal to
the common people. The crown itself is a symbol which, through ritual,
secures support and obedience. More than fifty years after Burke another British conservative, Walter Bagehot, (1826–1877) spoke of the
"symbolic" or "ceremonial" part of the Constitution (that is, the monarch) providing for the attachment of the common people and unifying

3. Ibid., pp. 139–40.

political society. The cabinet, the prime minister and parliament were the "efficient part," though this was understood only by an elite few, and hardly appreciated by the common people.[4]

If change, however, is to come, it must be natural and slow—one and the same thing for conservatives. Conservatives may even favor change in order to preserve. Change must reflect new needs and be the result of cautious adjustment with past practices. The British conservatives *allowed* for changes in the constitution, which they venerated: thus came about the gradual extension of the franchise, the ascendancy of the popularly elected House of Commons over the hereditary House of Lords, the development of a civil service based on merit, as well as economic and social reforms. But they did so often under pressure, and with the aim of preserving what they valued most. In their efforts to slow down reform, however, British conservatives remained firmly attached to the basic democratic principles of representative government, elections and the rule of law.

Leadership

The purpose of the State and its leaders is to balance the whole, to create unity and commonality of purpose out of diversity. Government leadership and decision-making should be entrusted to "natural leaders"—men or women of talent, high birth, property, with a stake in the interests of the country and in its fortunes. As late as the middle of the nineteenth century many argued in England that noblemen could own whole regiments in the army, outfitting and commanding them, and the explanation given was simple—they cared more about England's welfare than did the common people! They had a greater stake in the defense of the country.

As a conservative put it recently, "Government is instituted to secure justice and order . . . and . . . the first principle of good government allows the more energetic natures among a people to fulfill their promise while ensuring that these persons shall not tyrannize over the mass of men."[5] Quality and not election should therefore be the source of leadership. Conservatives fought against the extension of the franchise, acquiescing to it reluctantly, and did not accept the full logic of majority rule until very recently. The principle of one man one vote was unacceptable, and the notion that decisions could be made by simple arithmetic majority was considered "a violent fiction." The idea of decision-making by a majority could be entertained only when that majority, by long habits of obedience, had become self-disciplined. That would be when the majority had accepted the restraints that law and tradition had inculcated so as to act in accordance with the fundamental rules of the past.

4. Bagehot. *The English Constitution*. N.Y.: Oxford U.P., 1936.
5. Russell Kirk. "Prescription, Authority and Ordered Freedom" in F.S. Meyer (ed.). *What is Conservatism?*, p. 33.

The natural leaders hold the interests of the country in trust. They act on behalf of the people and the society. The trust, however, is almost a complete and blanket grant of power—it is not a delegation.

Another way of putting the same conservative notion of trusteeship is the theory of *virtual representation*. Today we agree that representatives represent their constituency, those who elect them, and the country in general. But their capacity to make decisions for us stems directly from elections and from the *mandate* they receive from their constituency or the electorate at large. Virtual representation, on the other hand, is the capacity to represent and make decisions by virtue of qualities other than mere election. Conservative thinking returns to the idea of birth and wealth. Persons who have one or both can represent the people and the nation by virtue of their position better than elected representatives. They are what in medieval times were called the *valentior pars* (the better part) of the community. This again shows the reluctance by conservatives to extend the franchise and accept majoritarianism.

Thus the natural leaders should govern, and the many should follow. All along and perhaps even until today this reflects the typical British conservative attitude. Many of the members and leaders of the Conservative Party still think that they are endowed with capabilities with which they can govern better than any other party and its leadership. They still believe that they can hold the interest of the country in trust better than all others. They also think that the government has autonomous and independent powers to govern, and that once elected it is free to exercise them. It is a government that once elected cannot be given instructions or be delegated to do some things and not others. So, there is an element of authoritarianism and elitism still lurking in the hearts of all good conservatives, together with a certain distrust for the "common people" or the "mass."

Paternalism

While conservatives believe that the propertied classes and the landed aristocracy have special privileges, they also agree that such privileges and their exercise have corresponding social obligations. There is here a strong element of paternalism, whereby the natural leaders have to cater to the well-being of the common people by providing them with relief when out of work and at other times improving their living conditions. Because of their organic theory of the society, conservatives tended to subordinate economic interests to the overall interest of the collectivity. Social solidarity and social cooperation are given precedence over particular interests. Finally, the purpose of "the whole" goes beyond simple material considerations. The State is an all-encompassing agency for providing justice and order. It has a moral purpose to which particularisms and economic interests must yield.

For all these reasons conservatives reject the utilitarian philosophy of economic liberalism. Self-interest, unrestrained competition, individualism and the very notion that the society is held together by competing claims and antagonisms is repugnant to them. They reject laissez-faire economics, or at best tolerate it on condition that individual effort and competition not be allowed to tear apart the fabric of the society. They accept economic individualism if it allows everybody to show his or her worth and capabilities; they reject it if it were to lead to sharp inequalities and social strife that would upset the balance of the whole. British conservatives have favored State intervention and welfare measures, unlike other conservative parties on the Continent and elsewhere.

Constitutional Government and Democracy

The British conservatives and their Conservative Party became strong advocates of constitutional and representative government. In contrast to the European conservatives they did not waver in their support of democracy and parliamentary institutions. Authoritarian and totalitarian solutions appealed to only a negligible number of their leaders and followers. In this way conservatism, while representing the status quo groups, recognized the realities of social change and the necessity of guiding it and reducing its speed rather than arresting it altogether. Classic conservatives appear something like a well-controlled dam in this way; not a bulwark against the forces of all change.

After the nineteenth century conservatives not only accepted major economic changes such as the establishment of Britain's Welfare State

The House of Commons in action. The Conservative leader Benjamin Disraeli addresses the members of the House, c. 1865. (The Mansell Collection)

and the nationalization of its industries. They themselves also *introduced* social and economic reforms. In 1951, when the Conservatives replaced the Labour government, they assumed the direction and the management of the nationalized industries and the welfare system Labour had built. The Conservative Party did not reject Labour's social economic and welfare legislation. It tried to slow their pace of reform until it judged society as a whole had time to adjust to it. Thus conservatived reconciles themselves to a new social and economic order.

The Conservative Party remains staunchly committed to democratic principles. While the authority of the leader of the party is given greater scope than in the case of other parties, notably Labour, the Conservative Party developed into a mass party with three to four million members. It holds annual conferences; allows its various organs considerable autonomy; holds free debates in which policy resolutions come from the floor and can be endorsed despite the opposition of the leadership. It now recruits its candidates for the House of Commons without consideration of their personal wealth and ability to contribute to their own campaign or to the party. In general, despite its affinities with the upper status groups and wealthier segments of the population, it has managed to appeal to and get support from many of the voters who belong to the working or lower middle classes. The marriage between the cottage and the throne that the great Tory leader of the Victorian period, Disraeli, had suggested, developed into strong ties between the people and the Conservative Party leadership. As a result the party has survived as one of the two major political groups in England. Since 1945 it has held the reins of government for some seventeen years. In May 1979 the Conservative Party won the general election and was returned to office again.

To sum up some of the basic characteristics of classic conservative thought: there is a belief that society is like an organism; that its parts are hierarchically arranged; that authority should be entrusted to natural leaders; a rejection of individualism and egalitarianism; a strong belief in custom and tradition and an aversion to change; emphasis upon religious and ritualistic symbolisms to solidify the union of the whole. Yet at the same time there is a strong commitment to a government under law guaranteeing individual rights, an acceptance of representative government, and with it an acknowledgment of the increased participation of all the people, an implementation of the Welfare State, and above all, a rejection of authoritarian solutions. Conservatism has thus legitimized itself as an ideology consistent with democracy.

People who like change and innovation and find themselves at odds with the conservative ideology should not be particularly hasty in rejecting it. Classic conservatism, as portrayed here, was and remains a brake to rapid change. But it channelled the well-to-do and, what is more, millions of voters, into accepting gradual and peaceful change.

Conservatives have been distrustful of human reason and majoritarianism. But they never attempted to control the first or to outlaw the second. They (like the British socialists) presented their position and policies in the context of democracy. The conservative ideology—the creature in a sense of the British ruling groups—tamed the class that formulated it and disciplined its followers to act within the logic of individual and associational freedoms and accepted free political competition without which democracy cannot exist. By creating an ideology that taught the British ruling classes how to bend in order not to break they legitimized not only gradual change but all change if and when the electorate demanded it; and they prepared their followers to accept change, if not always with grace, but at least without resorting to force.

Conservatives and Neo-Conservatives in the U.S.A.

Until World War Two the term "conservative" was virtually unknown in American political life. When used, it was considered a slur. Yet in 1978 an opinion poll revealed that 8 percent of a representative population sample considered themselves "very conservative," 31 percent declared themselves to be "conservative" and 31 percent called themselves "moderates." Only 19 percent called themselves "liberals" and only a small fraction, 4 percent, proclaimed themselves to be "very liberal." Either the terms have changed meaning or the American people have undergone a dramatic change in the configuration of their political beliefs and attitudes. A change, that is, in political ideology.

As we saw in our discussion of British conservative ideology, conservatives admire and try to preserve the past; they are elitist in that they believe in natural leaders; accept only gradual and incremental change; admire a well-balanced and hierarchically structured society and emphasize the need of authority. "Civilized man lives by authority," according to a (British-born) American conservative.[6] Conservatives believe that societies develop norms—that is, enduring standards of behavior—and that we obey them because of habit and tradition. "The sanction to norms," writes the same author, "must come from a source other than private advantage or rationality"—the two basic propositions used by liberals to explain our obedience to the State. The real source of authority and obedience "is tradition." For conservatives, "the good citizen is a law-abiding traditionalist."[7]

To most Americans these propositions are alien. "Man is created equal"; all of us are "endowed" with liberty. The American dream has been change, progress, the future and the manipulation of the environment in order to get more out of it. Human nature is perfectible

6. Ibid., p. 23.
7. Ibid., p. 31.

and a person's worth lies in achievement, not birth, inheritance or status. As for society, it has no meaning and reality outside of the individuals who make it and can remake it. There is no hierarchy and no organic quality about it, there is no fixed subordination of some to others, no structure of deference. The self-made person is still the symbol of Americanism, and of the constant restlessness, mobility and change of Americans and American society. Law is but a convenient external standard which we set up to accommodate our internal conflicts, hardly a norm maturing and gaining strength and respect with time until obedience to it becomes a tradition.

American history and practice have both shaped and strengthened these attitudes. The vast land to be conquered by individual effort in the days when the frontier was open to the west; the immensity of the resources available; the freedom of all (except, until recently, the blacks) to move at will since they were not bound to a lord or master; the relative weakness of the central government to impose law and order, allowing individual groups and vigilante organizations to do it— they all strengthened egalitarian and individualistic values and determined the spirit of liberalism. To quote the famous phrase of the Greek philosopher Protagoras, the individual remained "the measure of all things," in America.

Liberalism became the dominant American political creed, and virtually all social thinkers called themselves liberal. Few dared call themselves conservatives, until very recently. There was little to conserve and a lot to change and to conquer: more wealth to amass; greater material benefits to realize for all. Outside of individual effort and achievement neither norms or "tradition" or "wise prejudice," as Burke had put it, restrained the myth of material success and self-improvement that was the heart of the beliefs of Americans. When the labor leader, Samuel Gompers, was asked in the latter part of the nineteenth century what it was that American labor wanted, he gave the answer that all Americans understood: "More!" In a society holding such an ideal, genuine conservatives were likely to find themselves out of place or, what amounts to the same thing, there was no place for them.

American Conservatives and the British Model

The American political tradition has few conservative authors or leaders in any way comparable to the British ones. John Calhoun, Herman Melville, Irvin Babbitt and more recently Walter Lippmann are often mentioned. Calhoun, without any doubt, had a profound influence in the years until the Civil War. But his impact, any more than that of the others, has not been a lasting one. The real classic conservatives—the "humanistic value preservers"—who venerate tradition, order and natural law, have been very few indeed. The reason is that the American system and the American society were made in the name of human reason and individual rights, not tradition. Real conservatives in the

United States must either go directly to the British sources for inspiration, which they often do, or try to find the particular institutions and ideas that best correspond to the conservative ideology in the American experience, which they have tried to do. The only conservative ideology they claim to find is in the Constitution and in the thinking of the framers that produced it and, of course, in the political philosophy of some of them as it was expounded in the Federalist papers.

American conservatives have tried to draw their inspiration from the Constitution because of the limitations upon direct democracy that it embodies, and because of its emphasis upon law. The American republic is "a government of law and not men." It is a republic and not a democracy—a state in which separation and balance of powers makes it impossible for any single branch of government to concentrate in its hands enough power to endanger the rights of the people; a system carefully engineered to make it impossible for a numerical majority to control at one and the same time all branches of government and to establish its "tyranny"—one that is considered just as bad as the tyranny of a minority or a group of men or of one man. Restraints are built into the system not only against the governmental organs, federal and state, but against the people as well. It is in this that American conservatives find the "wisdom of the framers."

Similarly in the Federalist papers providing for a defense of the Constitution and embodying the philosophy of the "framers," notably Madison and Hamilton, references are made and institutions are defended in terms that are close to British conservative ideas and vocabulary. Thus, the "electoral college", that was supposed to be free, once chosen, to elect the president, is viewed and defended as a body of wise men—more reliable to make the proper choice than the people directly; the early mode of election for the Senate, by the state legislatures, again provides for an indirect mode of election whose purpose was to filter the popular choice. It is significant, however, that the electoral college has ceased to play the independent role it was supposed to play, and that the Senate is now elected directly by the peoples of the various states.

Emphasis upon law—a government of law and not men—remains an important ingredient of a conservative ideology. Yet only a careful examination of the jurisprudence of the Supreme Court, the ultimate custodian of the Constitution, can answer to what extent. Furthermore it should be remembered that nowhere does the Constitution grant power to the Supreme Court to declare acts of Congress unconstitutional and to set them aside.

This interpretation of the Constitution and of the intentions of its framers, as being essentially conservative and a reflection of a conservative ideology must be considered seriously. The framers were afraid of "the people" and of the majority; they looked for "natural leaders," and many had a profound respect for tradition. But this hardly makes them and the Constitution, as it developed, conservative. Conservatives in England believed in the wise exercise of power and extolled established authority; they put politics and political wisdom above everything else except religion and divine or natural law; they thought, as we have seen, that a political society was a living organism to which material and functional interests were subordinated. Wise leadership kept this organism together.

The framers of the U.S. Constitution, on the other hand, feared political power. It could be abused and might be abused by anybody and everybody, even by "wise rulers." They were skeptical about the possibility of legitimizing power and of creating a strong political authority. Their solution was to weaken authority as much as possible by fragmenting it and dividing it. The solution was a mechanical one—it reflected no belief in tradition, custom or in natural leaders. Like the Newtonian physics which influenced its framers, the policy was one in which at best an equilibrium of forces and of governmental organs would result.

This philosophy was fully consistent with the climate of opinion of the times. By downgrading the powers of the government and by providing for checks and balances for each and all of its organs, the framers hoped to liberate society (i.e., the individual, the economy, voluntary associations, the churches, etc.) from the State and from political domination. The best government was the one which governed the least, leaving individuals free to pursue in the best utilitarian manner their material interests, to maximize their pleasure and avoid pain as they saw fit. The "do-it-yourself man" of Benjamin Franklin was to emerge unfettered by political power, free of tradition and prescription, but also free from the wisdom of political elites and their natural leaders! This was and remains the very opposite of classic conservatism.

The American Neo-Conservatives: Who Are They?

Despite the foregoing, in the last twenty years the term conservative has gained respectability, and the conservative ideology many followers. There are many who proudly claim to be conservative. What is the meaning of the term? And who are these new conservatives? To begin with, conservatives today in the United States are very different from the British ones. They are in fact liberals, who subscribe by and large to the tenets of nineteenth century liberalism. They accept the institutions and policies of nineteenth century liberalism and want to preserve what in their opinion worked so well for this country. They believe in economic individualism, competition, the free enterprise system and are against State intervention. Until 1932 *they* were the liberals. Herbert Hoover called himself a liberal!

It was the economic depression of 1929 and the New Deal under Franklin D. Roosevelt that accounted for a change of terms. Roosevelt, who also called himself a liberal, introduced sweeping social reforms, most of which involved the direct intervention of the federal government in economic and social matters. These included public works, social security, insurance schemes, a minimum wage, legislation that favored the growth of trade union membership and gave them a new role in collective bargaining with employees, direct and indirect controls over agriculture and farm prices, unemployment compensation, production of electricity by a federal public corporation, federal loans to business and prospective house-buyers, stringent controls on banks and federal guarantees to protect people's savings, and so on. Without ever rejecting the free market economy the New Deal fashioned a system of controls and regulations unprecedented in American history. As a result, the federal budget swelled and taxes rose. The New Deal asserted the role of the State and the nation over the economy. Political power was used directly to compensate for the weaknesses of the market economy that was presumed to have brought about the depression, a depression that halved the national income, arrested economic growth and accounted for the most severe unemployment that the country had experienced. About ten million people were unemployed between 1929 and 1938.

With the "statism" and State intervention of the Roosevelt era in economic affairs the meaning of liberalism changed. Those who supported Roosevelt and favored the intervention of State controls in the economy and who endorsed the welfare measures became the liberals, or the "neo-liberals." From 1932 until World War Two and ever since, political leaders, whether Republican or Democrat, have accepted this general philosophy, and the federal government continues to expand and to spend more. Defense has been one reason, but welfare legislation is just as important. Education subsidies, loans and grants, anti-poverty programs, expansion of welfare benefits and of the number of beneficiaries, Medicare, more comprehensive old age and related benefits, hospital subsidies and health care, and an ever-growing expansion of the social security system to provide more to larger numbers accounted for this vast amount. Taxes increase accordingly.

The neo-liberals sought also to expand the basis of political power, and with it *their* power. Since the New Deal there has been a growing involvement of groups of people who had previously virtually been excluded from the political process. Labor was the first to assume a greater degree of power thanks to the New Deal legislation favoring the growth of trade unions and their role in collective bargaining. Ethnic and religious minorities came next—Catholics, Jews, Poles, Italians, Irish, Greeks, etc. Al Smith, running for president in 1928, faced strong and overt hostility in many parts of the country because he was a Catholic. But by 1960 the religious issue did not play a critical role when another Catholic, John F. Kennedy, was elected.

The assimilation of the blacks came in the late 1950s and 1960s, and by 1970 the federal government was actively intervening through a variety of programs to ensure that ethnic minorities were not discriminated against in employment or education. The 1970s saw, finally, the same protection extended to women in employment and education. The neo-liberals have been responsible both for the widening of political and social opportunities to all and for comprehensive economic controls and welfare measures. Equality has become, gradually, synonymous with social justice; it is no longer solely a matter of equality of opportunities, but of real equality in substantive benefits and achievements.

It is through this process that the meaning of liberalism has changed. Those who accepted the New Deal and its philosophy and policies were the neo-liberals, or welfare liberals, or collectivist liberals. However, the liberals who rejected it became known as conservatives, or, the term we use here, neo-conservatives. Paleo-liberals (old-time liberals), or autonomist liberals (believers in the independence and freedom of the economy and the market) are other terms used to describe them.

What do the neo-conservatives stand for? First and foremost, for individual initiative and freedoms. But they narrowly interpret both, to mean in particular *economic freedom*—freedom of enterprise, freedom to work irrespective of whether or not one belongs to a union, freedom of contract, a free market economy. One of the most sophisticated of the neo-conservatives, William F. Buckley, points this out:

> Conservatives have failed to alert the community to the interconnection between economic freedom and—freedom. . . . It is a part of the conservative intuition that economic freedom is the most precious temporal freedom, for the reason that it alone gives to each one of us, in our comings and goings in our complex society, sovereignty—and over that part of existence 'in which by far the most choices have in fact to be made, and in which it is possible to make choices, involving oneself, without damage to other people. And for the further reason that without economic freedom, political and other freedoms are likely to be taken from us.[8]

Thus neo-conservatives ask that the federal (and often state) government move out of the economy; that if and when welfare measures are needed they should be undertaken at the state and local levels and not the federal one; that the federal budget and federal expenditures be sharply reduced; that income taxes but also many other federal and state taxes be sharply curtailed. In effect, neo-conservatives ask for the dismantling of much of the New Deal legislation and of the Welfare State.

Many arguments favor the position of the neo-conservatives, and

8. William F. Buckley, Jr. *Up From Liberalism.* N.Y.: McDonnell, Oblensky, 1959, p. 166.

we are already familiar with some of them: bureaucracy leads to inefficiency; State controls and regulations stifle competition and are wasteful because they increase the cost of production. State controls lead to us becoming increasingly deprived of moral freedoms, and most importantly of the freedom to make our own choices and to assume our own responsibilities. We become dependent upon bureaucratic, impersonal services for which nobody is responsible. In 1946 Friedrich von Hayek, a professor of economics at the University of Chicago, wrote *The Road to Serfdom*, in which he sounded the alarm and set the tone for the neo-conservatives. State intervention and economic planning, he argued, and the end of individual economic freedoms, would result in moral degradation for all of us and the ultimate loss of our political freedoms as well. The bureaucratic state would make choices for us—what to produce and what to consume, where to work and where to live, what income to make, and so on. The same theme is repeated by Buckley:

> What all conservatives in this country fear, and have plenty of reason to fear, is the loss of freedom by attrition. It is therefore for the most realistic reasons, as well as those of principle, that we must resist every single accretion of power by the State. . . .[9]

What do neo-conservatives propose? Buckley provides a list of particulars:

> . . . to maintain and wherever possible enhance the freedom of the individual to acquire property and dispose of that property in ways that he decides on. To deal with unemployment by eliminating monopoly unionism, featherbedding, and inflexibilities in the labor market, and be prepared, where residual unemployment persists, to cope with it locally, placing the political and humanitarian responsibility on the lowest feasible political unit. . . .[10]

We can identify the neo-conservatives, then, in terms of a cluster of issues. Less taxation, reduction of the federal budget, withdrawal of the State from economic regulation and control, reduction of public expenditures (federal and State), sharp reduction in welfare services and in the size of the bureaucracies, more initiative and freedom to local government bodies. Yet neo-conservatives, irrespective of the positions they take regarding social and economic matters, have remained within the framework of constitutional democracy. At no time do they envisage the use of force or repressive tactics, in or out of

9. Ibid., p. 179.
10. Ibid., p. 202.

government. They believe in political competition and political freedoms and use the political process to gain support.

Neo-conservatives have been gaining strength. Increased taxation in the 1970s, coupled with inflation and unemployment, have turned the public away from the neo-liberals, whether Democrat or Republican. The middle classes feel threatened. Reduction in taxes is the slogan of many neo-conservative leaders, and the passage of Proposition 13 in California mandating an across-the-board reduction of state taxes and consequent reduction in state expenditures has set a precedent that other states may follow, and that may affect Congress and the federal government as well. The disillusionment with the neo-liberalism that the New Deal spawned seems to be strong.

While taxpayers seem in a state of revolt, the economic and business elites give their full support to policy changes along the lines of neo-conservative ideology. Thus the *New York Times* reports "The Economic Wind's Blowing Toward the Right—For Now,"[11] and indicates the direct entry of corporations into the promotion of university research to support the free enterprise system. "The prevailing theology of liberalism providing a common intellectual core of beliefs that many leaders in Washington could rally behind has broken up," the head of the American Enterprise Institute in Washington is reported to have declared. Others just note with pleasure the "crumbling" of the liberal center. Business corporations are actively engaged in promoting the dissemination of views opposing the neo-liberal "theology." According to some business executives, corporate gifts to universities should be guided by "corporate self-interest." Money, in other words, should be given to universities where professors are sympathetic to the free enterprise system, and denied to those where the academics teach different views. These may be only straws in the wind but they show that there is a genuine movement against neo-liberalism and in favor of neo-conservatism.

Neo-conservatives in the United States echo today the liberal voices of the nineteenth century. They stress the economic core of liberalism and remain attached to the moral and political core. Their growing strength derives from the disenchantment of many—and in particular the middle classes—with what now seems to be the deficiencies of State controls, public spending, high taxes and centralized decision-making through an ever-growing bureaucracy. But there is also the argument that public spending and public controls undermine the moral initiative of individuals and dull their incentives and inventiveness so that in the last analysis productivity and economic growth are undermined. The myth of "rugged individualism" so central to nineteenth century American liberalism remains remarkably strong.

11. The *New York Times*, July 16, 1978, and the *New York Times Magazine*, July 23, 1978.

So too is the notion that the character and moral fiber of a person can be tested only through competition and individual effort—a struggle in which only the best survive.

Bibliography

Burke, Edmund. *Reflections on the Revolution in France.* New York: Bobbs-Merrill, Library of Liberal Arts, 1955.

Cecil, Lord Hugh Richard. *Conservatism.* London: Williams and Nurgate, 1912.

Hayek, Friedrich von. *The Road to Serfdom.* Chicago: University of Chicago Press, 1946.

Kirk, Russell. *The Conservative Mind.* Rev. ed. Chicago: Henry Regnery, 1960.

Meyer, Frank S. (ed.). *What Is Conservatism?* New York: Holt, Rinehart and Winston, 1964.

Rossiter, Clinton. *Conservatism in America.* 2nd rev. ed. New York: Knopf, 1966.

Viereck, Peter. *Conservatism: From John Adams to Churchill.* Princeton, N.J.: Van Nostrand, 1956.

part two

COMMUNISM: FROM ONE TO MANY

In place of the old bourgeois society . . . we shall have an association in which the free development of each is the condition for the free development of all.

KARL MARX AND FRIEDRICH ENGELS
The Communist Manifesto

The conservative political ideology, as outlined in chapter 4, remains solidly within the constitutional and democratic tradition. It fully accepts individual freedoms, political liberties, political competition, representative assemblies and constitutionalism. This is not the case with totalitarian ideologies and regimes. They are anti-democratic; they extol leadership; they reject individual and associational freedoms; they use force as an instrument of governance; they rely upon a single party, excluding all political competition among parties and groups. Representative assemblies in these regimes are but a rubber-stamp, unanimously accepting the policies formulated by the leadership. Elections are controlled by the State apparatus and by party officials.

Totalitarian movements and the regimes which display totalitarian tendencies exhibit shared characteristics:

1. The ideology is total and comprehensive and everything becomes subordinate to it. Society is to be restructured in terms of the posited ideological goals.
2. All associations, all groups, all individuals become subordinate to the party, the State and the leader. There is no cultural pluralism. Education, literature, art, music, architecture—all must yield and conform to the overriding objectives and goals of the political ideology. Groups and individuals, the family life, the economy, schools and social life, even recreation activities, must be synchronized with the political regime. All must "march in step" with it.
3. The single party becomes a party to control, intimidate and to govern. It becomes the major vehicle of political mobilization and recruitment.
4. No political competition is tolerated.
5. The use of violence is institutionalized and applied through the police and other specialized instruments of coercion and intimidation.
6. The authority and power of the leader is absolute. He concentrates all powers and is the supreme legislator and umpire. Totalitarian systems do not establish, as some claim, hierarchical relations of command and execution. In totalitarian systems the will of the leader overrules everything else. He can change at will the lines of command and the established hierarchies.
7. There is, finally, an inherent expansionist tendency in totalitarianism, associated with the exaltation of the nation and nationalism.

Needless to say, these characteristics represent extreme or "ideal" types, helpful for the purposes of analysis. None of them are likely to be found in their pure form. Even in portrayals of the most extreme of totalitarian systems, like Huxley's *Brave New World* or Orwell's *1984*, the total conformity of the society and the individual to the ideology and leader are shown to be impossible. Dissent and nonconformity can never be eliminated entirely.

For some time the view of totalitarianism as an exclusively right-wing phenomenon was widely held. Marxists argued that it represented, in fact, the last stage of capitalism, with the economic oligarchy forced to jettison democracy in order to preserve its position, economic power, property and profits. Palmiro Togliatti, the Italian communist leader, defined fascism, for instance, as a revolutionary movement "for counter-revolutionary purposes." It was aimed at stopping the proletarian revolution and socialism.

As our preceding analysis shows, however, totalitarianism is a political phenomenon that subordinates individuals and their freedom to the political objectives of the party and the State. In this sense, communism and fascism are *both* totalitarian ideologies, having the same elements of personal leadership, elimination of all opposition, single-party rule, subordination of all activities to State and to party, and the use of police terror.

The Soviet Union, the People's Republic of China, and many of the regimes in new nations—Ethiopia, Mozambique, Cuba, Vietnam, for instance—are totalitarian regimes. They are elitist, politically exclusive, rely on one-party government and control, use force and repression, and attempt to unify the nation along strong ideological, often nationalist, themes.

Some Similarities

There is in fact a convergence between "left-wing" and "right-wing" totalitarianism. The similarities are best apparent in relation to their shared negative themes—that is, what they oppose. But they are close too in regard to the tactics they advocate for the conquest of power and with regard to the manner in which their power is institutionalized.

Both left- and right-wing totalitarian states reject economic and political liberalism, democracy, representative assemblies with genuine power to deliberate and decide, and economic and political freedoms and civil rights. In their tactics for the seizure of power both advocate force, and both prepare for it through a well-disciplined political party. Similarly, when totalitarian parties of either left or right gain power, both eliminate freedoms and political competition, both establish one-party rule, both promise to develop a planned economy and to replace the free market, both stress social and communitarian goals as opposed to individualistic ones. Both subordinate the individual, in fact, to State or party, and to the new ideology they establish, and whose orthodoxy they try to impose.

Some Differences

There are fundamental differences, however, between their ultimate goals. Totalitarian controls in communism are supposed to be temporary—they represent a historical phase before individual freedoms return. The "dictatorship of the proletariat" only paves the way to the disappearance of the State; the socialization of the means of production destroys the class structure of the society and makes the use of force unnecessary; production is not geared to profit but to need. A true communist system will become not only increasingly egalitarian but also more open and free. Finally, nations and national wars will give place to a fraternal and egalitarian international community.

Right-wing totalitarian movements on the other hand, such as the regimes established in Italy and Germany, project an entirely different set of goals. Domination of the few over the many is to be permanent: the elite will continue to govern. Property is respected, even if under State control, and so are profits. The role of the State as a coercive agency is strengthened. Inequalities on the basis of a number of factors that include race are considered natural and are legitimized. Finally nationalism is consolidated, thanks to the exaltation of the superiority of one nation over others.

Overriding these distinctions, and perhaps the most important of all, is the fact that communism as an ideology, a movement and a regime emerges in the name of and for the workers, the poor and underprivileged, while right-wing totalitarian movements have usually been directed *against* the workers, despite early promises and appeals made to gain their support.

These differences appear to be impressive. However, there is no assurance that the professed goals of communism will ever be realized. There is no clear evidence that they are being implemented in any communist regime, and especially not in the Soviet Union. Stalinism represented, as we shall see, a political movement that remained very remote from the professed doctrinal goals of communism. There is also no indication that communist regimes are immune either to war or nationalism. In fact, the appeal to nationalist myths, past or newly fabricated, in an effort to integrate the people, characterizes communist movements and regimes, just as it does right-wing totalitarian ones. Conflict seems to be very much in evidence today, pitting some communist regimes against each other while the prospect of expansion or domination of others is ever-present. The Chinese communists, for instance, are accusing the Soviet Union of a "hegemonic" foreign policy.

Thus until there is a clear indication that the professed ideological goals of left-wing totalitarian regimes are beginning to be implemented, we seem to be dealing with a similar *political* phenomenon in our discussion of the extreme right and left.

Communism
and Marxism

Marx was a genius; we others were at best talented. Without him the theory would not be by far what it is today. It, therefore, rightly bears his name.

FRIEDRICH ENGELS Selected Works (vol. 2)

Communism is, literally, the economic and social system whereby all the means of production are concentrated in the hands of the community or the State, and in which the production and allocation of goods and services is decided upon by the community and the State. Generally, however, communism has meant much more. It has been "an ideal, a political movement, a method of analysis and a way of life."[1] As an ideal it promises an egalitarian society with production geared to need—a society in which the dream of abundance will be realized. As a political movement it means the organization of men and women striving to attain freedom; as a method of analysis it sets forth propositions which explain the past and point to the future development of our societies; finally, as a way of life it portrays a new type of citizen for whom the communitarian and social attributes of human nature will gain ascendancy over egotism and private interest.

Whichever one of these ends we have in mind, and usually all of them are present, communism has been one of the most powerful myths

1. Alfred Meyer *Marxism*, p. 1.

and ideologies in history. It takes the form of a moral imperative—how to create a collective and social ethic that will override self-interest and do away with the demons of profit and private property which are seen as the cause of subjugation of the many to the few.

Ever since antiquity, the theme of the *moral* superiority of communal ownership, in contrast to private property, interest and individualistic aspirations, has been kept alive, with many variations and qualifications. It is defended in Plato's *Republic,* where no private property is allowed the rulers, the Guardians, in order that they can give their full attention to communitarian values and govern in the interest of the whole. The myth of communism appears and reappears in many religious writings in which property is viewed as the result of "man's fall". It is part of secular law, not existing through "divine" or "natural" law. The theme reemerges with particular force in the writings of many utopian socialists in the decades after the French Revolution, and well into the nineteenth century. After the Industrial Revolution, the dream of favoring collective ownership and eliminating all income inequalities and poverty has been particularly potent.

Not until the middle of the nineteenth century, however, did the ideal become transformed into a political movement; and not until the end of the century did the ideology take on flesh and blood with the formation of political parties. In 1920 communism gained ascendancy in one country, the Soviet Union, and spread thereafter with renewed vigor all over Europe. By World War Two the ideology had crystallized firmly into the Soviet political system; and after the war it had established itself in other countries—in Eastern Europe and China, with noticeable spillovers elsewhere. But at about the same time, under the impact of a number of forces, communism began to splinter into various sects (national or ideological) to such an extent that today a discussion of the movement has to specify *what kind* of communism we are talking about. Even more, the early fraternal cooperation among communist states has given place to rivalries.

Communism plays today two quite separate roles. In a number of countries it sustains a political system, being the official or, as we called it, the *status quo* ideology. This is clearly the case in the Soviet Union, Eastern Europe and some of the Balkan countries. In Asia, such countries as Republican China, North Korea, Laos, Vietnam and Cambodia have communist regimes. In parts of Africa and Arabia, such as Angola, Ethiopia, Mozambique and South Yemen, communism has gained a foothold. Even in the North American sphere of influence, there is, despite the vigilance of the United States, one fully established communist regime, Cuba. Today at least 30 percent of all peoples of the world live under communist regimes and the communist ideology.

In virtually all other countries communist ideologies and movements play *a revolutionary role,* seeking political power and domination through various means. There are powerful communist parties in France and Italy; moderately strong ones in Portugal, Spain and Greece and throughout the rest of Europe.

Almost a century and a half ago, Marx wrote in the opening sentence of *The Communist Manifesto* (1848), which transformed communism from only a theory into a strong political movement, that "a specter" haunted Europe—"the specter of communism." Today it is a reality. Communism, either in the form of established political regimes or as a powerful political revolutionary movement, inspires, mobilizes and organizes for political action a greater number of people than any other political ideology. But what kind of communism is it?

As with other ideologies, communism can be viewed in two different ways. Firstly, as a body of theory and philosophy. This requires us to examine and analyze it with one question in mind: how valid is its theory and underlying philosophic assumptions? Secondly, as a political ideology and movement. This requires us to examine the way in which its basic philosophic and theoretical propositions have been translated into an action-oriented movement (i.e., an ideology). While the first level of analysis is important, we shall emphasize communism here as a political ideology, a movement for political action, and stress some of its contemporary characteristics.

The Legacy of Marx

It was Karl Marx and his associate Friedrich Engels who provided us, not only through their writings but also with their political activities, with the foundations of contemporary communism. Of the two, Marx was the dominant intellectual figure. He published major theoretical works on economics and philosophy and produced a series of pamphlets on various aspects of political tactics. After his death in 1883, Engels synthesized, some might say simplified, some of his ideas. When we speak of Marxism, however, we are referring to the combined work of Marx and Engels.

Marx and Engels provide us with a comprehensive philosophy of economic, social and political life, which includes the rejection of capitalist society; the dynamics of a communist revolution; and the promise of a new society.

The Sources That Inspired Marx

Four sources combined to produce the overall synthesis that constitutes Marxism. They are:

1. Hegel's philosophy, especially his philosophy of history.
2. The works of the British economists, notably Ricardo, Adam Smith, Malthus, and others.
3. The French utopian socialists, even though they were criticized sharply by Marx and Engels.

4. The social and economic reality of the mid-nineteenth century, particularly in England.

The first of these gave Marx a dynamic and evolutionary theory of history based on conflict; the second provided him with a new objective analysis of economic phenomena in which all economic factors were viewed in abstract terms as commodities or variables relating to each other on the basis of demonstrable and quantifiable laws; the third provided hints on the construction of the future society.

As for the reality of British industrial society in the middle of the nineteenth century, it had a profound impact on both Marx and Engels. Working conditions were dismal, hours of work long, children and women were employed at starvation wages for twelve and fourteen and sometimes sixteen hours a day, living conditions were abominable and life-expectancy low. The miseries of the workers contrasted sharply with the well-being of those who had land, property and money (i.e., capital), and could employ others. Conditions like these provoked not only moral indignation, but also widespread protest. Workers rebelled and wrecked the new machines for fear they would deprive them of work; regimentation in the factory under the new industrial order was deeply resented; workers attempted to use their numbers against the employers, who in turn made use of the instruments of coercion available to them.

But this movement of protest against the early conditions of industrialization and capitalism was unorganized and diffuse. Marx and Engels provided a theory that gave an order and a direction to it.

The Rejection of Capitalism

For Marx, the rejection of capitalism is *not* based on moral or humanitarian considerations. It derives from what he considered to be the empirical reality of the capitalistic economy. It obeys certain laws. Understanding them and studying them leads to the unavoidable conclusion that capitalism is doomed. Marx's anatomy of capitalism is also its autopsy!

The key to the understanding of capitalism and also that of its inevitable demise is the notion of value, surplus value and profit. The student can easily follow the Marxist critique of the capitalistic economy by following Marx's own steps:

1. Only labor creates value.
2. Machines, land and all other factors of production create no new value. They pass on to the product a value equivalent to the portion of their value used as they depreciate during the process of production.
3. The capitalist (the entrepreneur) pays the worker only a subsistence wage.

KARL MARX (1818–1883)

HISTORICAL PICTURES SERVICE, INC., CHICAGO

Born in Germany, where he studied law, philosophy and history, Marx and his family settled in London when he was thirty years old. He began there a life-long cooperation with Engels to develop a communist ideology and to translate it into political action. In 1848 they produced *The Communist Manifesto,* urging the workers to rise and take over the means of production from the exploiting capitalist class. In 1864 he founded the First International, whose purpose was to unite the workers everywhere in a revolutionary struggle. A prodigious worker, a committed man, and also one of the most learned and creative minds of the nineteenth century, Marx, like Freud half a century later, suggested a new way of looking at social life and history. According to it, material and economic conditions are responsible for the shaping of our values, morality, attitudes and political institutions. Marx singled out property relations to be the key element and the exploitation of "have-nots" by the "haves" to be at the heart of liberal capitalism. It was at the same time the reason for a working-class revolution, and the vindication of communism. He wrote voluminously, but his major work is the analysis of the capitalistic economy in *Capital,* the first volume of which was published in 1867 and the second and third posthumously, by Engels, in 1885 and 1894.

4. The worker produces a value that is twice as much (generally speaking) as what he or she gets in wages.

5. The difference between what the capitalist pays the worker and what the worker produces is the *surplus value,* pocketed by the capitalist.

6. All profits derive from the surplus value, though the actual profit does not correspond to the amount of surplus value extracted by a given capitalist.

7. In the market there is a fierce competition among capitalists. Each tries to sell more; a large volume of goods sold, even at lower prices, will bring added income.

8. This incites the capitalist to modernize and mass-produce; to introduce better machines to increase the productivity of labor.

9. A modern firm manages with fewer workers to produce and, hence, sell more. So more and more workers are laid off.

10. Thus the modern firm can reduce prices by lowering its profit *per unit.*

11. Many firms that fail to modernize are gradually driven out of business. They employ more workers and they pay out more in wages, and thus cannot compete with the lower prices the modernized firms set.

12. As a result many firms have to close down. Capital becomes increasingly concentrated into fewer and fewer hands and in larger and more modern firms, in which more machinery and modern technology is introduced.

13. Capitalism reaches a point where a small number of highly modernized large firms can produce goods efficiently and cheaply. However, with a great number of people out of work there are not enough buyers for the products, so firms can no longer make a profit. Production becomes restricted.

14. Profit and private property, the great incentives of the Industrial Revolution, now become obstacles to the plentiful production of goods.

15. The legal forms of capitalism (private profit and private property) come into conflict with the means of production (efficiency, high productivity and potential abundance).

This is the Marxist scheme in a nutshell. Some explanations must be added.

The heart of capitalism and capitalist production is to be found in private property and profit. Capitalism emerged when landed property began to give place to capital and to the manufacturing of goods in the factory. The purpose of production is profit—that is, how the capitalist can get from the market a value for the product that is higher than all he spent to produce it, including the use of land, the cost of machines as they are amortized over the years, and, of course, wages. The difference between what the entrepreneurs spend to produce and what they receive for the product is *the profit,* one of the most dynamic incentives for capitalist production and growth.

Marx develops an ingenious theory to explain profit. It is *the theory of surplus value.* The worker is paid wages, which are determined by the market through the law of supply and demand. The daily wage corresponds to the price of goods the worker and his family need and consume in one day. During the same day, however, the worker has produced (since only labor can produce value) goods that have a much higher value. The difference between value produced (owned and sold by the entrepreneur) and what is paid out in wages is *the surplus value.* Marx contends that generally wages tend to correspond to not more than half of the value the worker produces. So, the other half goes to the entrepreneur—to the capitalist.

This is Marx's argument. There are, of course, qualifications. For instance, the increased growth of mechanization in the plant (what today we call technological advances) gives to some capitalists and firms the possibility of producing more with very few· workers. Take automation, for instance, and computers. The firms that make technological advances and invest in machines make the highest profit. Where does it come from? Marx answers by making a distinction between what he calls *constant capital* (technology, machines, etc.) and *variable capital* (workers employed). Since only workers produce value, the greater their number the greater their surplus value and hence the profit.

Yet the truth seems to be precisely the other way around. The more modern the firm, the more advanced its machines and technology, the fewer the workers, the higher the profit. The reason for this apparent contradiction is quite simple: competition among industrialists in the market is ferocious. The one who manages to improve the productivity of the worker through the use of machines, increasing the units the worker can produce every hour, manages to produce in the same given period of time twice as many goods as his competitors and is therefore able to sell the same product at a lower price. By selling twice as much, he will thus take in more than his competitors, even if his profit *per unit* is smaller. Industrialists are thus able to derive a profit from the surplus value their competitors make, compete with them successfully and, by selling cheaper, drive them out of the market. The margin of profit begins to fall on each item but as productivity goes up the fall is compensated by the volume of sales.

The Law of Capitalist Accumulation

The distinction between *constant capital* and *variable capital,* and the fact that the technologically advanced firms with the newest machines which increase the productivity of the worker make profit at the expense of the backward ones who rely upon a higher percentage of variable capital (workers), accounts for the trend towards technology and expansion. Many firms go bankrupt but the survivors accumulate in their hands an ever greater part of the capital. Fewer and fewer capitalists own the means of production, while more and more small firms disappear. The whole social structure becomes lopsided, with a tiny minority controlling production for the purpose of making profit, while the vast majority of the people have nothing but their labor to sell, exactly when it becomes less needed!

However, the capitalists who survive become the victims of their success. Having established firm control over the means of production the capitalist class now finds it difficult to find enough buyers for their products. This is implicit in the law of capitalist accumulation; or rather, it is the other side of the coin of the same law—the law of pauperization.

The Law of Pauperization

More and more people are dispossessed of the means to produce. More and more fall into the category of proletariat. Thus as the firms develop more sophisticated machinery, a greater number of people find themselves living in a state of misery. Many cannot find work. Many become "marginals" moving from one place to another, without a role, without skills, in a state of constant deprivation and humiliation. They are the *lumpenproletariat*—the army of the unemployed and also unemployable, people from the countryside or recently demoted from the middle or low middle classes. They become a permanent fixture of capitalist societies.

Unemployment, however, affects also qualified, skilled and semi-skilled workers. It becomes permanent. Capitalism therefore inevitably reaches a point at which it cannot utilize all resources and satisfy all needs, even basic ones. In fact a point comes when a given percentage of the population may not be part of the economic system—they do not work in it and they cannot buy and enjoy what it produces. Millions of human beings become "surplus labor," unwanted and useless.

To conclude: the profit motive—a driving and dynamic motive in the early stages of capitalism—becomes a drag and an impediment in its most advanced stage. It has pushed the capitalists to modernize and to accumulate capital and industrial equipment; it has indeed made production easier and much more efficient; *objectively speaking* it has made it possible for human beings in a society to supply all their wants and more. Capitalism thus achieves a most remarkable breakthrough by creating all the material conditions for the good life. Marx is full of praise for the bourgeoisie and for capitalism when he views its historical role:

> The bourgeoisie . . . has been the first to show what man's activity can bring about. It has accomplished wonders far surpassing the Egyptian pyramids, Roman aqueducts, the Gothic

FRIEDRICH ENGELS (1820–1895)

HISTORICAL PICTURES SERVICE, INC., CHICAGO

Karl Marx's companion, associate and collaborator. Born in Germany, he lived most of his life in England. He collaborated with Marx on many publications including *The Communist Manifesto,* and edited the second and third volumes of *Capital* after Marx's death. While he played an important role in the formulation of the communist doctrine, Engels himself admitted that the real theoretical inspiration came from Marx. Engels wrote *The Origins of the Family; The Condition of the Working Class in England in 1844; Socialism: Utopian and Scientific; Anti-Dühring* and a number of other less important essays. He took part in the founding of the First International in 1864 and the Second International in 1889.

cathedrals; it has conducted expeditions that put in the shade all former Exoduses and crusades. . . .

The bourgeoisie has through its exploitation of the world-market given a cosmopolitan character to production and consumption in every country. In place of the old wants, satisfied by the productions of the country, we find new wants, requiring for their satisfaction the products of distant lands and climes. In place of the old local and national seclusion and self-sufficiency, we have intercourse in every direction, universal interdependence of nations. And as in material, so also in intellectual production. The intellectual creations of individual nations become common property. National onesidedness and narrow-mindedness become more and more impossible, and from the numerous national and local literatures there arises a world-literature.

The bourgeoisie, by the rapid improvement of all instruments of production, by the immensely facilitated means of communication, draws all, even the most barbarian, nations into civilization. . . .

The bourgeoisie has created enormous cities, has greatly increased the urban population as compared with the rural, and has thus rescued a considerable part of the population from the idiocy of rural life. . . .[2]

Yet it is precisely at this point that the capitalistic economy can no longer provide for profits. By creating a chronic state of unemployment, by pressing heavily upon the middle class, the independent artisans, the small manufacturers and the small farmers, and by reducing them gradually to the ranks of the poor and the dispossessed, many have been deprived of the means to buy things and meet their needs. Demand goes down and with it comes lower profit. To keep the rate of profit the capitalist now is forced to produce less, to control prices, to develop monopolies in order to avoid competition and cartels to keep prices up. Whereas profit was a positive incentive to industrial growth and production, now it becomes a shackle. This is the point when capitalism has outlived its purpose—it can produce plenty but there is no incentive to do so. It is at this point that Marx pronounces its death sentence!

The student will note that thus far there has not been a single note of moral approbation or disapprobation. Marx gives us a "scientific" account, i.e. a description of what he sees happening, a description

2. In *The Communist Manifesto*. See Tucker (ed.) *The Marx-Engels Reader*, pp. 469–500.

which fits his basic laws of the capitalist economy. As capitalist production and the capitalist economy develop they begin to show contradictions that *inevitably*, that is to say for reasons inherent in the
system itself, will bring it down. The major contradiction which ultimately unfolds itself is the discrepancy between the productive capacities that the system has developed and the forms of production
(i.e. private property and profit). Capitalism will collapse because private property and profit become *dysfunctional*—they are no longer
adequate incentives for production.

The analysis, however, of the laws accounting for the demise of
capitalism do not amount to a "rejection" of capitalism. People must
become aware of something, dissatisfied with something and move
actively against something in order for there to be a rejection. Rejection
is a subjective phenomenon associated with a collective desire and
consciousness and with concerted action. *This is the revolutionary
side of Marxism.*

The Dynamics of the Communist Revolution

In contrast to his economic analysis, in which Marx set up theories and
hypotheses and sought their confirmation in the empirical world of the
capitalist economy, his whole notion of a revolution is the culminating
point of philosophic speculation, and is not amenable to the same rules
of scientific inquiry. It includes: (a) a philosophy of history, (b) a theory
of class struggles, (c) a theory of the State, (d) the historical act of
"revolution" and (e) the utopian world to follow. We shall discuss each
of them.

A Philosophy of History

History has been defined as a set of tricks that the living play upon the
dead. For Marx, there are no such tricks! For him, the living constantly
interact with the dead. Men and women are both the product of history,
bound by the conditions it creates, and also the makers of history in
reacting to those conditions and changing them. But this is only within
limits that history itself allows.

We can look at history in evolutionary terms—gradual changes
occur not only in our material world but also in human knowledge and
the way we think. The individual gets better and better control of his
environment. In this sense there is progress. Another method is to look
at history without any notion of direction at all—just as a matter of
chance. We can conquer war and misery but they can defeat us too!
The third view is that we move in circles, with a period of great achievement, material well-being and knowledge alternating with periods of
decay and ignorance. Our task in this case is like that of Sisyphus

(cursed by the gods to carry a rock to the top of the mountain and to tumble down with it the moment he reached the peak) but with the destiny of humankind, so to speak, on our backs. We rise and then crash down into the ravine, only to start again and again and again. This is the cyclical theory.

All these theories are interesting but none of them answers the question of why at all there is "history," why there is change and movement. Why do we change our ways? Why do we find out about germs? Why did we move from the Stone Age? Why did we invent a new language called mathematics and find out about regularities in the universe which surrounds us? Is it out of "love"? Is it because human beings are "rational"? Is it the divine will that pushes us? Marx answers this crucial question by using the ideas of the German philosopher G.W.F. Hegel (1770–1831) to develop a theory of history and change.

According to Hegel,[3] history moves through conflict—a conflict of ideas. He believes that there is something like a divine will, an Absolute, destined to finally unfold itself fully in the universe. But the process of unfolding is not evolutionary. It takes place through struggle between opposing ideas. The idea of beauty has opposing it the idea of ugliness, the idea of truth that of falsehood, the idea of liberty that of slavery, etc. Throughout history and its various stages there is a constant and Homeric battle between opposing ideas, called by Hegel *dialectical idealism*. It goes something like this: each phase in history corresponds to the manifestation of certain ideas or an idea. It is called the *thesis*. It includes, however, its opposite, its *antithesis*. Thesis and Antithesis struggle with each other until the antithesis manages to devour the thesis or to combine it in one form or another. This combination is called a *synthesis*, representing a new stage in history. Every synthesis in turn becomes a thesis that suggests automatically its antithesis which comes into conflict with it to lead to a new synthesis and so forth. . . . A point comes *when history will have exhausted itself—the best possible synthesis will have occurred*. God or the Spirit will have fully unfolded themselves in the universe!

This sounds abstruse, and it is. But the important thing to retain is that Hegel makes conflict the mother, father and the midwife of history. He is not an evolutionary, he does not believe in cyclical movements, he traces all change to conflict between ideas.

Marx maintains the dialectic (the notion of conflicting opposites); he maintains the whole scheme of historical movement in terms of thesis-antithesis-synthesis. However, he is clearly not an idealist. Writing in his preface to *Capital*, Marx tells us himself how he changed the very foundations of Hegel's philosophy of history while maintaining the basic structure.

---

3. Hegel. *The Philosophy of History*, N.Y., The Colonial Press, 1900.

My dialectic method is not only different from the Hegelian, but its direct opposite. To Hegel, the life-process of the brain, i.e. the process of thinking, which under the name of "the Idea," he even transforms into an independent subject, is the demiurgos (creator) of the real world, and the real world is only the external, phenomenal form of "the idea." With me on the contrary the idea is nothing else than the material world reflected by the human mind, and translated into forms of thought . . . With Hegel (the dialectic) . . . is standing on its head. It must be turned rightside up again. . . .[4]

In other words, Marx found in the material world of our senses and our working conditions the source of ideas and the source of conflict and change and not the other way around, as Hegel had done.

Dialectical Materialism

This is what, in contrast to "dialectical idealism," has become known as *dialectical materialism*. The stages of historical development, the specific contents of a thesis, an antithesis and a synthesis are not to be found in the not-so-easily observable world of ideas but in the empirical world—in our society. It is a momentous shift. It makes out of Marx a social scientist, an empiricist, one concerned with observable phenomena. The Hegelian abstraction becomes now a theory leading to hypotheses about human and social life that can be observed and tested.

Types of Conflict

What is the conflict that generates movement and change and accounts for history? There are two types of conflict according to Marx, the first between the human being as a social being (society) and the environment (the outside world). The second is between human social groups.

MAN AGAINST NATURE

Every social group, from the primitive tribe on, attempts to carve out of its environment, out of nature, as much as it can in order to live, and by so doing to overcome necessity. It is a basic struggle and human beings are affected deeply by it—their thoughts, their social institutions, their law and values are influenced by this interaction between themselves and the world in which they find themselves. They depend in part on it; they are its creatures and even its slaves. Yet they try to overcome it and survive in it; they try to change it and emancipate themselves from its mastery. Real freedom will come when they have

4. Marx. Preface to *Capital*.

fully conquered it. Marx believes that one day they will be able to do it. The whole of humanity will be free. It will conquer nature and necessity.

CLASS CONFLICT

The second conflict is that among individuals and groups in one and the same society. It is not an indiscriminate conflict haphazardly pitting individual against individual. It is highly structured. The conflict is between classes: it is a *class struggle*.

But what is a class? The word has been used to define nobility, riches, education, intellect and other characteristics of certain groups. Marx, however, gives a very precise definition to the term. *A class is defined in terms of the relationship individuals have to the means of production.* Very simply, there are two classes, consisting of those who own property and those who do not. This has been the reality of social life and the basic source of conflict and change. Class struggle is the motor force of dialectic materialism.

Property, however, has taken many forms. To each form corresponds a different "class." For each class there has been an "antithesis" corresponding to the emerging new class. The antithesis devours the thesis, borrowing from it what was most useful to its interests and purpose and discarding what was useless. In every case it is conflict— a revolution—that brings the antithesis—the emerging class—to power.

Each historical phase corresponded to new and different forms of private property. Landed property was the characteristic of the feudal period and the landed aristocracy. But within it money and gold and commerce made their appearance. Artisans, small manufacturers and merchants emerged and with them commercial capital and finally manufacturing and industry. They were destined to become a new class, an antithesis, *the bourgeoisie.* The French Revolution of 1789 epitomized, in a way, the end of the landed aristocracy and the coming of the middle class to power, emphasizing new types of property and new productive forces. But the moment the capitalists, and the various groups allied to them, emerged, the antithesis was already present. It was *the working class*, a small cloud on the blue horizon of bourgeois capitalism. With no property of its own, with nothing to sell but its labor, subject to the laws of capitalistic economy, the cloud of working class power grows bigger and bigger. The class struggle is on, presaging the storm and the inevitable revolutionary conflict between the workers and the bourgeoisie.

Infrastructure and Superstructure

In the constant interaction between society and environment, but also in the constant class struggle that corresponds to various historical stages, human beings develop particular forms of property but also change them. For each phase there is a particular set of ideas and norms, and these correspond to and are fashioned by the interests of the property-owning class. They rationalize and legitimize (i.e., make acceptable to all) the dominance of the ruling and property-owning class. This theory, which traces and attributes moral ideas and norms directly or indirectly to economic factors, is called *economic determinism*: it states that the way and place we live and work fashion our ideas about the world. Capitalists have a set of ideas about society and the world which correspond to their interests and to their dominance. The workers begin to develop theirs to express their needs and interests.

In the Marxist vocabulary the totality of factors that determine a person's relations to private property and work constitute the *infrastructure*: they are the material and objective social conditions. On the other hand, the way we look upon society—the ideas we have about it, in a word our ideology—is the *superstructure*. This includes religion, law, education, literature, even the State. This ideology is fashioned by the dominant class, the one that owns property, and its view of society is forced upon all (including the workers) until a moment comes when other groups begin to question it.

Objective and Subjective Conditions

Each phase of the class struggle and each form of property relations differs in content from the preceding one. Bourgeois capitalism revolutionalized the *objective economic conditions* of production. Division of labor, capital accumulation, technological progress, all these profit-inspired activities changed the world in the late eighteenth century and throughout the nineteenth. Marx, as we have seen, conceded this. But by also creating a vast proletarian army, by divesting the lower classes of property, and by concentrating capital in a small number of firms, individuals and banks, it made it easier for society to replace the capitalist class. A mass of people begin to demand the end of capitalist rule and are ready to replace it. These are the *subjective conditions*. Thus capitalism, at one and the same time, creates the conditions for greater productive effort, and lays the groundwork for expropriation of it by the community at large. A point comes when objective conditions (technology, concentration of capital, the capability of the economy to provide abundance) coincide with the subjective conditions, (i.e., the will and the consciousness of the workers to take over the industrial apparatus, created by the capitalist, and use it for the whole community and provide for abundance). When subjective and objective conditions converge, it is the moment of revolution.

Note this carefully. *The revolution is not, according to Marx, a matter of will, indignation or even leadership.* Conditions, both objective and subjective, must be ripe. The workers must gain full consciousness that they are a class and that they must demand the change in the existing property relations. Only then can revolution under the appropriate leadership be envisaged.

The Theory of the State and Revolution

The State is viewed by Marx as part of the "superstructure." It is used to keep the majority of the people, who do not own the means of production, under the control of the small minority who do. While many (including Hegel) see in the State the embodiment of noble purposes—rationality, an agency for social justice and protection, the equitable distribution of goods, an impartial observer keeping and adminstering the rules and laws equitably—Marx sees in it the instrument of the capitalist class. It is a repressive agency.

It is not alone in this, for the whole superstructure, as we have noted, is fashioned by the ruling class. Religion inculcates observance of bourgeois values and respect for property; the family and the laws of inheritance perpetuate the rule of property; the educational system socializes everybody to respect the capitalistic ethic and, most important, private property; art and literature extol the same virtues. No matter where they turn the workers and their children will confront the same values and principles and many of them will be brainwashed into accepting them. The peculiar characteristic of the State, however, is that it is the only part of the superstructure that can use force. Hence it is necessary to use force against it.

The Revolution

Revolution, therefore, is necessary and unavoidable. "But what about democracy?" the student asks. "What about free and equal voting, freedom of association and of trade unions, of political parties and even of socialist parties?"

The answer is complex. Firstly, when Marx wrote, trade-unions were only beginning to develop; secondly, there were no socialist parties or they were just making their appearance; thirdly, political parties almost everywhere were just about to become national parties with national organizations and members; fourthly, outside the United States, universal suffrage did not exist or could not be freely exercised. Most important of all, however, Marx did not really believe that a capitalist system and the capitalist State would ever allow socialist parties to gain ascendancy, nor did he believe that such parties would ever be allowed to directly challenge private property nor to control production and the allocation of goods and services. If they did the State would use force against them.

It is true that at times Marx wavered, and Engels even more so. On occasions they both conceded that it was possible for well-established democracies, in which the parliamentary system and universal franchise had gained deep roots—*where in other words the superstructure was genuinely democratic*—to radically transform property relations and socialize the means of production. This might happen, but it was very unlikely: the use of force against socialists would be virtually inevitable everywhere. The workers had to gain freedom from their oppressors, therefore, by force. They had to make a revolution when conditions were ripe, when and where there was a convergence of subjective and objective factors in the industrialized countries.

The Communist Society

Marx gives us only a sketchy account of the communist society to come. In fact, he provides us with what amounts to a two-stage scheme. The first corresponds to the transitional stage towards socialism, and the second is the ultimate one, the utopian level of communism.

In the first, the revolution is followed by the "dictatorship of the proletariat." The workers take over the State and all the instruments of coercion that it disposed and use them against the capitalist class. "The development towards communism," he writes, "proceeds through the dictatorship of the proletariat; it cannot do otherwise, for the re-sistance of the capitalist exploiters cannot be broken by anyone else or in any other way."[5] In contrast to all other dictatorships, however, this is one by the majority against the minority. It is necessary, he claims, in order to avert a counter-revolution. This is a dictatorship, therefore, that corresponds to, and gradually becomes, a democracy of the people and the workers. The few—the capitalists—are excluded and suppressed by force.

What are the measures to be taken during this stage? Marx advo-cates abolition of the ownership of land, heavy progressive income tax, abolition of all rights of inheritance, centralization of credit and all means of transport, extensive socialization of factories and all means of production, equal obligation of all to work, public education, etc. They are to pave the way for the complete abolition of property and to the full and comprehensive socialization of the means of production.

As the State is now being used by the workers against the capi-talists, its substance changes. It becomes the instrument of the many against the few. As the means of production become socialized classes disappear, since there can be no classes without property. Without classes there is no need for coercion. *The dictatorship paves the way towards its own disappearance and to the establishment of a classless and stateless society.* The State simply "withers away."

The second phase corresponds to communism. The economy, both production and distribution, is now in the hands of the community. Nobody can exploit anybody; "bourgeois rights" (individual rights) give their place to "common rights." The final and ultimate phase is

5. In *The Communist Manifesto.*

reached with the collectivization of all the means of production, with the harnessing of production to common purposes, with the transformation of the State from a coercive power to a purely administrative one. The objective conditions of production bequeathed to the new society from capitalism can now be used to make the slogan "From each according to his ability to each according to his needs" possible.

This is the apocalyptic or utopian element. And although Marx did not go to the lengths some earlier utopian socialists did, he shared their general optimism and was influenced by it. Crime would disappear, the span of life would increase, brotherhood and cooperation would inculcate a new morality, scientific progress would grow by leaps and bounds. Above all, with socialism spreading around the world, the greatest blight of humankind, war, and its twin brother, nationalism, would have no place. International brotherhood would follow. Engels waxes enthusiastic over the prospects and goes so far as to declare that with the socialist revolution humanity will complete its "prehistoric" stage and enter for the first time into what might be called its own history. Until the revolution, he claims, society submits to outside forces, while the majority of humans within a society submit to a ruling class. After the revolution a united classless society will be able for the first time to decide which way to go and what to do with its resources and capabilities. For the first time we shall make our own history! It is a "leap from slavery into freedom; from darkness into light," he announced.

The skeptics were now for the first time confronted with the anatomy of capitalism, a theory of history, a theory of revolution, a theory of the State—all of them pointing in the same direction, communist society. With it of course the laws developed by Marx would come to an end, for individuals and society would be free to make their own laws and shape their own future.

The Diffusion of Marxism: Success and Failure

Marxism represented the synthesis of many socialist writers and of movements that were active before the body of Marx's thought became known and disseminated. The first volume of *Capital*, incorporating Marx's analysis of capitalism, was completed in 1867; it was translated from German into French and English by 1886. Most of his other works, especially the many political pamphlets, including of course *The Communist Manifesto* of 1848, were translated, at least in French and English, almost as soon as they came out. They all were read, by socialists, anarchists, utopians, and the many other radical groups of the time. The work of Marx helped shape ideas, create a firm ideological orientation, and ultimately brought together various sects and factions into well-organized large socialist movements and parties. It became an ideology.

In 1864 the International Working Men's Association (the First International) was founded by representatives of English, French, Italian and German labor organizations. Marx wrote the basic guidelines for the International, including among others the need for a federation of all workers of various nations, the destruction of class domination and the emancipation of the working class. With its headquarters in London, the First International never attained a large membership, and most of its efforts were not so much devoted to the organization of the workers but to fighting a strong anarchist faction. It held a few congresses and gradually disappeared.

The spread of Marxism took place after his death in 1883, with the development and consolidation of socialist parties almost everywhere in Europe, but also in the United States. These were dedicated to the expropriation of the capitalist class, to class struggle and to internationalism. The German Social Democratic Party became the dominant socialist party of Europe, receiving in the 1912 elections 4,250,000 votes—almost 35 percent of the total. In France, after many internal struggles a Socialist Party was founded in 1904 and in the election of 1914, on the eve of World War One, received over one million votes. By 1904 the British Labour Party had been established—perhaps the only socialist party of the world, however, that did not owe much directly to Marx. It made appreciable electoral gains. In Russia a clandestine Social Democratic Party was founded in 1898. The Socialist Party of America was founded in 1901. It gained a million votes in the presidential election of 1920—while its leader, Eugene Debs, was in the penitentiary for speaking against the war.

Many of these socialist parties, and others from Italy, Belgium, Holland, etc., were represented at the founding of the Second International in Paris in 1889, called to organize all workers against anarchism, to prepare them to combat the dangers of war that threatened Europe at the time, to commit them to class struggle and, of course, to socialism and internationalism. "If war threatens to break out," the leadership of the Second International declared, ". . . the working classes pledge themselves . . . to use their utmost exertions to prevent the outbreak of war by using the means which seem most effective to them. . . ." If, however, war should break out they pledged themselves "to work for its speedy termination, and to exploit with all their strength the economic and political crisis induced by the war to arouse the people and thereby hasten the abolition of the class domination of capitalism."[6]

While socialist movements and parties were spreading all over the

6. Quoted in Max Beer. *The General History of Socialism and Socialist Struggles,*
Vol. 2. N.Y., Russell and Russell, 1957, pp. 157–58.

world so was trade-unionism. After the end of the nineteenth century, the freedom of workers to establish trade-unions, to bargain collectively, and in some instances to strike, had become assured in most of the western democracies. Millions of workers in the advanced capitalistic countries, notably Germany, France and England, became union members and engaged, legally or illegally, in strikes. Some theorists saw in the strike the special weapon of the working class—the ability to undermine the capitalist order. But others used it simply to extract local benefits from the employers. Still others saw in the trade-union movement a prerequisite for the development of working class consciousness. One Marxist leader, however (Lenin), was fearful that trade-unionism might divert the workers from revolution and limit them only to the search for immediate benefits within the capitalistic order.

Revisionism and Nationalism

The year of crisis for Marxism was 1914, as it was for socialism and for the Second International. There were at least two separate crises: revisionism and nationalism.

We have already discussed revisionism in regards to evolutionary socialism. It had abandoned revolutionary tactics to become increasingly gradualistic and reformist, and it accepted the principles of democracy and representative government. By 1914 virtually all socialist parties had become revisionist and paid only lip-service to Marxist formulas and slogans.

Nationalism was a different, and perhaps even more serious, problem. Its tenacity, both before, during, and also after World War One, indicated that the *class* consciousness of the workers was not as strong as their *national* consciousness. Although according to Marx the workers of all the countries shared the same predicament and should have united against their common masters everywhere, the German, French, British, Austrian and all other workers and socialists in all countries supported their government (with very few exceptions) and fought against each other in the war. Workers' international solidarity remained a dream, and the Second International was broken.

Revisionism and nationalism, the former dealing directly with the validity of the Marxist theory and blueprint, the latter denying explicitly its internationalist aspirations, were of course only two forces that undermined and weakened Marxism. Criticism came from many other sources, from the left as well as the right. Anarchists already objected to the Marxist scientific scheme that subordinated revolution to specific conditions. They preferred to stress individual and revolutionary political will. But they also rejected the blueprint of the "dictatorship of the proletariat" and the imposition of socialism through State controls. Anarchists felt that the society envisioned by Marx provided little prospects for individual freedom and initiative, and that the communist regime would substitute one form of tyranny for another. Similarly many socialists, as we have seen, shied away from the advocacy of force. They believed that change through persuasion and education would in the long run prove to be far more lasting and creative than one undertaken by force.

Many other philosophic assumptions and conclusions of Marx were criticized. Economic determinism came under attack by philosophers, and also by the Church and the many strong religious organizations. Religious leaders argued that it reduced men and women to passive instruments whose fate and actions, ideas and beliefs, were undermined by the material conditions of life. The individual was deprived of his vaunted "freedom of will." A strong reaction among intellectual and educational leaders against dialectic materialism developed, often leading them to the other extreme of proclaiming the complete and unfettered freedom of individuals to choose and shape their own lives.

By 1914 therefore, Marxism as a philosophy and a revolutionary political ideology had become increasingly isolated. Socialist parties had accepted parliamentary democracy, negotiations and compromises with their capitalist "masters," as well as the reality of the nation-states within which they lived. The hard core of the Marxist doctrine had been abandoned. It seemed like a monumental defeat.

But one man had recognized the reasons for the failure, had reflected on them, and was determined to revive Marxism. This man was Lenin; and to his efforts, and the establishment of communism in Russia, we now turn.

Bibliography

Avineri, Shlomo. *The Social and Political Thought of Karl Marx*. New York: Cambridge U.P., 1968.

Bernstein, Eduard. *Evolutionary Socialism*. Trans. E.C. Harvey. New York: Schocken, 1961.

Bober, M. M. *Karl Marx's Interpretation of History*. New York: Norton, 1965.

Burns, Emile. *An Introduction to Marxism*. New York: International, 1966.

Drackhovitch, Milorad M. (ed.). *Marxism in the Modern World*. Stanford, Ca.: Stanford U.P., 1965.

Gregor, James. *A Survey of Marxism*. New York: Random House, 1965.

Lichtheim, George. *Marxism: An Historical and Critical Study*. 2nd ed. New York: Praeger, 1965.

Marx, Karl and Engels, Frederick. *Selected Works*. New York: International Publishers, 1968.

McLellan, David. *Karl Marx*. Baltimore: Penguin, 1976.

———. (ed.) *The Karl Marx Reader*. New York: Oxford, U.P., 1977.

Meyer, Alfred G. *Marxism: The Unity of Theory and Practice*. Ann Arbor: University of Michigan Press, 1963.

Miliband, Ralph. *Marxism and Politics*. New York: Oxford U.P., 1977.

Plamenatz, John. *German Marxism and Russian Communism*. New York: Longmans-Green, 1954.

Tucker, Robert C. (ed.) *The Marx-Engels Reader*. 2nd ed. New York: Norton, 1978.

———. *Philosophy and Myth in Karl Marx*. 2nd ed. New York: Cambridge U.P., 1972.

Wolfe, Bertram D. *Marxism: One Hundred Years in the Life of a Doctrine*. New York: Dial Press, 1965.

6

Soviet Communism

The organization of the Party takes the place of the Party itself; the Central Committee takes the place of the organization; and, finally, the dictator takes the place of the Central Committee   LEON TROTSKY Our Political Tasks

With Lenin, Marxist ideology and revolutionary tactics were given a new sharpness and urgency. Lenin was able to take the theoretical Marxist blueprint and adapt it not only to the revolutionary movement of Russia in the early part of the twentieth century, but also to the independence movements of the colonial world. The first successful revolution in the name of Marxism, the Bolshevik Revolution, was made under his leadership in Russia on November 7, 1917.

Stalin succeeded Lenin in 1924 and became in a true sense the architect of Soviet communism. He remained in power for almost thirty years until his death in 1953. Collectivization, economic planning, rapid industrialization, the expansion of Soviet power but also one-man authoritarian government are associated with his rule. Since Stalin's death the same blueprint has been retained by the Soviet leaders, while at the same time a number of communist movements have emerged that differ sharply from the Soviet model.

Leninism

Lenin accepted faithfully the body of Marxist thought and devoted a good part of his life to defending it against its many critics. He accepted the idea of dialectic materialism, endorsed and developed Marx's theory of the State and sharpened and refined Marx's theory of revolution, and especially revolutionary tactics.

His two most important contributions to communist thought can be found in two pamphlets—*What is to be Done?* (1903), and *Imperialism, the Highest Stage of Capitalism* (1917). In the first, Lenin developed a new theory for the organization of the proletariat through the Communist Party; in the second, he attempted to show that the highest stage (and last stage) of capitalism was inextricably associated with colonial wars among capitalist nations. In a third long essay, *The State and Revolution* (1918), he elaborated on such key concepts as the revolutionary takeover of power, the period of the dictatorship of the proletariat and the final stage of communism where the State was to disappear and material abundance become a reality. But his most critical contribution as the head of the Russian Bolshevik Party, was to make a revolution and to preside over its consolidation.

Both because of Lenin's theoretical contributions to the works of the founding fathers Marx and Engels, and also because of the political tactics he developed as a revolutionary, Lenin's name has been permanently attached to theirs. The new term of orthodox ideology became *Marxism-Leninism.*

Lenin's Revolutionary Doctrine

The greater part of Lenin's life was devoted to the development of a revolutionary doctrine. In *The State and Revolution,* he summarized the Marxist theses: the State is the product of the irreconcilability of class antagonisms and the agency of the capitalist class; liberal democracy is another name for capitalism, ensuring domination of the workers; law and the State are instruments for the domination of the ruling class against the working classes; and, of course, revolution and the triumph of the working class is both desirable and inevitable.

The revolutionary stages Lenin envisages are the following:

1. The armed uprising of the proletariat, under proper leadership.
2. The seizure of political control by the workers in the form of a temporary "dictatorship of the proletariat," against the remnants of the capitalist classes.

   Lenin's concept of dictatorship was as succinct as it was brutal. "The scientific concept of dictatorship (of the proletariat) means neither more nor less than unlimited power, resting directly on

LENIN (1870–1924)

Vladimir Ilyich Ulyanov ("Lenin" was originally a pseudonym, but became the better known name) spent his childhood—a happy one according to all accounts—in the province of Kazan. After receiving his law degree he was arrested for revolutionary activity and exiled to Siberia. In 1900 he was allowed to go abroad where, as a professed Marxist, he pursued his revolutionary activity with remarkable energy. He formulated, and imposed on his followers, a program for a highly centralized party consisting of trained revolutionaries.

The collapse of the Tsarist armies and the democratic revolution of February 1917 found Lenin in Switzerland. He managed to negotiate with the German government for a passage across the front line between the German and Russian armies; on the night of November 6–7, 1917, the Bolsheviks seized power and Lenin was made chairman of the new government. By 1918, Lenin had established what amounted to a dictatorship. He dissolved the Constituent Assembly after the Bolsheviks failed to get a majority in the elections, but his main attention was given to the war against the Tsarist loyalists. Not until 1920 did the Russian Civil War come to an end with the victory of the communist forces.

force, not limited by anything, not restricted by any law or any absolute rules. Nothing else but that."[1]

3. The socialization of the means of production and the abolition of private property.
4. Finally, the slow "withering away of the State" as an instrument of coercion and class oppression, and the emergence of a classless, stateless society.

The Communist Party

What does Lenin mean by a revolution of the working classes under *proper* leadership? Marx's position was that objective economic factors and the class consciousness of the masses would move in parallel. The maturing of capitalism would mean the maturing of the social (i.e., revolutionary) consciousness of the workers.

Lenin posits from the very beginning, however, the need for leadership and organization, and stresses the inability of the masses by themselves to develop a proper social consciousness. The working class—and particularly the Russian working class—could never develop revolutionary consciousness by itself. An elite, organized into a Communist Party, would have to educate the masses, infuse them with revolutionary spirit and inculcate in them class consciousness, leading them toward the revolution and, ultimately, communism. *Dialectic materialism is brushed aside here to be replaced by a theory of voluntarism.* The Communist Party is based on the will and dedication of Marxists. They are the revolutionaries. They can make the revolution irrespective of the prevailing social conditions.

A number of consequences, both on the theoretical and tactical level, follow these assumptions.

ELITISM

The party is to be composed of gifted individuals who understand Marxism and therefore understand the direction of history better than the rest of the people. The leaders of the party are particularly endowed with scientific knowledge and foresight that the common people lack. Leadership is likely to come not from the ranks of the working class but from "outside"—from middle-class intellectuals who are able to comprehend the totality of the society's interests and hence promote socialism. They are trained in Marxist dialectics and can discern the historical pattern leading to socialism. This party is the *vanguard* of the proletariat. It speaks and acts on behalf of the proletariat.

---

1. Quoted in Bertram Wolfe, "Leninism" in Milorad Drackhovitch (ed.). *Marxism in the Modern World.* Stanford, Ca.: Stanford U.P., p. 69.

The rank and file of the party is united with its leaders by bonds of allegiance and common action, but also obedience and discipline. They must be prepared for any kind of action, legal or illegal, at any time. "The one serious organizational principle for workers in our movement," Lenin wrote, "must be the strictest secrecy, strictest choice of members, training of professional revolutionaries. . . ."[2]

The party, Lenin asserts, has to be organized on the basis of *democratic centralism*, according to which:

1. All decisions are to be made in an open and free debate by the representative organ of the party, the congress.
2. Once a decision is thus made it is binding upon all. No factions are to be allowed within the party and any minority within the party is permitted neither to secede nor to air its grievances in public.
3. All officers of the party—secretaries, the central committee and other executive organs—are elected indirectly from lowest membership upwards.
4. All decisions and instructions of the party executive officials are binding upon all inferior organs and officers.

Thus, the party can be democratic if the principles of open debate and elections are followed; but it can also become authoritarian, and even autocratic, if emphasis is put on the right of the superior officers to command and the obligation of inferior officers to obey.

The organization of the Soviet Communist Party became, in fact, hierarchical. Orders for action flowed from top to bottom. Throughout his whole life Lenin was able, despite opposition, to hold the supreme decision-making power in his hands, and to control the nomination of local party leaders.

The party did not tolerate dissent, and under Lenin's leadership indulged in purges in the years after the revolution. He invented the notion "enemies of the people." It was during this same period that thousands of so-called wreckers, saboteurs, petit-bourgeois and many others were jailed, and "thieves" and "speculators" sentenced to death.

From Lenin's modeling of the party, it is obvious that he had no respect for democracy. In his view, representation, universal and secret franchise, political parties and periodical elections had no value in themselves. If suitable to the revolutionary struggle they ought to be defended, but if they proved to be obstacles to the proletarian revolutionary movement at one moment or another, they should be brushed aside without a moment's thought.

2. Ibid., p. 78.

The second congress of the Russian Social-Democratic Workers' Party was held in Brussels in 1903. Writing of it, Sir Isaiah Berlin says: "There occurred an event which marked the culmination of a process which has altered the history of the world . . . Lenin and his friends [insisted] upon the need of absolute authority by the revolutionary nucleus of the party." When this concept was questioned one of the founders of Russian Marxism took Lenin's side with the statement that the "revolution is the supreme law." "If the revolution demanded it . . . everything—democracy, liberty, the rights of the individual—must be sacrificed to it."[3] Accordingly, Lenin had no scruples at all in dissolving democratically elected bodies whenever the Bolsheviks were in a minority in them.

TRADE-UNIONISM

One might have thought that Lenin would see in the growth of the trade-union movement a proper medium for the development of class and revolutionary consciousness. This was not so. From the very beginning Lenin looked upon trade-unions with apprehension. He feared that workers bargaining with capitalists through their trade-unions would increasingly tend to pay attention to their conditions of work, on how to improve them, and to their wages and benefits. If so they would gradually adjust themselves to the capitalistic economy and learn to act within it. Instead of gaining revolutionary consciousness they would on the contrary shed it in favor of opportunistic compromises and bargains.

There was also a second danger. If trade-unions represented only a part of the working class—usually the most favored one and the better organized—the working class would split and lose its solidarity. A situation would develop in which some workers would have a great deal to gain by staying within the capitalistic system while others would want to destroy it. One part of the working class would be pitted against another. Trade-union activity was therefore detrimental to revolutionary Marxism. According to Lenin, unionism is an infantile disease of the working classes, and the faster they are cured of it the sooner they will reach adolescence and revolutionary maturity.

Colonies and World Revolution

In *Imperalism: the Highest Stage of Capitalism*, published in 1917, Lenin attempted to show that the highest stage, and the last stage of capitalism ("monopoly capitalism"), corresponds to a period of control by the big banks and trusts, with investment in overseas colonies, the division of the world into colonial areas of domination and exploita-

3. Isaiah Berlin. "Political Ideas in the Twentieth Century" in *Foreign Affairs*, April 1950. Reprinted in Roy Macridis (ed.). *Political Parties: Contemporary Trends and Ideas.* N.Y.: Harper and Row, 1967, pp. 205–237.

tion, and wars. The most important thesis of the book, however, was that capitalist countries had divided up the world, and that as a result capitalism had become a world phenomenon despite the uneven economic development of the various countries and the backwardness of the colonies. From this he drew the conclusion that revolutions were advisable and tactically desirable irrespective of whether they take place in an advanced or backward country. Any revolution, anywhere, was legitimized because it was directed against capitalism as a world-wide phenomenon.

This account of *imperialism* appeared at a most opportune moment, shoring up the waverings of many Marxists. It explained why Marx appeared to be "wrong" in predicting the pauperization of the masses in industrially advanced nations. Now it was claimed that it was because of these nations' foreign colonies that this had not come to pass. Surplus values derived by the capitalists in the colonies was also shared in part by the workers of the imperialist powers. This in turn accounted for the delay in the development of working-class revolutionary consciousness and the successes of revisionism. It explained also nationalism and wars. But above all it vindicated revolutions in underdeveloped areas (including, of course, Russia). With this brilliant (no matter how inaccurate) pamphlet, Lenin revived Marxism—and, indirectly, justified the revolutionary takeover of power in Russia in the name of Marx.

TELESCOPING THE REVOLUTION

If capitalism had indeed become a world-wide phenomenon, if the imperialist nations had divided the world among themselves, and if

Bolsheviks on a makeshift armored car during the Russian Revolution. (Photo: Radio Times Hulton Picture Library)

they had managed to blunt the revolutionary class consciousness of the workers by providing them with benefits and advantages that were being extracted from the colonial peoples, where would the revolution come from? For Lenin, as we have seen, it would have to come from trained revolutionaries, well-organized and sharing a common will. But where?

One of the answers given by Lenin, with the support of Leon Trotsky, was that one should not wait for the stages of capitalistic development to unfold themselves. History could somehow be telescoped, so that even if capitalism had not matured and even if there were no strong working class, a combination of the peasantry and the workers could support a revolutionary seizure of power in the name of communism. The capitalistic stage could be combined with the socialist stage at an accelerated rhythm. It was possible, therefore, and indeed desirable, to push for revolutionary seizures of power anywhere in the world rather than wait until each and every country had reached the level of maturity required by Marx and Engels.

This analysis provided a theoretical justification and also a powerful tactical weapon for colonial revolutions. Capitalism was not as strong on its colonial periphery as it was at its center. The capitalistic chain which bound the world had some weak links, particularly its colonies, where it was vulnerable as colonial peoples demanded what many liberal bourgeois leaders had advocated for themselves—national independence, political rights, equality, etc. One part of the fight against the capitalists, therefore, was to try to snap their chain at its various weak links. Communists were asked, in the name of Marx, to promote revolutions in countries where the peasantry and not the workers represented the most numerous social group; and in the name of nationalism, rather than internationalism. From a tactical point of view every colonial independence movement that succeeded was a break of the capitalistic chain, and hence a victory for communist Russia.

It was a masterly tactical twist, designed both to defend communism in Russia (and in so doing defend Russia as well) against potential enemies, but also to expand and export the communist revolution made in Russia. At this point we enter the stage of ideology where communism as a political ideology becomes very closely linked with the interests of Russia as a nation-state. This was a phenomenon that became particularly pronounced under Stalin.

The Third International

But the colonies were not the major objective of the communist leaders. Even more important was the defense of the revolution at home and the defeat or neutralization of the capitalist countries that posed an immediate threat to communist Russia. The Third International, under communist leadership and dedicated to communist revolutionary objectives, was Lenin's answer.

The Russian communists, in the name of communism, now split from what was left of the Second Socialist International and asked all those abroad who subscribed to their objectives to form communist parties and to join the new and third International. Almost everywhere the response was strong and positive. By 1921 there were communist parties almost everywhere, and many trade-unions split into two camps—socialist and communist.

THE 21 CONDITIONS

What bound all these new communist parties and movements together in the Third International were the famous 21 conditions suggested by Lenin, and which were accepted. The same (or almost the same) characteristics of discipline, organization and loyalty which Lenin imposed upon his Bolshevik Party were required of all other national communist parties. Communist parties everywhere had to:

1. Accept absolute ideological commitment to communism.
2. They were to assume direct control over their communist press and publications.
3. They accepted the principle and practice of democratic centralism (i.e., the compliance of the rank and file to the instructions of the higher authorities and the obligation not to allow any factions to exist within their party. Reformists, revisionists, trade-unionists, were to be ruthlessly eliminated from their ranks).
4. Underground and illegal organizations and activities were to be established and party members should be ready for illegal work.
5. A pledge was taken to make special efforts to undermine and disorganize the national armies.
6. Pacifists and pacifism were not to be tolerated.
7. All communists understood the obligation to give aid and support to revolutionary movements of the colonial peoples.
8. They were ordered to break with all trade-unions affiliated with the Second International.
9. Communist members in national parliaments had to be subordinated to the Communist Party to which they belonged.
10. All communist parties in the world undertook to support the Soviet Union and "every Soviet republic."
11. The Communist Party program for every country had to be accepted by the executive committee of the Third International.

In this manner Lenin transformed the communist movement into a world-wide organization to counter the world-wide grip that he claimed the capitalists had established. Any threats on the part of the capitalists against socialist Russia would meet with the resistance of this well-organized force everywhere outside of Russia.

Conclusion

Emphasis upon political and revolutionary tactics, no matter what the objective conditions; reliance upon the human factor—that of will, leadership, organization—irrespective of its social contents; in fact, the subordination of everything else to political organization and political will and leadership to make the revolution, are the hallmarks of Leninism. Very often this is referred to as the theory of *substitutism*. With Marx, the working class develops the consciousness to make the revolution and establish communism, thus substituting itself for the whole of the society; with Lenin the communist party substitutes itself for the working class and speaks for the interest of the working class. Then thanks to the principle of democratic centralism it becomes the executive and higher organs of the party, the central committee, who speak for the interests of the working class, which speaks for the interests of the whole. But since the same central committee controlled the Third International it also spoke for the interests of all the communist parties, which spoke for their respective working classes!

It takes only one more step for the single leader to substitute for all the others in order to arrive at the logical outcome of such an organization—the subordination of *everything* to the leadership of *one* man. Such was the essence of Stalinism.

Stalinism

The name of Stalin is becoming as remote as that of Napoleon. But for many contemporary communists, Stalin and Stalinism remain important and highly controversial. A member of the Russian Communist Party and an associate of Lenin, Stalin succeeded him after his death in 1924. After five years, during which he managed to eliminate all opposition within the Communist Party, he became its absolute ruler. While Lenin was backed by his enormous prestige and was respected for his intelligence and writings, Stalin relied upon the organization he had built with the party and upon outright force. Stalin institutionalized in his own person the dictatorship of the proletariat: not bound by any law, indeed being above any law.

In 1929 Stalin undertook what became known as the Second Revolution, collectivizing agriculture, socializing all means of production, establishing a rigorous planned economy and attempting to industrialize the country as fast as possible through massive capital investment. He controlled not only all the instruments of coercion at home, but through the Third International managed to impose his will upon for-

JOSEPH STALIN (1879–1953)

BROWN BROTHERS

Born in Georgia, Stalin became the head of the Communist Party of the Soviet Union after Lenin's death in 1924. Though originally a lesser figure among the communist leaders who made the revolution, and lacking the literary, oratory or intellectual talents of many of them, Stalin nevertheless assumed a controlling position within the organization of the party, becoming its Secretary General, and his system prevailed. He launched what is generally called the Second Revolution, collectivizing agriculture and socializing all the means of production. His rule, which lasted until his death, saw the rapid increase of Soviet power, economically, internationally, and militarily. But it was in substance a personal dictatorship based upon the most ruthless application of force and terror, and is characterized by many to be a great betrayal of the original principles upon which the revolution was predicated. His regime brought about the most rapid industrialization any country has managed to achieve within such a short period of time.

eign communist parties. His personal rule emulated that of the tsars. Intellectuals, poets, novelists, scientists were forced to pay constant homage to him. During his lifetime the term Marxism-Leninism became transformed to Marxism-Leninism-Stalinism; an indication that he was considered one of the "founders."

With Stalin an important transformation in communist ideology occurs. From a revolutionary ideology it becomes the official *status quo ideology*. Even after the 1917 Revolution with Lenin trying to consolidate it, Marxism was still a revolutionary movement. He hoped that what he had started in Russia would be only a spark to ignite a worldwide revolutionary conflagration.

Stalin succeeded Lenin at a moment when the revolutionary spirit in Russia, and everywhere else, was at an ebb. Long years of strife, civil war and economic hardships had disillusioned a number of revolutionary leaders and undermined the morale of the rank and file of the party. The inability or unwillingness of the European working classes to follow the Bolshevik Revolution left the Soviet Union in a precarious economic and international position. Times called no longer for the revolutionary, but the administrator and the organizer. The period needed stability and reconstruction.

Stalin's rise to power reflected this basic desire. A party organizer above all, with all the qualities and limitations of an administrator, Stalin was able to succeed Lenin because of his administrative functions and position within the party. Patiently he wove within the central committee of the party and within the regional and district committees at large a web of personal and organizational contacts. He controlled the appointments of Communist Party members to local and district administrative jobs; he was in charge of party admissions; he was asked to reorganize and purge the administrative apparatus of the State. He used these powers to the best of his ability in order to consolidate and promote his own personal position.

Almost a year before his death, Lenin dictated the following in his political testament:

> Comrade Stalin, having become secretary-general, has boundless power concentrated in his hands, and I am not sure whether he will always be capable of using that power with sufficient caution.[4]

A man of rather limited philosophic and speculative capacities, Stalin did not share the broader outlook of other communists. He set for himself the task of reconstructing the economic and political institutions of Russia, without concern for world-wide socialism. Neither did he share the faith of the other party leaders in the possibility of a

---

4. Richard Tucker (ed.). *The Lenin Anthology*. N.Y.: Norton, 1975, p. 727.

proletarian revolution in Western Europe. In fact he had a deep distrust, even enmity, for the western world about which, in contrast to the other Russian communist leaders, he knew and understood little.

Gradually the terms Soviet Union and Russia came to be identified with communism, and the survival of communism became identifiable with the well-being of the Soviet Union. Loyalty to the one meant also loyalty to the other. With Stalin what was a revolutionary ideology and a revolutionary movement became State and party orthodoxy. Speculation, argument, debate gave place to imposition and dogma. Arguments or mere disagreement were magnified to mean treason. Persuasion gave place to force—and the State and the party became the agencies to administer it. Marxism (so rich in speculative thought, and claiming to be a rational and scientific doctrine), was now presented in simple didactic terms to settle every dispute—especially when the presentation of the ideas involved was made by Stalin himself. It became a catechism repeated through all the socializing mechanisms available to the party—the party agitators, the press, the schools, the radio, the universities, the trade-unions, etc.

Socialism in One Country

The first element of Stalinism is a nationalism closely associated with the traditional patterns of Russian history. Stalin decided to forge ahead with socialism in Russia without much concern for the fate of communist revolutions in Western Europe, though he continued to exert influence over all communist parties in Europe, China and Southeast Asia. He set before him the task of building "socialism in one country" (a phase first used by Lenin) in Russia. His decision, though made in the name of socialism, evoked a genuine patriotic response among the members of his party and part, at least, of the Russian people. Russia was backward when compared to the West. The assertion that Russia alone could perform the miracle of building socialism was in itself an expression of faith in the strength of Russian society, a defiance of the West, and a proclamation of Russian independence and self-sufficiency.

THE ORGANIZATION OF THE COMMUNIST PARTY

The organization and functions of the Communist Party under Stalin represent the ultimate development of what Lenin had started. The party remained an *elite* composed of loyal and energetic members. Its mission was to maintain and further the cause of Soviet socialism and to educate the masses into socialism. Its membership continued to be relatively small. Sometimes it was described as the "chief of staff of the proletariat" and sometimes as "the teacher" of the Russian masses and the "vanguard of the working class and the masses." It grew into an exclusive organization which controlled every aspect of governmental and social life of the Soviet society.

The Leninist conception of the hierarchical relationship between leadership and rank and file hardened into an institution. The role of the leader began to be expounded upon in a semi-religious, semi-Byzantine manner: he was omniscient and omnipresent, he was the father of the people, his word was law. There was in Stalinism a marked similarity to the despotic paternalism of the tsarist regime.

The development of this concept of leadership is also related to the internal development of the party organization. Decision-making powers became concentrated exclusively in the hands of the executive organs of the party, and any semblance of democratic centralism was abandoned in favor of rigid centralization and control from the top. Nominations to party posts were made from above and not by the rank and file. Criticism was allowed only when leaders would permit it, and only on subjects selected in advance by them; periodic purges accounted for a constant turnover of the rank and file and middle-echelon officers and organizers.

NO INTERNAL DEMOCRACY

Another indication of the demotion of the status of the party was the lack of any genuine free deliberation and criticism among its assembled delegates. Congresses, whenever they were convened, spent their time in giving their approbation without any debate to the resolutions of the leadership. After 1927 not a single protest was raised; not a single dissenting voice or vote expressed. The slate of candidates for the various executive organs was prepared in advance by Stalin and his immediate associates, and was always approved unanimously.

THE POLICE

The new organ that in effect replaced the party was the police, operating directly under Stalin. It was the duty of the police to maintain communist legality. Lenin had used it to first operate against "deviationists" and "dissenters," but it was always understood that it was to be an adjunct of the party acting on its behalf. But by 1935 the secret police became, in the hands of Stalin, the instrument of control and intimidation not only of society as a whole but also vis-à-vis the party. Party members were totally at its mercy and so were high-placed party officials. The secret police gradually became the most feared coercive and punitive force, with its own private army (including tanks), a huge network of spies and informers, and in command of the forced labor camps where the inmates—variously estimated to range from three to four million to as many as ten million over the whole Stalinist period— were interned. Terror thus became an instrument of government.

STALINISM AND THE SOCIAL ORDER

When the revolution took place in Russia in 1917, the attention of all intellectuals, socialist leaders, and that of the people of Western Europe was directed to the first genuine revolutionary experiment to be made in the name of Marx. Expectations and hopes ran high for many, and the leaders of the revolution shared them. Trotsky for instance, on becoming Minister of Foreign Affairs, claimed that all he had to do was to publish the various secret (and imperialist) treaties signed by the victorious powers in World War One, issue some revolutionary proclamations and then "close shop": national boundaries would melt away and internationalism would come about! The early policy of war communism—a blanket socialization of all property and the direct control by the socialist state of the economy—would pave the way to the transitional stage leading to communism. Throughout these first years, these social developments were carefully watched. Lack of democracy was consistent with the idea of the dictatorship of the proletariat, but it was fully compensated by the prospect of economic equality, many argued. The argument was repeatedly made that the West protected political (formal) rights while the Soviet socialist system was ushering in economic (substantive) rights.

INDUSTRIALIZATION

Reality, however, differed sharply from expectations based on ideology. Communism failed to initiate any economic recovery, just as national boundaries had failed to melt away. Lenin, a masterful tactician, was the first to retreat. His New Economic Policy of 1921 reestablished freedom of commerce, agriculture, and manufacturing, but the State kept in its hands what he called the "commanding heights" of the economy—banks, steel, iron, coal, transportation, energy. The rest went back to private hands: private employers who could hire labor and presumably get surplus value and make profit, private tradesmen and individual farmers who owned farms could buy land and employ farmhands.

This was the situation that Stalin had inherited and decided to resolve in 1929. All means of production and all private property were socialized and agriculture was collectivized. Marxism-Leninism became the convenient political instrument for controlling society and bending it to the task of rapid industrialization. This entailed a rigorous centralization and bureaucratic control of the national economy. Economic targets were formulated over five-year periods (the Five-Year Plans) with priorities and specific quantitative quotas. Capital investment—the building of factories and industrial equipment—and the training of the labor force took precedence over consumption. Education became an indispensable part of industralization, for technicians, scientists, skilled workers, engineers, and service personnel such as doctors, administrators, accountants, etc., were vital to economic growth. A crucial problem was to find the human resources to train, and Stalin's answer was a massive transfer of the population from the farm and the country into the new industrial urban centers.

The overall effort amounted to a radical overhaul of Russian society. In the name of socialism the task was to create what socialism should have inherited, an industrialized society. Three basic incentives could be used. The first was propaganda and persuasion: to extol the myth of socialism and incite people to communal efforts and sacrifices. But ideological exhortation has limits. Stalin had therefore to fall back upon the two classic means of encouraging compliance: the carrot and the stick. The carrot was monetary incentive; the stick, force.

He who did not work would not eat. Income was to be proportionate to the quality and quantity of work done: inequality of income was declared to be unavoidable. Trade-unions who had favored equality of pay were put in their place—their leaders arrested and eliminated, the right to bargain abolished and the right to participate in the decisions of the plant manager withdrawn.

The differences in pay created a salary structure that began to resemble that of the capitalistic societies, with the right of certain individuals to save and get interest, to pass on some of their gains to their heirs, to provide their children with better education, with special advantages for vacation, leisure and travel. There was even status—the recognition that they belonged to an elite class consisting of the top group of the *intelligentsia* (the Russian word implies a very large class of people, comprising all groups other than workers and farmers). In recognition of their services and as an added incentive, they were allowed membership within the party, thus bestowing upon them political status as well. The percentage of workers and farmers within the party decreased correspondingly.

Force took a number of forms and served many purposes. It was used against those who did not work or did not work regularly and failed to live up to the quotas assigned to them. These found their way to labor camps, and their disappearance was only a reminder to others of what they might have to face. Force was also used directly to create regiments of workers in labor camps who were responsible for tasks that nobody else would take (except for very high pay) such as mining of gold, lumber cutting, road construction. In a more comprehensive sense, force was also a constant reminder even to those who received a good pay for their work that any relaxation or negligence would be followed by swift punishment.

The Impact of Stalinism

Stalin and Stalinism can be viewed from three different points of view. Stalin can be considered, in line with Marx and Lenin, to be one of the chief exponents of communist philosophy and practice. One may also attribute to him the consolidation of the revolution in Russia. As communist dictator in charge of the party he expropriated the farms, socialized the means of production and established economic planning. Finally, he may be viewed as a great modernizer. He started Russia on the road to economic modernization. As Isaac Deutscher puts it, he found Russia with the wooden plough and left it with atomic weapons.[5]

Stalin in fact may go down in history as another Peter the Great, as one of the great modernizers. Under his rule and in a short period of time the Russian economy and society underwent a great change with an emphasis on education, technology, mass production, urbanization, the movement from the farm to the city, the development of science and above all, a rapidly increasing gross national product.

It was inevitable that rapid economic and industrial development would be linked to socialism, and that in the process the political aspects of Stalinist rule would be glossed over. It was also unavoidable that the modernizing aspects of socialism would be emphasized and presented as the most attractive side of the Stalinist regime.

But the great loyalty to Stalin during his lifetime and to the Soviet system in general by other communist parties and so many intellectuals in Western Europe and elsewhere is due to the profound impact of Marxism. As an ideology, it provided simple answers to the three most fundamental questions we ask about our society and our lives. Where are we going? How do we get there? What will it be like?

By answering them, Marxism, like all great ideologies, gave a particular meaning and therefore direction of history: it is not haphazard; it is not indefinite; it is not aimless. We are moving in the direction of freedom, equality and abundance to fulfill the ultimate goal of our nature, as individuals and social beings. We can get there when conditions are ready but only by an act of our own will or by revolution.

History and its purpose may be realized through the most unexpected or repugnant agencies, but it moves inexorably to its predetermined goal of communism, and Man's salvation! Stalin is thought of as a dictator, as a perpetrator of inhuman acts, as the murderer of friends and relatives. He is considered to have deprived millions of their freedom and their lives—and all of this is true. But to some he incarnated history. Jean-Paul Sartre spoke of the "monster dripping with blood," but still remained very sympathetic to the Soviet ideology and with it of course to Stalin. To attack *him* would have been to endanger the citadel of communism and with it the future of humankind. There *was* no alternative. Belief, a powerful ingredient of all ideologies, came to stifle critical inquiry.

As we pointed out, an ideology is a lens through which some people share a view of reality. Reality cannot prove or disprove them since for them reality is what they see in terms of the ideology. It is

5. Isaac Deutscher. *Russia, What Next?* N.Y.: Oxford U.P., 1953.

only in the last years that intellectuals from the left—even communist ones, in Spain, France and Italy—are beginning to raise embarrassing questions about Soviet communism and Stalinism.

Milovan Djilas: A Critique

The most scathing critique of the Stalinist system, and also more generally a critique addressed against virtually all communist systems, has come from a Yugoslav Communist, Milovan Djilas, in a book entitled *The New Class*. It was written only three years after Stalin's death and published in the U.S.A. in 1957. "Everything," writes Djilas, "happened differently in the U.S.S.R. and other communist countries from what the leaders—even such prominent ones as Lenin, Trotsky, Stalin and Bukharin—anticipated."[6] They expected, he points out wistfully, that the State would wither away, democracy would be strengthened, the standard of living would go up, and internationalism would supplant nationalisms. Exactly the reverse has happened; neither industrialization nor collectivization has accounted for economic improvement, let alone plenty. And the dream of a classless society remains a dream. In fact a new class has developed, the Communist Party and "the Communist Party State," with a huge bureaucracy. In the process of industrializing, and even after industrialization had been in part achieved, "the new class . . . can do nothing more than to strengthen its brute force and pillage the people. It ceases to create. Its spiritual heritage is overtaken by darkness."[7]

The new class legitimizes itself the way all classes have done in the past. It uses indoctrination and force, relies upon handouts to secure loyal supporters and develops a nationalist ideology to appeal to the same forces on which the bourgeoisie had relied in the past. The party oligarchy and its bureaucratic apparatus maintains not only a monopoly of political control but allocates to itself a disproportionate part of the national wealth and income. Despite their rhetoric, the communist regimes thus far, and Soviet communism in particular, have continued to perpetuate class rule.

Soviet Communism After Stalin

In 1956 Nikita Krushchev, having replaced Stalin after a short power struggle as General Secretary of the Party and Chairman of the Council of Ministers of the Soviet Union, gave a "secret report" to the delegates of the Soviet Communist Party at its twentieth Congress. He criticized Stalin sharply for the many crimes committed during his long stay in office.

6. Djilas. *The New Class: an Analysis of the Communist System*, p. 37.
7. Ibid., p. 69.

Comrades! . . .

After Stalin's death the Central Committee of the party began to implement a policy of explaining concisely and consistently that it is impermissible and foreign to the spirit of Marxism-Leninism to elevate one person, to transform him into a super-man possessing supernatural characteristics akin to those of a god. Such a man supposedly knows everything, sees every-thing, thinks for everyone, can do anything, is infallible in his behavior.

Such a belief about a man, and specifically about Stalin, was cultivated among us for many years . . . Stalin acted not through persuasion, explanation and patient cooperation with people, but by imposing his concepts and demanding absolute submission to his opinion. Whoever opposed this concept or tried to prove his viewpoint and the correctness of his position was doomed to removal from the leading collective and to subsequent moral and physical annihilation. . . .

Arbitrary behavior by one person encouraged and permitted arbitrariness in others. Mass arrests and deportations of many thousands of people, execution without trial and without nor-mal investigation created conditions of insecurity, fear and even despair.[8]

The Nobel Prize novelist, Aleksander Solzhenitsyn, in his *Gulag Archipelago* describes the utter capriciousness behind the terror that Stalin used. One of the inmates is asked for how many years he was sentenced in the labor camp. "For ten," he answers. "What did you do?" "Nothing." His companion seems surprised. "Nothing!" he ex-claims. "People usually get five years for doing nothing."

Since the time of the Khrushchev report, but particularly since 1961, Stalin's name has been virtually removed from every corner of Soviet life. Streets and villages and towns no longer bear his name. He is no longer part of the Marxist-Leninist-Stalinist trinity, and no longer regarded as a founder of the communist ideology. Occasional efforts to "rehabilitate" him have failed but similar efforts to rehabilitate some of the Communist leaders who were put to death or "disappeared" during his reign have also failed. The regime has attempted to liberalize itself but few, if any, significant changes in the overall ideology of the communist leadership and its practices are noticeable.

8. Krushchev's "Secret Report" to the Twentieth Congress of the Communist Party of the Soviet Union, in Bertram Wolfe. *Krushchev and Stalin's Ghost*. London: Atlantis Press, pp. 88–100.

The control that the Soviet leadership once exercised over the other communist parties in the world has declined. First it was Tito in Yugoslavia, then Mao in China, and then Eurocommunism, together with various "deviant" forms of communism that emerged in a number of countries, all of which we discuss in our next chapter. They all differed or claimed to be different from Soviet communism. The Third International was abolished in 1943 and the Cominform (the Communist Information Bureau) which was to maintain links with all communist parties, which was disbanded shortly after it was founded in 1946. References were now made to polycentrism, with multiple and independent centers of communist rule; to "national communism" where communist parties would follow a path dictated by specific national conditions and not by the Soviet leadership according to the Soviet model. The ability of the Soviets to impose their course of action declined.

Peaceful Coexistence

Communist leaders had posited the inevitability of a conflict between communist and capitalist blocs. After Stalin's death it was abandoned in favor of "peaceful coexistence," which assumed conflict between the two blocs but denied that it would inevitably lead to war. Such an admission in itself weakened Soviet control over other communist parties since war was no longer considered inevitable. Peaceful coexistence allayed the fears of many communists and gave them time to develop their own individual strategies and domestic politics. It is only within the Eastern bloc—the Warsaw Pact countries—that Soviet control has been maintained, by virtue of the presence of Soviet military forces.

Domestic Developments

Stalin's rule has come under increasing criticism both with regard to the political practices he used and also with reference to the overall kind of socialism that had developed. The state had not withered away—on the contrary, many pointed out that it had blossomed forth in the form of excessive centralization and bureaucratization; freedoms virtually disappeared; the development of a consumer-oriented economy was still far off; inequalities increased and coercive practices were still prominent even if more incentives were introduced.

Why was this so? many asked. Was Stalinism a phenomenon peculiar to Russia? Did it obey characteristics embedded in the Russian political culture and history? Was the continuing backwardness of the Soviet economy the inevitable result of its manifest backwardness at the time the revolution was made? As we pointed out, many communists and socialists considered that Stalinism was a temporary phase—inevitable, but destined to pass. Many hoped that democratization would be possible after Stalin's death. The disappearance of the cult of personality; the downgrading of the role of the police; the growth of intraparty democracy; the development of some degree of pluralism and a more tolerant attitude to dissent—all of them would indicate that liberalization was at long last on the way.

THE CULT OF PERSONALITY

Stalin, as the leader—omniscient and omnipotent—was replaced by "collective leadership." The General Secretary of the Party, however, continues to have ascendancy. Yet the servile adulation and deference is gone. Through the party, Stalin's successors continue to exercise control but it is no longer the direct and personal iron grip that Stalin held through the police and through outright intimidation.

SUCCESSION

The problem of succession seems to have been resolved in a manner that allows for the peaceful removal of a leader and the designation of another. The organs of the party—the Central Committee and the Politburo—are consulted. The ousting of top leaders does not lead to their

Stalin's one-man rule gave peace to "collective leadership." Here, the top Soviet leaders confer in the Supreme Soviet (Parliament) in 1974: from left to right Podgorny, Kosygin and Brezhnev. But it seems to be Brezhnev who has had the first and last word! (Wide World Photos)

physical extinction. There will be jobs for them in Uzbek or in Georgia . . . or in other remote parts of the Soviet Union.

THE POLICE

The police and their arbitrary practices have come under party control thanks to the development of some general rules and procedures. To be sure, Soviet legality may be a very flexible concept but some search for legality has been going on, and efforts to curb the police and to subordinate it to procedural and legal requirements have been made. People no longer disappear overnight; they are not sent to labor camps without proper investigation and "trial." Intimidation is not as pervasive as it used to be.

DISSENT

There has been a great interest in dissent and dissenters abroad, with the obvious conclusion that it is still not open to Soviet citizens, Jewish or non-Jewish. Yet despite harassment and persecution, dissenters remain active; they give interviews to foreign reporters and they seem to be protected by the interest world opinion has focussed on them. Some are allowed to leave. Others are not. The Nobel Prize winner Andrei Sakharov is active—something impossible to imagine under the Stalin regime. Others, however, less fortunate, have been sentenced to long years in jail and some to death. The regime continues to show its reluctance to allow for freedom of criticism, even the kind of freedom that does not question the foundations of the socialist system, but rather attempts to reconcile it with political freedoms and civil rights.

BUREAUCRATIZATION AND CENTRALIZATION

Nor is the regime sensitive to demands for decentralization in the economy. Economic centralized planning remains the general rule, despite some efforts to give more autonomy to firms. It applies to industry, trade and agriculture. No efforts have been made to provide for genuine autonomy or to allow for the participation of trade-unions in the decision-making process. The system remains, therefore, inflexible to consumer demand and needs.

All in all, little seems to have been modified in the official ideological orthodoxy of the party. The "dictatorship of the proletariat" continues to be proclaimed necessary and as long as there is a capitalist sector in the world it is to be maintained. The period of genuine communism as envisaged by Marx and Engels is still far off. Society is still going through a process of adjustment, allegedly to prepare the conditions for a truly classless society. The State in the hands of the Communist Party maintains its coercive traits and is likely to continue to do so.

It is in the social composition of the Communist Party and the bureaucracy that many begin to detect changes which may affect the official ideology. With industrialization and socio-economic modernization there has been a proliferation of new social groups—engineers, scientists, intellectuals, teachers, various types of experts such as the military, the managerial, and so on. These groups begin to develop their own particular interests and to become conscious of the special roles they play within the society. They, as a result, tend to express these interests in order to promote them or to safeguard them. They begin to act like all interests do in trying to influence policy decisions. The result is a certain degree of pluralism that affects the decision-making and the deliberative processes of the system. Interests begin to influence and even to colonize the party, the huge bureaucracy and other organs of the State. There is a constant pull and tug among them which breaks the monolithic structure of the state and of the party apparatus. Concessions have to be made; compromises are negotiated. Ideological requirements often yield to pragmatic considerations. The totalitarian structure begins to soften up.

Connected with this development is the effort on the part of many groups and their spokesmen to defend their positions. A defensive posture grows that in effect does not allow the State and the party to intervene consistently in dictating policies or shaping and reshaping the values of those who operate within their assigned roles and expertise. Limitations upon the totalitarian State begin to develop. This should, *logically,* lead to the granting of freedoms and privileges and autonomies that were denied in the past. The groups and interests must be given representation and their views should be voiced.

It is in such a development, consistent with the industrialization and the modernization of the Soviet society, that some authors find the seeds of its liberalization. But the seeds have not quite broken through the soil yet, and it will be some time before they bring forth the promised flowers—if ever. The Communist Party will be the first to feel them, for inevitably interest and other groups will have to begin to operate within the party in order to gain representation in it and to change its internal organization from democratic centralism to one of relative freedom to criticize and deliberate on different policies.

For the present the Soviet system continues to remain highly centralized and bureaucratic. The party and the police maintain their rule. A class consisting of party members, government officials, members of the intelligentsia—experts, scientists, defense personnel and officers, loyal authors and writers, top managers, is well off as compared to the average citizen. Among *them* the Russian minority is in a privileged position compared to the other nationalities, and Russian nationalism remains strong. The critique of Milovan Djilas published more than twenty years ago remains substantially very pertinent.

Bibliography

Borkenau, F. *The Communist International*. London: Faber, 1938.

Conquest, Robert. *The Soviet Political System*. New York: Praeger, 1968.

Deutscher, Isaac. *Stalin*. New York: Oxford U.P., 1949.

Djilas, Milovan. *The New Class: An Analysis of the Communist System*. New York: Praeger, 1957.

Lenin, V.I. *What Is To Be Done?* New York: International Publishers, 1969.

———. "Imperialism: The Highest Stage of Capitalism" and "The State and Revoluton" in *Lenin: Selected Works in One Volume*. New York: International Publishers, 1971.

Medvedev, Roy. *On Socialist Democracy*. New York: Knopf, 1975.

Meyer, Alfred G. *Leninism*. New York: Praeger, 1957.

———. *The Soviet Political System: An Interpretation*. New York: Random House, 1965.

Schammell, Michael. *Russia's Other Writers: Selections From Samizdat Literature*. New York: Praeger, 1971.

Schapiro, Leonard. *The Communist Party of the Soviet Union*. Rev. ed. New York: Vintage, 1978.

Shub, David. *Lenin: A Biography*. New York: Penguin, 1976.

Simon, Gerhard. *Church, State, and Opposition in the USSR*. London: C. Hurst, 1974.

Solzhenitsyn, Alexander. *The Gulag Archipelago*. Three volumes. New York: Harper and Row, 1974–1979.

Stalin, Joseph. *The Essential Stalin*. Edited by Bruce Franklin. New York.: Anchor/Doubleday, 1972.

Tucker, Robert C. (ed.). *Stalinism: Essays in Historical Interpretation*. New York: Norton, 1977.

Ulam, Adam B. *The Bolsheviks*. New York: Macmillan, 1968.

———. *Stalin: The Man and His Era*. New York: Viking, 1973.

Wolfe, Bertram D. *Three Who Made A Revolution*. New York: Delta/Dell, 1964.

Communist
Variations

*The most successful, and the most fanatically revolutionary
and communist, group of followers . . . found itself compelled to defy the claims of the Kremlin to dominate uncon-
ditionally every Communist Party of the world.*
ADAM ULAM   Titoism and the Cominform

The aftermath of World War Two accounted for the consolidation of
the Soviet Union as a world power. In the name of socialism, and
thanks to the presence of Soviet forces, most of Eastern Europe established communist regimes and came under the control of the Soviets:
Eastern Germany (the German Democratic Republic), Hungary, Czechoslovakia, Rumania, Bulgaria, Poland, together with the small border
states of Latvia, Estonia and Lithuania. Yugoslavia had already made
its own socialist revolution while the war was going on thanks to the
organization of a strong partisan army which fought the Germans under
communist leadership.

In Asia, it took only a few years after the end of the war for nationalist forces and the Chinese warlords to give way to the communist
forces led by Mao. Though they had received some Soviet help, these
forces were home-made and home-grown and as in Yugoslavia there
was no direct Soviet military involvement.

Would the communist bloc act as one? Would ideological ties
overcome national rivalries? Would the Soviets manage to maintain

their hegemony over the communist bloc—over its "satellites," as they came to be known, in the name of ideological unity, and power? Would they be able to extend their influence over other parts of the world, and especially among the new nations?

A brief glance at two dissident movements, Titoism and Maoism, indicates the emergence of ideological conflicts and national rivalries *within* what we called the communist bloc. Eurocommunism too may be viewed as the beginning of a new ideological movement among Western European communist parties claiming independence from the tight bureaucratic, organizational, ideological, even financial control that the Soviets had managed to impose in the years of Stalin and down to the 1960s.

The result has been a break in Soviet control and in the monolithic kind of communism that many, especially American political leaders, have taken for granted.

Titoism

Titoism is the label given to the prevailing communist movement and ideology of Yugoslavia. It began to develop after the German occupation of the country in 1941. Throughout the war, the Yugoslav Communist Party under Tito assumed the leadership of the resistance and organized and fought a sustained guerrilla war against the Nazis. In 1945, the party assumed political control of Yugoslavia, but in 1948–49, Communist Yugoslavia and the Soviet Union disagreed on a number of issues. Ever since, Titoism has been synonymous with a national communist regime that has declared itself independent of the Soviet Union, and that differs on a number of domestic and international questions.

Adam Ulam writes that Titoism is " . . . a proper name for the historical moment of the break between Tito and Stalin, but not for an ideology. . . ."[1] Yet he points out also that "Titoism . . . has a broad meaning [that] might be translated as resistance on the part of a communist party to the domination of the Russian communists." We shall not be concerned here with the specifics of the historical moment— that is, of how Tito defied Soviet leadership and control, nor of the circumstances surrounding it. We shall discuss rather the development of an ideology in terms of which the Yugoslav political and social and economic experiment seeks an identity separate from that of Soviet communism.

The Nationalist Urge

As we have seen, it was Lenin's genius which knit together the various Marxist groups and parties into an international organization, the Third

1. "Titoism" in Drachkovitch (ed.). *Marxism in the Modern World*, p. 137.

JOSIP BROZ TITO (b. 1892)

Josip Broz was born on May 25, 1892 in Croatia. Wounded in World War One and captured by the Russians in 1915, he eventually joined the Red Army and married a Russian woman (whom he later divorced). In 1920 Broz returned to Yugoslavia and joined the Communist Party. After serving a five year prison sentence received in 1928 for subversive activities, he went to Moscow to work for the Communist International. In 1937 he became Secretary-General of the Yugoslav Communist Party. In June 1941, after the invasion of the U.S.S.R. by the Germans, Broz returned again to Yugoslavia under the name Tito to organize resistance against the occupation forces there. It was one of the most successful partisan operations of the War. In 1945 Tito became prime minister of Yugoslavia. His independent, nationalistic brand of communism eventually brought verbal attacks, along with threat of military invasion, from Stalin in 1948.

International. This was accomplished at a time when communism was still a movement whose chances of survival, even in Russia, were dim. How would the international proletariat react when communism had triumphed in a number of countries? Would they disregard their national borders in favor of cooperation? Or would they follow the way of the socialist parties on the eve of World War One and put their country above proletarian brotherhood and solidarity?

Stalin's answer was simply to subordinate the communist ideology and the communist movements to the national interests and needs of Russia. One might argue this was only a tactical move, and that if and when communist regimes spread in other countries, then, indeed, cooperation among them would be spontaneous and would be carried out on a footing of equality. Again Stalin gave the answer: the communist regimes that emerged in Eastern Europe in the wake of World War Two were imposed and controlled by the Soviet leadership. They were consolidated in the period of the Cold War to answer the needs of the Soviet Union. Their leaders were handpicked; their economies controlled; their relations with each other and with the Soviet Union fully dominated by the latter. There was no semblance of international communism on a footing of equality, only the control of the Soviet Communists.

Tito and his Yugoslav Communist Party, as they emerged from the war, felt they merited special attention, and looked forward to genuine cooperation with their Soviet comrades. More than any other country in Europe there was in Yugoslavia a strong Stalinist faction in the Communist Party. It had waged war against the Germans, tying down a number of their divisions and keeping them away from the Russian front. It was able to lead the resistance successfully enough to force the Germans out without the intervention of the Soviet army. Tito's communist Yugoslavia was a home-made product with proper communist credentials, its own cadres, its strong popular support, its own roots and, therefore, free to claim its "own road" to the building of socialism.

The historical moment for breaking with the Soviets came after the end of the war, when the Yugoslav leadership showed remarkable unity in resisting attempts by the Soviet Union to dictate their policies. The leaders took exception to Soviet spying and machinations; to the lack of open and fraternal discussions; to Soviet "arrogance" and "interference." They asked the Soviet technicians and advisers to leave. The conflict which had been muted for some time came out into the open in the spring of 1948 and the Yugoslavs stood alone. It was like a mouse taunting the big bear . . . and the mouse survived.

The ability of the Yugoslav communists to resist was due to the strong national base that the Communist Party had developed as a *national* party. Some time after the split, the Yugoslav communist leaders began to search for their own ideology, and to take a foreign policy that differed from that of the Soviet Union. It was only then that Titoism became transformed into the *Titoist ideology*. This took at least two new directions: the establishment or at least the effort to establish political and economic institutions that differentiate Yugoslavia from the Soviet Union; and the search for a foreign policy that differed from and was independent of that of the Soviets.

New Institutions

The Yugoslav Communist Party numbered only some 15,000 members in the years before World War Two. It was a Stalinist party like all other European communist parties: tightly organized and disciplined, committed to revolution, but always ready to follow the tactical shifts and changes that Moscow ordered. By the end of the war—within a matter of six years—it numbered 120,000 members, and had made a revolution at home by destroying the industrial and financial elites, expropriating the land of the landowners, reducing the middle classes and gaining the support of the peasantry and the overwhelming backing of the workers. It also gained the support of the ethnic minorities. It was a remarkably youthful party, recruiting primarily from among those who had entered the partisan forces and were waging war against the Germans. Thus the party developed a solid base which gave it the independence to defy the Soviets and the strength to maintain its separate course and ideological orientation.

Tito's partisans took the lead in fighting the occupying German forces in Yugoslavia. The struggle was hard but the successes often spectacular: here, partisans lead large numbers of enemy prisoners down from their mountain hideouts. (Photo: Yugoslav Press and Cultural Center)

Nowhere in Europe was communism so deeply associated with national resistance against the Germans and, hence, with patriotism as in Yugoslavia. The communist leaders were the leaders of this resistance. They organized the partisans, provided for political and military direction and gradually gained the support of many of the social strata of the population. The more brutal the German repression, the greater the support for the partisans, and the greater the influence and control of the communists over the countryside. Young men and women fled to the mountains to join the partisans. As the predominance of the communist leaders asserted itself, and as they gained greater popular support, the elimination of opposition became easier. Rival partisan formations, and groups which collaborated, were destroyed in what amounted to a civil war fought alongside the guerrilla war against the Germans.

In this manner a social revolution took place in the context of a vast patriotic uprising against the Germans and the collaborators. The Communist Party emerged after the war with few enemies at home and with the backbone of the conservative forces broken. It had gained wide popular support.

FREEDOMS, LINKAGES AND PARTICIPATION

The Yugoslav Communist Party grew during the period of the occupation of the country.[2] It built its support by encouraging and directing the mobilization of the population. Given the nature of the guerrilla warfare against the Germans, however, it was not always easy to establish a centralized direction. It had to rely upon local initiative and effort. Thus at the local and village levels and often at the regional level the partisan forces had to be given initiative to act. A certain quite considerable degree of freedom was left, in other words, to the regional cadres and to lower echelons. It would not be an exaggeration to say that the party was built from bottom upwards. Inevitably a certain degree of democracy within the party developed, based upon common effort and mutuality of trust. The camaraderie of the partisans and their relative degree of isolation from the leaders strengthened this.

The partisan war necessitated also the building of solid links with the population and its various strata—peasants, workers, students, intellectuals, even some of the units of the army as well as various religious and ethnic groups. The communists created a National Liberation Front as an umbrella organization designed to be as inclusive as possible. In so doing they had to build links with as many groups as possible, and to exclude virtually none. The need for repressive tactics

---

2. This is fully developed in B. Denitch, *The Legitimization of a Revolution.* As mentioned in my preface, I am indebted to the author for many of my observations in this section.

was secondary and slogan appeals to class hatred superfluous. These linkages not only provided and strengthened support but created a more open and conciliatory attitude on the part of the communist leaders to all population groups, excluding only those who collaborated with the Germans.

Communist and socialist slogans were of course used, and the program of the Communist Party was to establish socialism and to deprive the established groups of political and economic power. But again, this was done (at least in part) by the Germans. The Yugoslav Army had been discredited after its defeat, and the financial, industrial and commercial elites that collaborated with the Germans were also discredited: those among them who refused to collaborate were destroyed by the Germans. The "class enemy" had been vanquished. The churches—Orthodox, Catholic and Moslem—lost their influence. They simply lost their base in the peasant and village populations, and, especially, the young people who left the countryside to join the partisans.

Almost a whole generation of people between the ages of eighteen and thirty-five came under the guidance of the Yugoslav Communist Party. They were the people most willing to embrace new ideas and turn their backs on old values and attitudes. The more they participated in the war the more committed they became to the liberation of their country *and* to communism. Communism assumed the character of a "generational revolution" bringing together the most enthusiastic and dynamic age groups of the population.

All the prospects, therefore, for the emergence of a national communism, open and populist in character, based on broad cooperation among the various social, regional and ethnic groups and with strong links between the party and the people, were present. The Communist Party relied less upon repressive and police measures than anywhere else. It had disposed of its actual or potential enemies or, more accurately, saw them disposed of by their own enemies, the German occupying forces. No better conditions could be found for the establishment and the consolidation of a communist regime.

AFTER THE SPLIT: A NEW COMMUNISM?

This brief account of the role and of the conditions under which the Yugoslav Communist Party grew explains not only why the party managed to survive the split with the Soviet Union but also may explain the split itself. The party emerged with grass-roots support, with faith in its own ability to lead, and with few enemies at home. The split with Soviet Russia forced it to consider alternative models of communist rule, and in fact, it triggered a search for a new model of communism which began to emerge some ten years later, by 1958.

The model is by no means complete. Yugoslav communists have been moving, and are still moving, into uncharted waters in attempting to build a new and different kind of socialism. The political regime and the ideology to sustain it have also been going through numerous modifications as they adjust to national and international pressures, demands and counterpressures. How the present regime will evolve is uncertain since the very symbol of legitimacy, Marshall Tito, who has played and continues to play the role of unifier and ultimate arbiter, is over eighty years old.

A Communist Society. Yugoslavia is a socialist society. Property belongs to the State, and to various State agencies and to the people. Except for the farmers who own their farms (nobody is allowed to have more than sixty acres of land) and small artisans and shopkeepers, the rest of the conomy is owned by the collectivity. Industry, manufacturings, mining—over 90 percent of the total non-agricultural economic activity—is in the hands of public bodies. Even in agriculture, publicly owned farms account for a significant percentage of the total production of some crops.

A Modernizing System? Yugoslav communist leadership emphasized from the very beginning economic modernization. One of Tito's associates wrote:

> It was necessary after the war to undertake a number of measures that had been requested by the people . . . It was necessary to raise the country from its semi-colonial position, to develop its vast natural resources . . . Plans were made for the industrialization of the country, so that it should no longer be a country of muddy roads and general backwardness . . . Foreign capital in Yugoslavia held the key positions . . . It was in a position to pursue its own economic policy . . . [It] increased the inequality of development in our country. It was necessary to eliminate the glaring inconsistencies between different sections of the population: abundance on one side and wretchedness on the other . . . The land was redistributed . . . These tasks . . . were accomplished with relative ease, because during the war the majority of the people had declared themselves for their enactment. That was why our People's Front readily accepted nationalization after the war: if the Communists had been alone in seeking to carry out this task, they would have been in a minority and civil war would have been inevitable.[3]

To modernize, one needs capital, ample supplies of labor, technical cadres (which means education) and of course the elimination of the traditionalist forces and values that impede change. In all these, the situation of Yugoslavia was a propitious one for modernization. For if capital was difficult to find, the other required conditions were present: the will to modernize, shared by the communist leadership and the

3. Dedijer, Vladimir. *Tito Speaks.* London: Weidenfeld and Nicolson, 1953 pp. 257–8.

communist-led elites; a great supply of labor, consisting of young men and women who had already left their villages; an adequate supply of technicians and cadres, at least for the initial phase of industrialization and modernization. The traditional elites had been virtually eliminated, so no resistance was possible. The broadening of educational opportunities, one of the first tasks of the regime, gradually provided the required expertise and skilled workers. Finally, when after the split with the Soviets the hope of getting economic aid from them disappeared, Yugoslavia profited from its independent status and received economic aid directly from Western Europe and the U.S.A.

The indicators of economic growth have been impressive. Gradually the number of people employed in agriculture has diminished from about 65 percent before the war to just about 38 percent. The number of workers and semi-skilled and skilled workers, but also white-collar workers and technicians and managers, has increased rapidly. Economic growth has been one of the highest in the world, averaging over 7 percent a year since 1960. There has been also a remarkable increase among university students—from eleven out of every thousand young people aged eighteen to twenty-five before the war to seventy-six out of every thousand in 1960, a percentage that has remained about the same since. What is more, the social composition of the student body showed a remarkable influx of students from poor or previously disenfranchised groups—21 percent came from working-class families and 39 percent from white-collar.[4]

Economic Democracy? By 1958 Yugoslavia had definitely abandoned the Stalinist model of modernization involving State control and subordination of economic activities to a highly centralized bureaucracy. Instead, it put the premium on *decentralization* through the development of quasi-independent units of production with grass-roots controls. This is in essence the principle of self-government in industry and the economy. The bureaucratic model has been turned upside down and economic activity has been returned, so to speak, to the producers. State socialism of the Stalinist model fixes production in advance, in the form of quotas, and controls prices, wages and consumption. The "socialist model" of Yugoslavia allows for competition among firms and decentralizes decision-making on what and how much to produce. It allows therefore for self-regulatory mechanisms, (i.e., for a market economy that generally determines prices, production and consumption). The system allows for a great degree of freedom for each and every individual firm. It encourages competition among enterprises and allows some to earn more while the others strive to do the same. Though property is "socialized," it is managed by thousands of separate firms and public enterprises. Efficient management brings higher profits from which everybody within the firm benefits.

4. Figures from Denitch, op. cit.

Institutions of Self-management: Workers' Councils. The major institution through which a decentralized socialist economy functions is the workers' council. Decentralization simply means that decisions are not made by one single central authority but are left in the hands of individual units and firms. Self-management, on the other hand, refers to the institutions and procedures under which decisions in a firm or in any other economic unit are made by all those who work in it.

The most important institution, which allows for such an internal democracy, is the workers' council in industry and in all other branches of the economy. The representatives elect the managers and have the right to dismiss them, and they review and deliberate on all aspects of the firm's decisions—what to produce, how much, how to distribute income, how much to allot for capital formation. They have a strong and at times the definitive voice on policies of hiring and firing, promotions, and standards for promotion.

No doubt tensions between managers and the workers' councils exist; firms everywhere may be run with an eye to profit, like capitalistic ones, at the expense of other social considerations. But Yugoslavia provides the only case of such a widespread participation of workers, and perhaps the unique case of workers' control. It is the only society that claims to have managed to embark upon industrial democracy.

What are the advantages of this system? They are social, economic and political. Politically the workers are increasingly allowed to participate. Even if it is for economic matters only they are drawn into the system and, therefore, the more they benefit from it the more they are likely to support it and to support the political regime as well. From a social point of view, workers' councils and workers' control may overcome the sentiment of alienation and powerlessness that afflicts workers in industrial societies, including the Soviet one. They have a voice and a stake in what is being decided and what is being produced, and they benefit or suffer directly because of the decisions they make. Furthermore, in making decisions of an economic nature, they have to balance their own direct and immediate self-interest against the interest of the collectivity where they live and work, and those of society as a whole. The system, in contrast to bureaucratic ones, presumes that the workers may be able to learn how to balance these various interests and to gradually shed the selfish motivation that "economic man" displays.

But one of the advantages of the system is that it does not do away with economic man. On the contrary, it allows for the expression of self-interest and, within limits, legitimizes it. It gives to the worker a sense of direct economic responsibility for his own well-being, since bad decisions may well mean less income. From a more general point of view the system allows competing self-managed firms to seek the highest possible efficiency in order to show a profit.

Towards a Political Democracy? The present regime appears to be relatively open and free, to a far greater extent than the Soviet Union and any of the Eastern European regimes. The country is open to millions of tourists every year and in turn Yugoslavs are free to travel abroad. The press is not censored; books—their publication and sales—are not subject to controls; university students and intellectuals write freely and express their own viewpoints.

Within the various representative assemblies debate is free and many policies are not agreed upon until an elaborate process of compromise has yielded agreement. The constitution provides for federal organs: a government and a parliament where national policies are hammered out; six individual republics and two autonomous provinces, each representing different ethnic and religious populations. The federal bodies represent the country and the "nation" as a whole. Every effort has been made to avoid the domination of one nationality (i.e. Serbian) over others.

The overall purpose is to create a multinational political society in which all ethnic groups have equal representation and participation and have freedom to use their own language and to enjoy their own ways, including the expression of their religious beliefs. The same is the case with another national institution, the army. Whereas in the past, 100 percent of the officer corps was Serbian, we find today not more than 60 percent. Only 46 percent of the generals and only 33 percent of the members of the high command are Serbian.

The League of Communists. Yugoslavia has a one-party system. The League of Communists of Yugoslavia (the new name for the Communist Party) is a national organization with a membership of over a million and a quarter. It is both a horizontal organization cutting across republics and a vertical one reaching down into every republic, region, locality, firm, and social institution. Elective office is generally limited to the members of the league, for at election time candidates for office must be approved by it. Thus, the league remains a monopolistic organization and competition for elective office is controlled by it.

There are three important considerations regarding the composition of the league that should be kept in mind. Over 65 percent of its members have joined it since roughly 1955. They are still relatively young, and all came into the party *after* the Yugoslav-Soviet split. Their entry coincides roughly with the shift away from the centralized model of Stalinism in the direction of self-management. To them, the institutions of the workers' councils and direct participation and control *is* socialism. Secondly, every effort has been made, despite the inevitable growth of white-collar and managerial groups, to keep the league a working-class party. Thus 31.2 percent are workers, 12.3 percent administrative personnel, 11.2 percent general intelligentsia, 7.4 percent private farmers, 11.6 percent managers and technical intelligentsia, 3.3 percent are students.[5] Workers, white-collar workers, technicians, managers and students comprise a majority and are considerably

5. Ibid.

over-represented in comparison to their population strength. These are
the more dynamic groups of the population, interested in continuing
modernization and anxious to maintain and enlarge their opportunities
and advantages in the regime. Thirdly, every effort has been made to
make the league as faithfully representative of the ethnic composition
of the country as a whole as it is possible.

What is the major function of the league today? "The League,"
writes Bogdan Denitch, ". . . even though it renounces the role of direct
shaper of day-to-day policy and defines itself primarily as the leading
ideological guardian of an essentially self-managing society and economy, is a key factor in the social changes taking place in Yugoslavia. . . ."
"It is hard," he points out, "to imagine an active citizen . . . who is not
a member of the League." The league "is the active vehicle for active
political participation in the system as a whole." Finally, "The League
functions as the representative of the new values of industrialization
and modernization."[6]

One might add that the league is also the major instrument for the
organization and integrity of a multinational political society both
against internal disruptive forces and external enemies. It is the custodian, in other words, of the nation, the State, and of the official
ideology.

The elite that constitutes the league is drawn from the population
on the basis of their ability and achievement. It is an elite that believes
in rapid modernization and progress, and takes it for granted that the
communism they practice is the best way of bringing it about. The
leadership is quite conscious that it needs widespread support, and
that force may be both costly and ineffective. Support is inculcated not
only through education, socialization and propaganda but through participatory mechanisms and rewards. Self-management and the workers'
council promote participation, and the modernizing sectors and strata
of the population, whether in industry, among engineers, white-collar
workers or managers, are rewarded with prospects of social mobility
and higher material benefits. The league acts as a catalyst in providing
and encouraging participatory politics and seeing to it that rewards
will be channeled in the name of modernization and socialism to the
more active and productive segments of the population—something
that *both* motivates them and secures their support.

It is conceivable, however, that self-management and participatory
politics may lead the citizenry to a point at which the basic values of
the regime may be questioned; in other words when persuasive politics
give place to confrontation politics. The league stands as a guardian
against such an eventuality. If dissent spills over the limits set by the
ideology on which the regime is based then it is inevitable that there
will be a sharp confrontation between the league and the participatory

6. Ibid.

and self-managing institutions it has created. The league, in other words, remains the only watchdog of the existing values and together with the army may have to protect them, even by force. In the meantime it acts as the nervous system of a highly complicated organism, promoting the acceptance of common values, facilitating compromise and decision-making, reconciling ethnic or group antagonisms, supervising from a distance the effective application of self-government in industry and in all other social local institutions, while making sure that no rival force develops.

It is precisely this openness, within the limits that a socialist regime can allow, that has been for the Yugoslavs both a source of pride and a lever of criticism against the Soviet Union. The words of Tito show why Yugoslavs are led both to glorify their own regime and to criticize the Soviet system. To explain the Soviet-Yugoslav split Tito wrote: "Progress toward socialism has been arrested and the Soviet Union has become an enormous terror state. . . . The fundamental question on which Stalin failed is the problem of freedom of the individual in socialism, for there can be no socialism without freedom. These two concepts are identical."[7] But freedom and openness are tolerated only within a socialist context, where most property has been socialized and the communist party enjoys a political monopoly.

Foreign Policy

An ideological profile is beginning to emerge; one of relatively open and democratic socialism, of participatory democracy, of decentralization and industrial democracy, of socialism with a market economy. It is a system, however, whose democratic credentials depend in the last analysis upon what the League of Communists (i.e., the Communist Party) will or will not allow.

It was far more difficult for Yugoslavia to develop a new image in the international world. Tito's image remains what it was when he split from the Soviets and managed to survive in the name of national communism. He planted seeds then that have continued to grow, and are now thorns that plague the Soviet Union. The most important one is the concept of "national communism." It means that nations, despite their acceptance of communism, are fundamentally and irrevocably committed to their full independence and reject any intervention in any form. "Titoism" as national communism spread all over Eastern Europe throughout the 1950s, and necessitated direct Soviet countermeasures.

A second effort by Tito to find an image was his sponsorship of "non-alignment"—that is, the effort to organize nations, mostly in the Third World, which refused to become dependent politically, diplo-

7. Dedijer, op. cit.

matically or militarily upon either the western world led by the United States or the communist world led by the Soviet Union. While these nations constitute numerically a large bloc, they are generally poor and torn with internal disputes and conflicts. They have been unable to organize thus far and have failed to agree on any basic foreign policy objectives. In their last congress, held in Belgrade in June 1978, they could agree on nothing except on the holding of the next congress in Havana. The implementation of even this decision, however, is doubtful.

Faced by the Soviet power, Tito and the present Yugoslav leaders have fallen back discreetly on the only possible course of action left to a small state—support from the United States. Also, more recently, there has been the establishment of closer relations with China. There was no alternative. It will have to be so until Titoism develops elsewhere in Eastern Europe, and until fellow-communist China, whose concerns and ideological posture parallel those of communist Yugoslavia, takes a more active part in European affairs. For the time being the assertion of an independent stance by a communist state in the name of national communism, and its consolidation, remain Tito's most enduring contribution in international affairs.

Maoism

Like Titoism in Yugoslavia, Maoism is the label for the communist movement and its ideology that developed in China under the leadership of Mao Tse-tung. "Chairman Mao" was for more than forty years the undisputed leader of the Chinese Communist Party and the head of the communist government in China after the civil war (1946–1949) until his death in 1977.

Maoism represents the first, apparently successful, communist revolution in an underdeveloped non-European society and the first viable non-European communist regime. As did Yugoslavia, China broke off from the direct political and economic oversight of the Soviet Union to follow its own path to communism. But the reasons for the break can be traced to the very beginnings of the Chinese communist movement, as expounded by Mao Tse-tung.

Background

Two powerful forces dominated pre-communist Chinese society: the landlords and the warlords. The first owned and controlled the land and squeezed out of the peasantry whatever they could, keeping them at a bare level of subsistence if not starvation. The second controlled the means of coercion. Military commanders in various regions and provinces, however, asserted their independent authority and engaged frequently in war with each other.

MAO TSE-TUNG (1893–1977)

Mao Tse-tung was the son of a peasant family from Hunan. In 1918 he became a librarian at Peking University where his socialist leanings were strengthened as a result of contact with the works of Marx and those of Li Ta-chao and Ch'en Tu-hsiu, two professors who with Mao were to help found the Chinese Communist Party in 1921. Although attaining leadership positions in the CCP, Mao's devotion to the peasantry as a revolutionary force, and his theory of guerrilla warfare rather than urban insurrection, alienated him from much of the party leadership. After the persecution and elimination of the communists in 1927, Mao proclaimed a "soviet republic" in southwestern Kiangsi Province. In 1934 he led his forces on the two-year "Long March" to regroup in Northwestern China. The Chinese Communist forces finally triumphed over their nationalist opponents in 1949 and established the People's Republic of China, which Mao served as President, in addition to his post as Party Chairman. Among Mao's major works are *On Contradictions, On Practice* and *Quotations From Chairman Mao,* an anthology which served as the textbook for the young Red Guard cadres of the Cultural Revolution.

There were at least three other important forces: the rich merchants, acting on behalf of foreign firms and exporters, British, American, French, Japanese; the foreign governments, who controlled with their own military forces many of China's eastern seaports, including a great part of Shanghai (these were the "concessions" that had been granted to foreign powers); and, finally, there were the Japanese, who after taking Taiwan in 1898 began to eye Manchuria and the eastern part of China. After World War One they too were given special concessions in Shanghai.

Foreign presence fanned the flame of a growing nationalism precisely when the internal quarrels of the warlords, the speculation and manipulations of the landlords and the merchants, the overall corruption of the elites, and the weakness of the political regime deprived the country of unity and direction. The circumstances, therefore, seemed propitious for the development of a new party such as a communist one, with unified direction and clear ideological goals. It could harness at one and the same time the widespread discontent, and give direction to the spirit of nationalism and the demands for national independence.

The Chinese Communist Party, founded in 1921, at first accepted fully the 21 conditions imposed by the Third International. It accepted the "dictatorship of the proletariat" and subscribed to the concept of revolutionary class struggle. Yet at the express insistence of the Soviet leadership, the Chinese communist leaders abandoned their party's revolutionary position and gave their support to the leader of what appeared to be a middle-of-the-road coalition of political forces in China—the Kuomintang, led by Chiang Kai-shek. Almost immediately Chiang turned against the communists, arrested and imprisoned thousands of leaders, cadres and members, and shot many of them. The Communist Party was destroyed in virtually all urban centers where it was supported by workers and intellectuals. Its proletarian base was wiped out. Perhaps it was from this moment on that the peasant base of the Chinese Communist Party became indispensable in the eyes of Mao. He and many communist leaders withdrew into the vast countryside to develop intimate relations with the peasantry.

They gathered in strength in one of the relatively poorer provinces of China, Kiangsi, where they established a Communist Republic and ruled the province from 1931 to about 1934. It was at this time that the Red Army, later to become known as the People's Liberation Army, was founded. But through their "Kiangsi experience" the Chinese communists under Mao learned what they had to do if they were to receive support from the peasants. They realized that they had to relate their strategy and goals to the expectations of the peasantry. "The peasants came to see that the communists worked for their interest. Their army was perfectly disciplined, neither plundered nor commandeered. What it needed it bought for cash and if it could not be supplied it went elsewhere."[8] Good relations with the peasantry, and the support they gave to the communists, was an important element of Mao's famous theory of guerrilla warfare.

But the communist republic in Kiangsi was gradually surrounded by Chiang's forces, while in the northeast, Manchuria fell quickly to the invading Japanese. It was at this juncture, aware of Chiang's determination to liquidate the communists, that Mao made a momentous decision, which both saved the Communist Party and consolidated its peasant base. The whole Red Army and the Communist Party in Kiangsi moved, in what became known as the "Long March," some seven thousand miles across the country to establish its headquarters in the Yenan Province relatively close to Manchuria and Peking. It first moved west, then north and then east. It was a monumental achievement, and its success was not only due to the perseverance of the leadership and of their followers, but to the general support given to it by the population—by the peasantry. From Yenan the communists were able to confront the Japanese between 1936 and the end of World War Two, thus emerging as the champions of Chinese nationalism and independence.

The Pillars of Maoism

It was the support of and identification with the peasantry, as well as the increasing assumption by the communists of a nationalist posture, which accounted for their ultimate victory. But it was to a great extent

8. Fitzgerald. *Mao Tse-tung and China*, p. 39.

Part of the Red Army, preparing for what came to be known as "The Long March." (Photo: Radio Times Hulton Picture Library)

also due to the development of a new revolutionary strategy—*guerrilla warfare.*

THE PEASANTRY

The peasants invariably play a crucial role in all revolutions, and their grievances have been exploited by conservative, liberal and communist leaders at different times. Lenin's slogan "land to the peasants" on the eve of the Bolshevik Revolution either directly rallied many of them behind the communists or, and even more important, neutralized them. But Marxists believe that while the peasantry could at times be helpful it was only the working class and its leaders, the Communist Party, which could develop the proper class and revolutionary consciousness, make the revolution and establish socialism. Peasants' major preoccupation is the ownership of land: they are considered, therefore, to be fundamentally an obstacle to the building of socialism.

At the second congress of the Third International in 1920 the role of the peasantry had been explicitly recognized as being side by side with the working class. It was Mao who for the first time went beyond this to attribute to the peasantry a genuine revolutionary role and to build his revolutionary movement on a peasant basis. The revolution would be made in close association with the peasantry and in great part by the peasantry.

It may be argued that Mao's strategy was dictated by the circumstances. Since the urban centers were controlled by Chiang and the proletarian ranks of the Communist Party were decimated, the communists had no alternative but to turn to the peasants. But there seemed to be more important reasons. Mao, the son of a fairly well-to-do farmer, had spent years in his native province of Hunan, studying peasant conditions.[9] He described their miseries, deprivations and the manner in which they were exploited by the landlords, but he also expressed his admiration for their stoicism, shrewdness and courage. There was a genuine populist streak in Mao: an admiration for the innate goodness and spontaneity of the peasants. He also saw that the decades of deprivation and exploitation and the constant strife against the hated landlords made the Chinese peasantry a potentially powerful revolutionary force. All that needed to be done was to mobilize it under the proper leadership. Doing this was Mao's major achievement. Without forgetting the importance of the proletariat, he built the Chinese Communist Party on the basis of the peasantry and from the peasantry.

NATIONALISM

The slogans of the Bolshevik Revolution were both anti-national and anti-war. They were addressed against the top oligarchy. The Bolshe-

---

9. "Report of an Investigation of the Peasant Movement in Hunan" (1927). In *Selected Works of Mao Tse-tung.*

viks simply overthrew it and replaced it almost overnight. The revolution amounted to a swift replacement of the ruling elite by a revolutionary one. It was almost like a *putsch* though it had the most far-reaching social and economic consequences.

The situation in China was vastly different. First and foremost the revolution took place over a long period of time in a two-front war against both the Japanese military forces that had occupied the greater part of Eastern China, and against the Nationalist forces of the Kuomintang led by Chiang. The communists claimed to be the only truly national force, fighting not only the Japanese but, indirectly, the British and the Americans who were supporting Chiang. Gradually Chinese nationalism and China's independence became associated with the Communist Party and Mao's People's Liberation Army.

The Communist Party broadened its appeal to include in fact almost all those who were fighting the Japanese but who also favored full and unqualified independence from all former imperialist forces, most notably the British and the Americans. Not only did they dig deep into the rich substratum of the peasantry, but, their appeal was irrespective of class. The base of the revolution was broadened therefore to include not only the workers and the peasants but also the middle classes, the intellectuals, the lower middle classes. The "people" were defined in the broadest possible terms to include virtually all groups. The only "enemies" were the landlords and those who served the interests of the foreign powers, including of course those who collaborated with the Japanese.

Mao theorized on "contradictions." He claimed that all contradictions within the people could be resolved: they were supposed to be "non-antagonistic," that is, not inherently leading to conflict. "Antagonistic" contradictions, on the other hand, were limited only to inherently conflictual situations which pitted the people against landlords and collaborators. The first could be reconciled without force; for the second, force was unavoidable. In this way all Chinese fighting together for their national independence against the common enemies were welcomed into a vast nationalist front led by the Communist Party and Mao.

GUERRILLA WAR

In classic Leninist theory and practice the revolution is an act of force made by a trained, organized and a highly disciplined revolutionary party (the Communist Party) acting in the name of the working class. The revolution is ruthless, just as it has to be swift. If successful, it will impose itself upon the society and the Communist Party will assume all powers.

The broader definition of the "people" given by Mao, on the other hand, and the particular circumstances of the struggle for power in China, differentiate Maoism from this Leninist model. Mao relied upon popular support and sustained collective effort and put a premium on

the motivation and the initiative of the masses, more than on organization and discipline. Furthermore, he could not envisage a revolution
in a single uprising replacing the ruling elite in China. The double
struggle against both Japanese and Chiang could not be sustained without broad support. The Communist Party could not monitor, let alone
lead, every skirmish and every confrontation with its enemies. A certain
degree of voluntarism and a great degree of decentralization were necessary and perhaps unavoidable. (We have noted that the same was the
case with the Yugoslav Titoist movement when the partisans fought
both against the Germans and the various collaborationist forces.)

Mao and his Communist Party relied therefore far more than did
the Bolsheviks on shaping "the minds and the souls" of the people, so
that they would support his Liberation Army, and provide the fighting
forces with shelter, food, information and new soldiers. In the long
struggle which ultimately led to victory, a vast network of connections
between the Communist Party and the People's Liberation Army with
the peasants and all other sections of the population was built. The
Communist Party spearheaded the movement, but the thrust of the
spear depended on the strong links to social groups and the solidarity
of supports that had developed.

Under these circumstances, then, the revolution in China was to
be made over a long period of time. It was not to be simply the expression of force at a particular moment. To be sure, force is to all revolutionaries what the Bible is to missionaries: Mao's famous statement
"Power comes from the barrel of the gun" shows that he had a great
respect for force. But his theory of guerrilla warfare shows also that he
understood the limitations of force and of the gun when it does not
take into account human factors: will, motivation, cooperation, initiative, moral support and commitment. The barrel is empty without
them: this is the basis of Mao's theory of guerrilla warfare. There must
be the broadest possible participation, for unless the population is
prepared and willing to give their support, fighting is impossible.

Mao's realization that no revolution could really succeed without
popular support derived in part from a teacher of his who admired the
British idealists—philosophers who put particular emphasis on the
development of individual motivation and purposive action. Without
such individual understanding and voluntary participation, no governmental reform or action and of course no revolutionary overhaul of
the society could be sustained. A revolution that did not bring forth
conscious individual effort was doomed to turn against what it professed to build: collective but conscious and voluntary support and
cooperation.

The Communist Regime

It took time after the defeat of the Kuomintang forces under Chiang in
1949 for the communist regime to take shape. When it did, the major
organizational lines were not unusual. First there was the predomi-

nance or rather the monopoly of political power and control in the hands of the Communist Party; secondly, the nationalization of the economy and the collectivization of the land.

As with other communist regimes the three basic organizational pillars of government were: (1) the State and its institutions; (2) the party and its ideology; (3) the army—the People's Liberation Army. Constant modifications of structures and reallocation of powers make anything but some general remarks difficult.[10]

THE STATE

The State is organized along familiar lines. There are the national organs for the whole of the country with some fifty departments and a large civil service. There is a head of state, the Chairman. He directs the activities of the governmental organs and is technically responsible to the National People's Congress, a large assembly meeting infrequently, consisting of over four thousand members. This congress is, only technically again, the supreme legislative and constitution-making body. It consists almost exclusively of Communist Party members.

Below the national organs are the provincial and communal organizations. These have varied in size and number over the last twenty years, governed by provincial and communal executive bodies—again controlled by the Communist Party, either directly or through provincial or communal congresses in which the Communist Party has a majority.

THE COMMUNIST PARTY

The second and supreme pillar of government is the Communist Party, consisting today of over forty million members. The principle of democratic centralism applies, with local authorities expected to abide by the decisions of the central organs, while the selection to such organs proceeds, in theory if not in practice, from the lowest level upwards. A National Party Congress representing all the party members "elects" the central committee, which in effect is the supreme collective body of the party. It, in turn, elects the Politburo, consisting of thirty-two members, which in turn elects the highest authority within the party— the Chairman. Since Mao's death the Chairman is the head of the government and also the commander-in-chief of the army.

THE ARMY

The People's Liberation Army is under the Ministry of National Defense, which in turn is under the Politburo and under the chairman of the central committee. It is of course thoroughly supervised by political commissars, all of them trusted communists. For every military unit, from the general staff down to company level, there correspond polit-

---

10. For a good account of the organization of the State and the Communist Party, see Townsend. *Politics in China.*

ical departments or officers. Most of the army officers themselves are members of the Communist Party.

Every effort has been made to avoid the development of hierarchies within the army. There are no insignia indicating rank; officers have to do, once in a while during the year, the tasks allotted to the soldiers. Morale seems to be high, the organization excellent and the fighting capabilities high enough to make it difficult for any power, including the Soviet Union, to contemplate an invasion of Chinese territory. In 1951 the Chinese confronted American forces in Korea, drove them back and were able to hold them off. In border skirmishes with Soviet forces, the Chinese have held their ground. There were no defections and no indication of any organizational or morale problems. In 1979 the Chinese were able to move into a strongly fortified area of Vietnam, administering what they termed "a lesson" to an ally of the Soviet Union.

The Regime in Flux

As some commentators have pointed out, what characterizes the communist regime in China thus far is a constant tug and pull between "institutionalization" and "transformation." The ideological goals of the regime remain the transforming of social relations and of the individual by establishing communism. Yet to do so new institutions must be established in education, governance, the economy and the army. However, institutionalization slows down change and inertia sets in; quite often vested interests develop which become obstacles to change. How to avert this? By once more launching forth in the direction of transforming what is just barely institutionalized! The regime, founded on the commitment to change, becomes endangered by the very change to which it is committed.[11]

To allow a process of institutionalization that fosters and crystallizes hierarchical relations and a bureaucracy which becomes uncompromising towards popular needs, is to abandon hopes for transformation and change. Even more, it is going against the high hopes of Mao that popular participation and the tapping of the ingenuity and spontaneity of the people is the only safeguard of socialism. It is also to gradually give in to bureaucratized controls and directions similar to those existing in the Soviet system, and by so doing to resort increasingly to force rather than relying on popular support.

There has been a high degree of fluidity, and at times downright instability if not chaos, in the development of the Chinese communist system. With the death of Mao and the virtual disappearance of all those who were in one way or another associated with the Long March

11. The thesis of institutionalization versus revolution is developed in Townsend's *Politics in China*. As I mentioned in my preface, I am indebted to the author for many of my observations in this section.

and the civil war, a new generation may put the premium on institutionalization, stability and rapid industrialization and modernization.

The following main ideological and institutional stages of the Chinese communist regime since its inception can be outlined:

1. A period of consolidation but also of education and mobilization in the principles of socialism (1949–53).
2. The move in the direction of economic planning and socialism (1953–56), followed by a period of liberalization.
3. A massive effort to industrialize—known as the "Great Leap Forward" (1957–60).
4. A subsequent period of retreat from the goals of rapid industrialization that lasted until 1965, to be followed by
5. The "Cultural Revolution" (1966–69), again followed by a period of consolidation until 1972.
6. The period since Mao's death when after a brief conflict between "moderate" leaders and "revolutionaries" (who hailed from the period of the Cultural Revolution and claimed to be Mao's intellectual heirs) the moderates have gained the upper hand. Their emphasis has been upon stability, industrialization and modernization, with the help of capitalist countries in Western Europe, and even the United States itself.

Thus the unfolding of the Chinese communist experiment moves in waves that flow and ebb. Socialism began in earnest with the first Five-Year Plan initiated in 1953. Like the first Soviet Five-Year Plan launched more than a decade after the Bolshevik Revolution, its target was to industrialize the country rapidly. Emphasis was put on capital development and on heavy industry. Individual businesses and plants were taken over by the State and, as in Russia, State centralized bureaucratic planning mechanisms began to develop. Also as in Russia, a rapid effort was made to collectivize the land by amalgamating peasant households and plots into communes and cooperatives of varying sizes.

But economic planning and the socialization of the economy and the collectivization of agriculture put heavy demands upon the State organization and apparatus. They led to centralization and to State controls that assumed coercive character. They endangered popular support and participation. In 1956 Mao initiated a period of controlled liberalization. He and the party leadership inaugurated what became known as the "Let a Hundred Flowers Bloom" movement, in which an open debate on all matters was encouraged. It revealed that there was discontent among the peasants; that the workers resented centralized management and managerial direction; that bureaucratization was indeed feared; and that many leading party organizers and cadres had abused the powers that centralized planning and direction had put in their hands. Intellectuals began to criticize many aspects of socialism while searching for new formulas that would reconcile communism with freedoms.

Just as suddenly as it began the Hundred Flowers campaign was abandoned. In 1957 Mao returned to the imperatives of industrialization, and seemingly resolved to out-Stalin Stalin's achievements. The new period, known as the "Great Leap Forward," began at the same time as the second Five-Year Plan was introduced in 1958. During the Leap, collectivization moved ahead with the merging of smaller co-operative and communal units into large communes that became the production and administration units in the countryside. They developed their own schools and factories, built mess halls that were used in common, provided for militia, hospitals, roads, etc. There were about 24,000 such large communes for the whole of China.

The Leap did not prove successful. Within two years progress came down to a crawl. Central controls were modified in favor of greater local autonomy, work in the communes was made lighter, the size of the communes was reduced and the total number of communes was increased from about 24,000 to about 75,000. Private plots were returned to the individual peasants and "trade fairs" (another name for free markets) reappeared.

In 1966 a new revolutionary drive was mounted—the Great Proletarian Cultural Revolution. It lasted almost until 1970 and it affected virtually every aspect of the State, the administration, the party, and the economy. It was in effect a revolution of the masses and the rank and file of the Communist Party—especially strong in the cities, the factories and the universities—against *their leaders* and *organized by some of them!* Its targets were broad and diffuse, thus providing for as wide a mobilization of the people as was possible. Old ideas, customs, habits, prejudices, selfishness, greed, authority and hierarchy—all came under a sweeping attack.

The revolution was characteristically enough spearheaded by the very young: high school students who were apparently organized and moved from one place to another by the army. They became known as the Red Guards. In some instances the youthful rebels seized power. Otherwise they invariably brought down many of the local, State, administrative and even party officials. More than 30 percent of the members of the central committee fell; many top leaders resigned. All in all there was a vast purge of the State and party cadres that, in contrast with Stalinist methods, did not take place in the dark through the secret police, but in the open through powerful pressures from below (even if carefully orchestrated from the top). Its ultimate purpose was to maintain the participatory and popular character of the Maoist regime.

As was the case with the Hundred Flowers and also the Great Leap, the Cultural Revolution came to an end as dramatically and suddenly as it had broken into the open. And as in the past, it was followed by

rivalries that followed his death did not affect the regime. Within a
relatively short time the Communist Party managed to reestablish its
unity and to select a new chairman, who is also now the Head of State
and the army.

Conclusion

All regimes that spring from revolutionary ideology and which take
power through revolution are shaped by the way in which they first
managed to acquire power. The Bolshevik Revolution was in effect the
work of a handful of men and women who believed in organization
and for whom the party was a paramilitary instrument for the conquest
of power. The Russian communists, once in power, used the party as
an arm of a highly centralized political organization, governing the
country from the top down through a highly centralized and bureaucratized apparatus.

The Chinese Revolution, on the other hand, and the communist
takeover of power in China, was the work of a vast popular movement,
of guerrilla warfare that involved in one form or another virtually the
whole of the countryside and many of the urban populations as well.
Victory was won thanks to popular support and participation. To maintain their leadership, therefore, the communist leaders and the party
have had to go back to the people, so to speak, to mobilize them,
organize them, and work with them and for them. Coercion has been
widely used but it could not in the long run succeed. It is education
in socialism and mobilization for socialism which is best able to bring
forth popular support.

This is perhaps the distinctive trait of Chinese communism.[12] Its
ultimate goal is to provide and generate incentives and participation;
to fashion men and women who ultimately become convinced of the
advantages of a communist society. The building of socialism and the
transformation of the individual must go hand in hand. But what if
individuals begin to turn away from the socialist framework? And what
if individual criticism and dissent begins to question the very citadel
of power—the Communist Party and its leadership?

The constant shifts and changes underlined by massive appeals to
the party rank and file, and the people, together with the frequent
attacks against bureaucratization and centralization, indicate that the
system is seeking a middle ground between freedoms and constraints,
between participation and repression, between orthodoxy and experimentation. It is still going through a period of change and transformation. The Chinese regime is still in flux.

12. For a general discussion of Mao's political ideology and its implications, see Schram.
The Political Thought of Mao Tse-tung.

Eurocommunism

The term Eurocommunism has been used to describe and identify new common trends, ideological and political, which have appeared since 1975 (sometimes earlier) among some European communist parties within the western democracies, and particularly in France, Italy and Spain. The term itself suggests that a European type of communism, different in both doctrine and tactics, may be emerging within the Western European democracies that differs from the Soviet one and from that of the Eastern European satellites. The phenomenon however, it should be pointed out, is neither comprehensive nor precise. All European communist parties do not act in the same manner, have not agreed on a common doctrine and do not espouse the same policies. Furthermore, there is no common forum or organization. Meetings between the heads of European communist parties have occasionally taken place, but there is no inter-European machinery for the communist parties to provide for deliberation and to formulate common guidelines.

After 1920 all European communist parties, having seceded from the socialist parties and the Second International, accepted the doctrinal and policy guidelines embodied in the 21 conditions. Notably:

1. Class struggle was unavoidable and desirable, with the communists acting on behalf of the working class.

2. Revolution was the way to attain power.

3. The dictatorship of the proletariat was the necessary instrumentality for the liquidation of the counter-revolutionary forces and the consolidation of the revolution.

4. Collectivization and nationalization of the means of production would follow.

5. The preservation of the fatherland of socialism—the Soviet Union— against all "imperalist" forces was the duty of all European communists.

The relationship between the national communist parties and the Soviet Union hardened in practice into a pattern of subordination to Moscow and control by the Soviets. Many of the tactical switches of the national communist parties could be traced directly to the national and strategic interests of the Soviet Union. Sometimes these called for a revolutionary and militant stance on the part of national communist parties, and sometimes for cooperation with their national governments.

Eurocommunism is supposed to represent a departure from these basic doctrinal and tactical guidelines, particularly with an assertion of an independent stance vis-à-vis the Soviet Union.

Eurocommunists are beginning to reconsider the principle of class struggle, which, as we saw, is of crucial importance to the thinking of Marx and Lenin. The reasons are many. The distinction between the working class and "capitalists" is not as marked in advanced industrialized societies as it has been in the past. The vast majority of the gainfully employed are salaried—they form a large new middle class. The composition and income of the working class has changed radically to allow for relatively high incomes for skilled and white-collar workers, whose mentality and outlook also becomes increasingly middle-class. The democratic process also bridges the gap between workers and capitalists, and allows the communists in combination with other parties to seek, and hopefully to obtain, political power. Eurocommunists therefore increasingly take a reformist attitude, advocating change, compromise, "advanced democracy," a "popular union" with other left-wing parties—not in order to establish socialism but in order to form a government to prepare the conditions from which socialism will develop.

Revolution

Electoral politics, the agreement of the communists of European countries to seek power, in combination with other left-wing forces, peacefully and through the ballot, makes revolution obsolete. Eurocommunists no longer wish to take power by force, or to impose one class upon the rest of the society. They prefer to cooperate with other groups to form a majority in parliament. Antonio Gramsci, the Italian communist leader and theoretician, advocated the tactics of a broad penetration of various socio-economic groups by the communists to gain popular support and acceptance. French communists over recent years have abandoned in their pronouncements their commitment to class and revolutionary politics, in favor of a broad "popular union." Such efforts may give to the communists and their allies a majority, or at least adequate parliamentary strength to participate in government, or to cooperate closely with other major parties as coalition partners. In Italy, from 1974 to 1979 the famous "historical compromise" amounted to the political cooperation of the communists with their formal arch-rivals, the Christian Democrats.

Parliamentary Democracy?

Many Eurocommunists therefore seem to accept the logic of majoritarianism and the principles of democracy. The Italian communist leader Enrico Berlinguer has even gone beyond this, stating that even if the Italian Communist Party got 51 percent of the vote they could not govern against the other 49 percent! He admitted the tactics of compromise and the necessity of getting support from as wide a sector of the population as possible.

French communists have accepted the principle of governmental "alternation," promising that they would accept the popular verdict: there can be no question of dictatorship. The Spanish communist leader (but not the Portuguese one) has committed himself to electoral and democratic politics, and has gone so far as to accept the monarchy in Spain. They all agree to respect the freedom of association and parties as well as individual and political freedoms.

Democratic Centralism and Avant-Gardism

The principle of democratic centralism, as we noted earlier, makes for hierarchical and leadership control within the communist party and does not allow the formation of factions. The party thus assumes a paramilitary character, stressing obedience of lower-ranking organs to superior ones, and ultimately to the leader of the party. It is this democratic centralism that differentiates the communist party from all other political parties, including the socialists. It is a practice that safeguards unity and militancy, necessary for a party committed to revolution and a dictatorship. The party is the "avant-garde" of the proletariat and the masses, leading them to socialism.

It would have seemed natural therefore for the European communist parties with their new profession of faith in democracy to have relaxed a rigorous application of democratic centralism and to allow for an open and free debate within their ranks. This has not come to pass. In fact the French Communist Party silences all internal criticisms and does not allow its daily newspaper to publish articles of party members critical of the leadership and suggesting new policies. The same has been generally the case with the Spanish and the Portuguese Communist Parties, and even of the Italian Party. The Eurocommunist parties do not seem ready to abandon their tight organzation, discipline and leadership control.

National Communism?

Ever since the death of Stalin the control of the Soviet Communist Party over all European communist parties has progressively weakened. National forces, as we have seen, with Tito first, weakened Soviet control until it had to be reaffirmed through military intervention—in Hungary in 1956 and again in Czechoslovakia in 1968. But Western European communist parties, the Italian one first and foremost, began to reassert their own intellectual and political independence to develop their program and their course of action. Communism should manifest itself in its national colors, independent of Moscow.

Will Eurocommunist parties in the name of the rediscovery of their "national colors" defend foreign policies independent of Soviet ones, and even contrary to them? Or will they stay close to their previous line by identifying the interests of communism and the working class with the interests and policies of the Soviet Union? This may well be the ultimate test of the genuineness of the professed independence of the communist parties. No clear answer can be given as yet. While there are occasional signs of difference between the policies of the national communist parties and the foreign policies and actions of the Soviet Union, most European communist parties continue to agree with the Soviet foreign policy objective and tactics.

Conclusion

On many of the basic ideological and policy issues, Eurocommunism does not represent as yet a unified body of doctrine and practice. It is unclear whether we are confronted with a new phenomenon, a genuine transformation which will overhaul the doctrinal bases of the communist world in Western Europe to such a degree as to enable us to talk of a genuine "democratic communism" or "national communism"; or, whether it is a mere tactical shift to accommodate the communist parties to the realities of the democratic industralized societies in which they live.

Can the communist parties in Western Europe be trusted to act independently of the Soviet Union in foreign policy matters? Can we believe that once in government they will accept fully the rules of democracy and allow political competition in free and open elections which might oust them from power? It is still very doubtful. The communist parties—*all* Eurocommunist parties—are tightly controlled by their leadership. There is no guarantee that once in government the leaders will not attempt to impose the same control upon society as a whole. It is also difficult to believe that good communists will ever abandon their faith in the superiority of their doctrine and allow for genuine pluralism in ideas, political parties, publications, and so on.

Communism and the Third World

It remains now to discuss the appeal of communism and the extent of the adoption of its political and economic organization by the leaders of new nations, mostly in Africa and Asia.

There are a number of reasons which lead one to expect a rapid spread of the communist, especially the Leninist, model among new nations. It provided a way to rapidly mobilize the population. It suggested a way to industrialize and modernize, as Stalin had done, through collectivization, nationalization and economic planning. So in the 1950s and 1960s many colonial leaders claimed to be Marxists and Leninists. The revolution was a matter of political organization, they claimed—a matter of leadership capable of exploiting and marshaling the moral indignation of the colonial peoples against their masters. Both Castro and Che Guevara felt that this should be the basis for revolution in Latin America, where the proximity of the U.S.A. and its "colonial" practices, in cooperation with despotic and corrupt regimes, accounted for a spirit of moral indignation and deep resentment. Some of the more sophisticated of the colonial leaders began to look beyond Lenin into some of the early works of Marx, where revolution had its sources in a moral protest against deprivation and exploitation.

Emphasis upon will and organization, the appeal to moral imperatives, the support of the peasantry—all led to the concoction of a "doctrine" in terms of which some colonial revolutionary leaders called themselves Marxist and Leninist and waged war to gain their independence. In so doing they were of course cooperating fully with other social and political groups and leaders for whom national independence, not communism, was the primary consideration. The question of the applicability of the communist model came therefore with special urgency *after* independence had been proclaimed and after the colonial powers in India, Burma, Malaysia, Indonesia, the whole of Africa and most of the Middle East, had withdrawn. In some of these countries communism has been a negligible force; in others, lip service has been paid to the communist doctrine; only in a few has a fairly strong and politically conscious communist leadership and an organized Communist Party developed.

A communist regime that was an approximation of the Soviet model established itself only in very few countries. Vietnam is one; Castro's Cuba is a second—but it is only an approximation. So is the China regime—there are, as we have seen, basic differences from the Soviet model. In Indonesia the Communist Party came close to assuming a controlling position in the government and establishing a one-party rule, but was crushed. In the whole of the Middle East, the only country with a legalized Communist Party is Israel. In Africa there is hardly anywhere a communist party, though some political leaders call themselves Marxists. In Burma and Malaysia the communists have been outlawed.

In most of these countries the doctrine proclaimed favors the establishment of some form of "humanistic" or "democratic" socialism in which the State claims to control the major economic activities without, however, eliminating the market economy. But in virtually all of them there is a one-party system representing, as we pointed out, "democratic" unity and "communitarian" values.

Thus one might conclude that the Soviet model, important in shaping the doctrine and the organization that led to guerrilla warfare and to independence, has not been adopted by most of the new nations, nor has it been radically modified to suit specific circumstances. The reasons are many. First and foremost was the problem of national integration and consolidation after liberation. The Stalinist model, based upon indoctrination, a well-organized party and force, could not be used. There were, simply, no well-organized communist parties, it was difficult to indoctrinate illiterate and apathetic groups, and, finally, because the very use of force might split the population of the new nations into their tribal or ethnic, linguistic or religious components, rather than uniting it. "Nation-building" can be accomplished by force only when there is a powerful group or party that can use it and impose it.

Secondly, communism as a set of tactics developed by Lenin was welcome to many, but not as a way of life. Most of the African elites viewed their struggle for liberation in moral and religious terms, and sometimes even in the liberal terms in which nationalism had been couched in Europe in the nineteenth century. Marxism-Leninism was "materialist" and "atheistic." It was, according to some Asian, African, and Moslem leaders "another religion" that would not tolerate the existing ones. It was therefore unacceptable.

Finally, there were practical considerations stemming from the international political situation and the willingness on the part of the U.S.S.R. and the U.S.A. to offer economic aid. Former colonies maintained ties with the colonial powers: France, for instance, very quickly renegotiated economic, cultural and military accords after the independence of its African colonies. The same applied to some of the British colonies in Africa in their relations with Britain. American business groups, but also the American government, had every reason to invest or to give aid so that the new countries would not turn to the Soviet Union. Whatever the affinities were, therefore, between the new leaders of the new nations and the Soviet Union (and there was a debt to the Soviets for the moral and often material support given to them during their independence struggle), it would have been unwise to abandon the ties with the capitalist and democratic west. In fact, as the years went on after independence the Soviet leaders did not show themselves to be particularly generous nor did they provide aid, whether economic or military, without attaching strings. Aid was often clearly subordinated to Soviet strategic considerations.

Ideologies and institutional practices are not easy to import. Democracy has been reinterpreted by the new nations almost out of its original meaning; so, in many instances, has communism. Democratic institutions virtually do not exist in the Third World, but similarly, the one-party system adopted by many of the new states has no resemblance to the Leninist conception of the party, nor to Stalinist practice. The new nations are still in the process of developing their own political ideologies by adapting western ones to their own needs, and their own political culture.

Bibliography

Bicanic, Rudolf. *Economic Policy in Socialist Yugoslavia.* New York: Cambridge U.P., 1973.

Denitch, Bogdan. *The Legitimization of a Revolution: The Yugoslav Case.* New Haven: Yale U.P., 1972.

Carrillo, Santiago. *Eurocommunism and the State.* New York: Lawrence Hill, 1978.

Dedijer, Vladimir. *Tito Speaks.* London: Weidenfeld and Nicolson, 1953.

Drachkovitch, Milorad (ed.). *Marxism in the Modern World.* Stanford, Ca.: Stanford U.P., 1965.

Fitzgerald, C.P. *Mao Tse-tung and China.* New York: Homer and Meir, 1976.

Griffith, Samuel B. *Mao Tse-tung: On Guerrilla Warfare.* New York: Praeger, 1961.

Griffith, William E. (ed.). *Communism in Europe.* 2 volumes. Cambridge, Ma.: M.I.T. Press, 1967.

Kaplan, Morton A. *The Many Faces of Communism.* New York: Free Press, 1978.

Mao Tse-tung. *Selected Readings from the Works of Mao Tse-tung.* Peking: Foreign Languages Press, 1971.

Schram, Stuart (ed.). *The Political Thought of Mao Tse-tung.* New York: Praeger, 1963.

Townsend, James R. *Politics in China.* Boston: Little, Brown, 1974.

Ulam, Adam. *Titoism and the Cominform.* Cambridge, Ma.: Harvard U.P., 1952.

Urban, G.R. (ed.). *Eurocommunism: Its Roots and Future in Italy and Elsewhere.* New York: Universe, 1978.

part three

THE TOTALITARIAN RIGHT

No shepherds and one herd! Everybody wants the same; Everybody wants to be the same; Whoever feels different goes voluntarily into a madhouse!
FRIEDRICH NIETZSCHE   Thus Spoke Zarathustra

Nazism and fascism, and the other totalitarian regimes that developed in Europe and elsewhere after World War One, had deep roots. They did not spring from the wickedness of a leader such as Hitler; they were not the product of deviant personalities; they were not initiated by adventurers and veterans of World War One seeking redemption from defeat or boredom. In fact they were well-organized and well-structured political movements representing at one and the same time a very powerful reaction against both liberal democracy and communism and the communist parties that had developed in the wake of the Bolshevik Revolution. They were movements that reaffirmed, in the strongest possible terms, national solidarity and unity, order and discipline. They drew heavily from the body of anti-democratic and anti-liberal thought, but also from the ideology and practice of Leninism.

In other words, right-wing totalitarian movements and regimes cannot, any more than communist totalitarian systems, be dismissed as exceptions to the democratic norm. They drew their inspiration, whatever the specific historical circumstances that brought them to power, from deep roots that had been planted in fertile soil. These roots have not yet been fully removed. We must not consider Nazism and fascism something that happened in the past and should be forgotten, but as a political ideology which is still with us.

Nazism and Fascism: The Background

(Fascism) . . . is the general reaction of modern times against the flabby materialistic positivism of the nineteenth century. BENITO MUSSOLINI The Doctrine of Fascism

Right-wing totalitarian movements like those of the Nazis and fascists developed everywhere in Europe soon after World War One. They spread to Central Europe, Portugal, Spain and the Balkans in the 1930s. They affected countries with strong democratic traditions like France, and even England. Liberal democracy was everywhere threatened.

The new regimes did away with some of the most basic freedoms that the civilized world had built-up over many centuries. They proclaimed force at home, and war in the international community, as the highest of values. Their discrimination against certain races, nations and creeds was taken to the point not only of advocating, but actually implementing, their methodical destruction.

Right-wing totalitarianism, as has often been pointed out, is couched in terms of negative themes—it is "anti" so many things: against liberalism, against individualism, against reason, against equality, against parliamentary institutions, against democracy, against international law, against the bourgeois society and its culture, against big cities. The twentieth century right-wing movements signified a culmination and a synthesis of a multiplicity of "antis," most of which were developed throughout the nineteenth century, side by side with the development of liberal democratic thought and democratic regimes. They are also based upon a body of thought that is deeply anti-rational, stressing the importance of emotions and intuition as opposed to scientific inquiry and reason, and seeking to find in communitarian values and solidarity the key to political obligations and stability.

The Intellectual Roots

Many authors and philosophers, and scientists sociological, anthropological, and political, as well as political activists, contributed to the formulation of an anti-liberal and anti-democratic body of doctrine. Some would have taken pride in the movements and regimes that borrowed from their thinking; others would have rejected them outright as a gross distortion of what they had thought, written and taught. The major ideas used by the right-wing parties were elitism, racialism, Social Darwinism, irrationalism, the exaltation of violence, the notion that the group has a reality superseding that of the individual, and nationalism. Lenin's conception of a revolutionary party based upon will played also an important role. The reaction against industrialization by many social groups who felt threatened by it, and also a widespread reaction against the impersonality of a mass society, were also strong contributing factors.

Elitism

Liberal assumptions of equality and participation had not been accepted by many conservatives. The latter spoke in terms of natural leaders, persons with special endowments and with a special stake in the country due to which they would have special leadership roles. Throughout the nineteenth century, a number of authors advanced new arguments to justify the rule of the few, whether by government or by an elite: but the majority was simply incapable of self-government. The distinction between an elite and the people was a reflection, they claimed, of the natural endowments of some, and the lack of endowment by the many.

Elites derive superiority from intelligence, or knowledge, or manipulative skills, or from sheer physical courage. One sociologist distinguishes between gifted individuals and the mass of mediocrities who follow them.[1] He asserts that competition takes place only among elites; the people follow like sheep. Democracy, he claims, is nonsense: a better name for it would be mobocracy. Robert Michels, in a much-quoted book on political parties, has observed and documented the same phenomenon of elitism within socialist parties that claimed to

1. Vilfredo Pareto. *The Mind and Society.* N.Y.: Dowe, 1963.

be open, egalitarian and democratic.[2] They were run by an elite. In all such organizations there is an "iron law" of oligarchy.

The German philosopher Nietzsche reached even more extreme conclusions. He identified leadership with the "heroic man" who has the will to power and the desire to dominate. The "superman," he predicted, would emerge and rise to power to impose his law and his will upon the "spineless multitude" with its Christian "slave morality." The future belonged to heroes unconstrained by law and conventional morality who would set their own morality and make their own law for all to follow. Lenin, too, as we noted, without subscribing to the "superman" theory, emphasized that only a few, an elite, could organize the Communist Party and speak on behalf of the workers and lead them to the promised land of communism.

Irrationalism

Early in the nineteenth century another German philosopher wrote a book characteristically enough entitled *The World as Will and Idea*.[3] It began with the ominous phrase, "The world is my idea. . . ." What this means is that rational and scientific discourse is inadequate to provide us with the understanding of the world surrounding us and that "knowledge" is a matter of intuitive communication that alone can provide full "understanding." Knowledge thus becomes entirely subjective. Much later, the French philosopher Bergson stressed also the intuitive aspects of learning—the mystical communication of the subject with the outside object.[4] It is thanks to intuition that we "know" an object by "entering into it." Science, reason, measurements, observation give us only a relative, partial and fragmented knowledge; intuition, an "absolute" one.

Myths and Violence

But what is the relevance of intuition or instinct to politics? Simply that logic, persuasion and argument cannot move people and cannot sustain a political system. In politics the counterpart of intuition is the "myth," that is, an idea, a symbol, a slogan that moves people into action because it appeals to their emotions. They become attached to it and they feel for it. The "crowd" or "the masses" act and can be much more easily moved when their emotions are aroused. They act in terms of stereotypes, prejudices, instincts, not in terms of reason and proof. The myth unites them and gives purpose and meaning to

2. Robert Michels. *Political Parties*. N.Y.: Free Press, 1962.
3. Arthur Schopenhauer. *The World as Will and Idea*. Translated by E.P. Payne. N.Y.: Dover, 1968.
4. Henri Bergson. *The Two Sources of Morality and Religion*. Notre Dame, Ind.: University of Notre Dame Press, p. 177.

their lives far better than logical exposition and reasoning. After all, it was the great philosopher Plato who had defined a myth as a "golden lie" to be propagated by the philosopher king in order to keep the people united and under control. All people were to be taught that they were brothers and sisters because they had the same parents, and were to accept inequalities as natural. Myths can take a variety of forms—racial supremacy, racial purity, national superiority and strength, the dictatorship of the proletariat, the resurrection of ancient empires, the reassertion of tribal bonds, the coming of the superman, and so on.

Georges Sorel, the French revolutionary syndicalist, used the myth explicitly as a vehicle for moral, economic and social revival.[5] The myth that he considered as potent as the Christian belief in the Second Coming, was that of the general strike, by which he meant the development of a state of mind among the workers favoring the violent destruction of the existing social order. Violence would organize the workers, form the battle-lines and marshal them to war against the society. Their "sentiments," properly aroused by an elite, would force their resolution. The myth of the general strike, therefore, called for a state of permanent violence. Violence, Sorel argued, is ennobling in itself, but it also helps people develop the moral courage and the proper emotions to distinguish them from bourgeois cowardice and rationality. He wrote:

> Proletarian violence, carried on as pure and simple manifestation of the sentiments of class war, appears . . . a very fine and heroic thing; it is at the service of the immemorial interests of civilization . . . It may . . . save the world from barbarism.[6]

Lenin never accepted Sorel's overall philosophy, but he nonetheless endorsed the need for violence.

Social Darwinism

Charles Darwin's theory of evolution and the notion of the survival of the fittest was quickly, and unwarrantedly, transferred to the social and the international order. In its new setting it became known as Social Darwinism. According to Darwin, "survival" means that some species survive while others perish in the course of adjusting, or failing to adjust, to the environment and to each other. Transposed to human society the term was taken to mean that those who manage to survive or to succeed are superior or better than those who are unsuccessful or perish. Conflict between individuals, groups, and especially races

5. Georges Sorel. *Reflections on Violence.* N.Y.: Macmillan, 1961.
6. Cited in Lane W. Lancaster. *Masters of Political Thought.* Vol. 3. Boston: Houghton Mifflin, p. 296.

and nations, was declared, therefore, to be a natural and necessary process for the selection of the best and the elimination of the weak and incompetent. The elites in power arrive in their position through struggle; but they are likely to be displaced through struggle if they begin to lose the qualities that brought them on top. The struggle for survival is likely to affect them just as it affected the dinosaurs.

Social Darwinism had been used by liberals to justify economic competition and economic individualism. Right-wing totalitarianism used it to justify competition and conflict especially among elites, races and nations, and to legitimize the supremacy of some individuals on grounds of biological superiority. Some nations are superior to others and need more territory than others; some races are superior to others. There are "master races" and "slave races."

Racialism

Throughout the nineteenth century, sympathy for racial theories such as this was widespread, and Social Darwinism reinforced previously developed racist theories. French and British authors had discoursed on racial differences, concluding with the establishment of criteria of superiority and inferiority—cultural, biological, moral. They concluded that the white race, and various of its branches, was superior. This was the rich background from which the Nazis could draw to develop racist theories and to proclaim their own superiority. It came to the most horrifying conclusion with the attempted extermination of the Jews, but there were plans, too, for the elimination of other ethnic groups.

The Group Mind

As we pointed out, liberalism freed individuals from all attachments to groups and status which defined and structured their activities. The individual became the driving force within the social and political system. The formation of associations and even the existence of the State was traced ultimately to contractual and voluntary relations and individual consent. There was nothing "real" outside of the individual, to whose will, consent and rationality all economic, political and social institutions were traced. Throughout the nineteenth century, however, this position was strongly contested by those who argued that "individuals," as such, were a mere fiction, and that their ideas and values and ultimately their reasoning derived from group values. Marx argued, too, that individual attitudes and ideas were determined by the class to which an individual belonged.

Anthropologists and sociologists claimed to have discovered the "group mind" in tribal groups. People living in tribal societies could not clearly distinguish between "I" and "we"; individual morality, value judgments and attitudes coincided fully with tribal or collective values and attitudes. In this way, the group was larger than its parts, the individuals, and preceded them. Even more, group and collective ideas had a coercive character: the individuals were constrained by them, and their lives were to be understood only in terms of conformity and compliance to such groups. It was group solidarity not individual morality that counted most.

Thus, studying and understanding groups was a better way of understanding society than studying the individual, who was nothing else but the sum total of the group images and pressures weighing upon him. Only the group was real. It took but one step to move to larger collectivities, notably the nation. The nation was real, not the individuals who made it; the morality of the nation was the morality of the individual; individual judgments had to yield to national judgments and imperatives. Thus the nation and nationalism became a superior moral force.

Escape from Freedom

Erich Fromm published a melancholic book in 1941, entitled *Escape from Freedom*. He claimed that there was one basic psychological need that liberalism had ignored. It was the individual's desire to belong,

The "group mind" in action: the Führer arrives at a mass rally, Nuremburg, 1935. (Photo: Wide World Photos)

to be attached to groups or to hierarchies that make decisions, to be part of the whole with fixed obligations to it and fixed rights deriving from it. Feudalism had provided such a setting, and its destruction had uprooted the individuals from their traditional groupings. Individuals found themselves desperately in need of similar ties to anchor their existence—ties that liberalism and industrialization had broken. Totalitarianism was, in essence, a return to group values and to authority; it was a response to the intense need for "belongingness," which, he claimed, was much stronger than reason and self-interest. Liberalism, therefore, and the historical phase of liberalism were nothing but an interlude between the structured life of the feudal society of the past and the subjection to the totalitarian regimes of the future. The latter amounted to a revolt of the individuals against the burdens of freedom and free choice that liberalism had imposed upon them.

Against the Bourgeois Mentality

Bourgeois values were a major target of criticism throughout the nineteenth century. The peaceful but unheroic existence of the citizen; the constant search for material gains and satisfactions; the compromising spirit that democratic liberalism fosters; the smugness of the wealthy and their ability to manipulate representative institutions to their advantage, while paying lip-service to equality and freedom; the subordination of all values to material considerations—all this was repugnant to many intellectuals and philosophers, as well as workers. In a reaction, many writers extolled courage, violence, emotions and instincts. They sought to find new binding ties in common adventures that liberalism downgraded and to help the "true" individual realize himself or herself; to find a way of life that was closer to nature but farther away from reason; closer to instinct and intuition but farther away from material interests; closer to feeling but away from science. It was in essence an exaltation of bygone romantic values of valor and adventure and physical strength.

The Historical Setting

As we have pointed out, ideas may hibernate for a long time until the right conditions bring them back to life and transform them into political ideologies and movements. This was the case with the antiliberal and anti-democratic ideas outlined above. Until World War One, democratic liberalism and democratic liberal regimes remained strong. Even socialist parties had joined, for all practice purposes, liberal democratic parties and regimes. Right-wing extremist movements received only little support.

It took two major upheavals to transform totalitarian ideologies into powerful movements and for liberal democracy to find itself on the defensive almost everywhere.

World War One

World War One accounted for an unprecedented destruction, loss of life and socio-economic and political upheavals throughout Europe. It spawned bitterness and distrust in the political institutions of almost all countries involved, both the defeated and the victorious, with the possible exception of England and the United States. In Russia it created the conditions that accounted for the triumph of the Bolshevik Revolution in November 1917. In Germany the semi-authoritarian system collapsed to give place to a democratic constitution, but conditions remained chaotic and democracy was never given a genuine chance to gain respectability. Defeat haunted many Germans, and the democratic constitution established in 1918 was for them the symbol of defeat. In France a strong communist faction emerged and divisions between the left and the right became sharper. Italy (a latecomer in the war on the side of the victorious powers) felt betrayed by its allies when it came to the final settlement at the Treaty of Versailles. In Central and Eastern Europe, extreme left-wing radicalism, often supported by Russian communism, alternated for a while with right-wing authoritarian reactions.

The war brought forth new popular demands and had serious political implications. The peoples of all nations had been mobilized into the war effort. They fought for four years in the trenches, where a new spirit of egalitarianism and camaraderie had been fashioned, and where distinctions of birth, wealth and education had been blurred. Wartime sacrifices were translated into demands for a better life and more comforts, and these were pressed hard on national governments. Failure to provide them brought quick political reaction, and more often direct and violent action. Resentment increased and took the form of left or right-wing extremism. In some countries, as in Russia, the "system" broke down; in others, notably in Germany, inflation deprived a great number of people (and particularly the middle classes) of their savings and their pensions, and dislocated economic activity. The liberal democratic states seemed unable to cope.

The Great Depression

It is against this background that the Great Depression of 1929 should be assessed. The depression was particularly severe in Germany, where almost half the labor force found itself without jobs. But throughout the whole of Central Europe, as well as in France and England, unemployment spread.

The faith in liberal economic and political institutions was severely shaken. For the left, depression was a clear indication that Marx had

*In post-World War One Germany, inflation wiped out peo-
ple's savings and earnings. A bread peddler, Berlin, 1923.
(Photo: Wide World Photos)*

its contradictions. For the right-wing, the depression was an equally
clear manifestation that liberal economic and political institutions
could no longer function. A new formula was needed, avoiding both
Marxist revolutionary politics and putting an end to economic liberalism.

The remedy suggested was that of a strong State which would
overcome internal divisions and cleavages, with a new economic system that would set aside private interests and even private profit in
favor of unity and cooperation with common social and national goals.
It was the formula used in Italy by the fascists and the Nazis in Germany,
and by all other right-wing nationalist movements throughout Europe.

Thanks to the depression it appealed to a growing number of people
and voters. Unemployed workers, farmers, the lower middle classes,
and particularly the middle classes, war veterans, university students,
and in general those between twenty and forty found the combination
of nationalist and unifying slogans, together with the promise of economic reform, irresistible. Status quo groups, fearing loss of status,
joined forces with the disaffected, the romantics, the nationalists, and
the unemployed. During the depression, right-wing extremism swelled
into powerful political movements everywhere.

Special Reasons

There were other reasons for right-wing totalitarianism's victorious emergence in Italy and Germany. In both countries, but also in many others that followed their example, democracy had never gained legitimacy. Elites, intellectuals, associations and interest groups, never developed a strong working attachment to democratic regimes. They had not become integrated into the system. The educational system and the family did not socialize the young into the principles and practices of democracy. As a result, both the Italian Republic and the German democratic constitution were faced with hostility and indifference rather than with affection and support. Nationalism in both countries (which became nation states only in the 1870s) remained a powerful force. Germany's defeat and the non-realization of national claims for Italy intensified the two countries' search for nationalist solutions.

The economic difficulties facing these countries right after the war and the inability of their political institutions to cope with them, to provide employment and to arrest inflation, further undermined whatever attachment the people had to democracy.

Similarly, the existence of strong communist parties in both countries played a dominant role. A sharp reaction against them was couched in strong nationalist terms. There was also a strong resentment against the settlement of the war, the Versailles Treaty which imposed heavy reparation payments upon Germany and gave the victorious powers—England, France and the U.S.A.—a dominant position in world affairs.

If we review the various factors that accounted for the coming and spread of right-wing totalitarianism in a number of European countries, we find the following:

1. Defeat or feeling of deprivation in and after World War One.
2. Intensification of nationalism because of the relatively late national unification (Italy and Germany).
3. Inflation, unemployment and in general economic depression.
4. Loss of status among middle classes or fear of further deterioration of their position.
5. Fear of strong communist and revolutionary movements and parties.
6. Reaction against the international order and the settlement after World War One.
7. Lack of legitimacy of democratic institutions.

Thus the stage had been set for the eruption of powerful anti-democratic and anti-liberal totalitarian mass movements. The individual and the individualistic ethic, which had hardly come into their own, were shoved aside in the name of the group, the party, and the nation. What Aristotle had termed "reason without passion"—the law—for the regulating of human intercourse and the safeguarding of peaceful and stable relationships, was to become a laughing stock, subject to the whim and caprice of political leaders and tyrants.

Bibliography

Adorno, T.W., et al. *The Authoritarian Personality*. New York: Norton, 1969.

Arendt, Hanna. *The Origins of Totalitarianism*. New York: Harcourt Brace and World, 1968.

Delzell, Charles F. (ed.). *Mediterranean Fascism 1919–1949*. New York: Walker and Co., 1971.

Fromm, Erich. *Escape From Freedom*. New York: Avon Books, 1965.

Gregor, James A. *The Ideology of Fascism*. New York: Free Press, 1969.

Laqueur, Walter (ed.). *Fascism: A Reader's Guide*. Berkeley: University of California Press, 1976.

Mosse, George C. *Crisis of German Ideology: Intellectual Origins of the Third Reich*. New York: Fertig, 1978.

Nietzsche, Friedrich. *Beyond Good and Evil*. New York: Vintage, 1956.

———. *Thus Spoke Zarathustra*. Baltimore: Penguin, 1961.

———. *The Will to Power*. New York: Vintage, 1968.

Oakeshott, Michael. *The Social and Political Doctrines of Contemporary Europe*. New York: Cambridge U. P., 1942.

Talmon, J.L. *The Origins of Totalitarian Democracy*. New York: Norton, 1970.

Weber, Eugen. *Varieties of Fascism*. New York: Van Nostrand, 1964.

Woolf, S.J. (ed.). *European Fascism*. New York: Vintage, 1969.

9

Nazism and Fascism: Ideologies and Regimes

For the Weltanshauung *(the ideology) is intolerant . . . and peremptorily demands its own, exclusive, and complete recognition as well as the complete adaptation of public life to its ideas.* ADOLF HITLER Mein Kampf

The intellectual background of anti-liberal and anti-democratic thought and the particular historical circumstances of Europe after World War One affected all nations, but particularly Germany and Italy. It is in these two countries that the special reasons we mentioned triggered powerful totalitarian movements. It is to these two movements and regimes, the Nazis and the fascists, that we turn now.

I discuss the Nazi movement and regime first, despite the fact that the Italian fascists came to power a decade earlier, because it was far more "successful" in accomplishing what it professed. Italian fascism was less comprehensive and far less effective in mobilizing society. But the Nazis managed to bring virtually all Germans and all elements of German society under their control. Germans were made to "march in step" to the tune of the Nazi Party. This was the meaning of the famous term *gleichschaltung*—the "synchronization" of all aspects of social life with the political ideology and objectives of the Nazi Party. Not so in fascist Italy. Many did not march at all, while others dragged their feet, and still others marched to different tunes than the one played by the Fascist Party. It was said that the Italian fascists made the Italian trains run on time; Hitler and the Nazis, notwithstanding internal rivalries and often bad management of the economy and the war, made the nation march in unison.

German Totalitarianism

A historian of Germany entitles his chapter on German National Socialism—the Nazi movement and regime—"Germany goes berserk."[1] It is only a mild comment on what occurred in one of the most advanced and civilized nations of the world.

Nazism shows better than anything else the immense power of ideas, and the degree to which citizens can be manipulated not simply into submission but into frenzied action. It should be a constant reminder to all of us—no matter how special the conditions in Germany appear to have been—of how fragile the bonds of reason and law are, and how vulnerable, under certain circumstances, we *all* may be to political fanaticism.

German right-wing totalitarianism became a political reality when the leader of the National Socialist Workers' German Party, Adolf Hitler, came to power in January 1933. Hitler immediately set about organizing the new system, the Third Reich,[2] implementing many of the promises he had made. Most notably these included the abolition of the institutions of democracy and the preparation for an expansionist war to establish German world-wide domination.

The Road to Power

The beginnings of the Hitler movement can be traced directly to the aftermath of World War One, and also to the rich background of German anti-democratic literature, and right-wing political extremism. Nazism was both nationalistic and racist, and also had a strong streak of a populist appeal that was both communitarian and egalitarian. Many nationalists traced the political system they favored to the early Germanic tribes, where direct democracy had been practiced among warriors bound together by ties of common blood and common sacrifice and effort.

Defeat in World War One caused a great disillusionment, and in time a desire for revenge, focused on the Versailles Treaty which had stripped Germany of its colonies and imposed a heavy burden of reparations. But there were other factors. First, the galloping inflation of the early 1920s was unprecedented in the economic history of any nation. The inflation wiped out savings, pensions, trust funds, and

1. K.S. Pinson. *Modern Germany* 2nd ed. N.Y.: Macmillan, 1966.
2. Third Reich was an expression intentionally used to indicate continuity with the German Empire (1871–1918) and the Holy Roman Empire.

made salaries and wages dwindle with the passage of every day, week and month. It created a state of acute panic among the middle classes.

A second important factor was the reaction to communist revolutionary movement. Revolutions actually took place right after World War One, and communist regimes were installed temporarily in parts of Germany. Private groups and armies, led by officers and war veterans, took it upon themselves to stop the leftists. Often aided by the police and whatever remained of the German army, they began to wage war against the communists and their sympathizers. Many of these veterans and their organizations rallied to the Nazis and formed the hard core of the Nazi Party.

The Nazi Party was founded in 1921 as the extension of the German Workers' Party (DAP) over which Hitler had managed to gain control. Its original program included the usual nationalist and racist themes but promised also social and economic reforms which were downright socialist: land reform, nationalizations, the "breaking of the shackles of capitalism." It also attacked the political and economic elites, and identified the "domestic" and "outside" enemies of Germany as the victorious powers, (notably England and France) and Jews and "international Jewry." It was a small party at first, a sect, with not more than a few thousand members, quite typical of many other extremist nationalist groups. Few paid attention to its founding. When the economic situation improved, it seemed destined to oblivion, particularly so after 1923, when Hitler attempted to take over power by force in Munich. The coup failed dismally and Hitler found himself in jail and the party was outlawed.

In 1924, running in the legislative election under various camouflage labels, the Nazis managed to get thirty-two deputies elected in the legislature and received 6.5 percent of the national vote. Thereafter its electoral fortunes declined: in the presidential election of 1925 the party's candidate, General Ludendorff, received only 200,000 votes, and in the legislative election of 1928 the party seemed to have been virtually wiped out, receiving only 2.6 percent of the national vote. After 1928, however, and especially after the depression of 1929, the Nazis began to make rapid gains, soon emerging as the strongest single party, as table 9.1 indicates. There were a number of reasons for the rapid growth of the Nazi Party. The party had managed not only to survive, but become the sole spokesman of all right-wing extremist groups. Hitler had paid particular attention to its organization and managed to create what amounted to a paramilitary party. Leadership was consolidated in the hands of the leader—the Führer. Uniforms, a special salute, pomp and ritual, but above all, discipline and activism appealed to many, especially the young. In 1931, some 35 percent of the party members were below the age of thirty. Party membership began to grow, especially after 1928–29 when there were about 100,000

ADOLF HITLER (1889–1945)

The Führer, ironically enough, was a non-German. Hitler was born in Austria in 1889. A poor student given to prolonged moods of melancholia and day-dreaming, he found himself in the army where he served with the rank of a corporal with apparent diligence and courage. Defeat enraged him and he sought scapegoats in the "cowardice" of the civilians and the "conspiracy" of the Jews. Without any formal education—he wanted to be an architect and had tried painting—he was widely read in German nationalist authors.

After World War One he found himself in Munich, capital of Bavaria, where he founded the NDASP (the Nazi Party) in 1921. After the abortive effort to seize power in 1923, he received a light sentence and spent the nine months of his imprisonment writing what became the political bible of Nazism, *Mein Kampf* (My Struggle). It was the Depression and the frustrations and political conflict associated with it that provided the climate for his ascent to power. On January 30, 1933, President Hindenburg asked him to become Chancellor of Germany and he assumed full powers until his "Thousand Year Reich" ended with his suicide in the ruins of Berlin on April 30, 1945.

TABLE 9.1 *Elections and the Nazis*
(From K. S. Pinson, *Modern Germany*, 2nd ed. N.Y.: Macmillan, 1966)

LEGISLATIVE ELECTIONS

1924 (May 4)	1,918,300 (32 deputies)	6.0%
1924 (Dec. 7)	907,300 (14 deputies)	3.0%
1928 (May 20)	810,000 (12 deputies)	2.6%
1930 (Sept. 14)	6,409,600 (107 deputies)	18.3%
1932 (July 31)	13,745,800 (230 deputies)	37.4%
1932 (Nov. 1)	11,737,000 (196 deputies)	33.1%
1933 (March 5) (Nazis in power)	17,277,200 (288 deputies)	43.9%
1933 (Nov. 12) (Nazis in control)	39,638,800 (661 deputies)	92.2%

PRESIDENTIAL ELECTIONS

1925	200,000 (Ludendorff)	
1932 (March) 1st ballot	11,339,288 (Hitler)	30.1%
2nd ballot	13,418,051 (Hitler)	36.8%

members, to 1,200,000 by 1933, and up to about 2.5 million at the beginning of World War Two.

Special shock formations were established. The SA (Brownshirts) and, after 1934, the SS (Black Guards) grew in numbers to almost equal the German army. At the slightest provocation they engaged in street fights, attacks against leftists and opposition leaders, whose headquarters they sacked and burned. Anti-Semitic demonstrations and acts of violence were common. All this was testing the will of the Nazis, preparing them for further action and intimidation.

Yet Hitler and his associates pledged to respect "legality" and, in effect, promised not to use violence in order to come to power. Many political leaders, especially among the conservative and centrist groups, believed him, thus allowing the Nazi Party to operate, convinced that it would never receive a majority and that even if allowed to form a government it would abide by the constitution and act according to the rules and procedures of the parliamentary assemblies. When after the 1932 election the Nazis, 196 strong, entered the legislature, Hitler left no doubt at all as to what he meant by "legality."

"We come as enemies," he wrote. "Like the wolf coming into a flock of sheep, that is how we come!"[3]

A number of front organizations were created to strengthen the party's appeal and to recruit more members and sympathizers. The Hitler Youth in 1931 numbered only about 100,000.In 1933–34 it was close to about four million members and at the outbreak of the war almost nine million. In addition, there was a Hitler Student League, an Officer's League, a Women's League, a workers' Nazi organization (the Labor Front), and many others, representing every academic, social and professional group in the country. The party, gradually, became a state within a state, with its private army, tribunals, police, military formations all spreading far and wide the Nazi doctrine and creating within Germany a strong Nazi sub-culture. It had its own cult, slogans, and morality—anti-republican, racist and nationalist.

With the economic depression and the renewed fear of leftist revolutionary moves, the Nazis made the breakthrough that led them to power in 1933. They became a mass party, as the election results show. But they also attracted the attention and support of the conservative forces and of the army. The business community and the financial elites opened up their purse, and the party's treasury was again full. The Nazis and their leader broadened their appeal to catch, if possible, every group, every section and every occupation and profession.

Nazi Pledges

To the farmers, the Nazis promised "green democracy" and "soil-rooted" pure communitarian values, but also protection and subsidies. They pledged to uphold the rural values and traditions that were menaced by urbanization.

To the workers, they promised jobs. Between 1928 and 1932, unemployment had shot up from one million to six million. Many workers and unemployed workers began to join the party and to vote for it. The depression had weakened the trade-unions and left-wing workers were hopelessly divided between socialism and communism.

To the army, the Nazis promised rebuilding and an end to the Versailles Treaty.

To the middle classes, they promised special measures to arrest the decline of their income and give them security; above all, they promised to do away with the dangers from the left by eliminating communism. These promises appealed also to many in the lower middle classes—merchants, artisans, shopkeepers, civil service personnel, clerical personnel, etc.

---

3. Cited by Bracher. *The German Dictatorship*, p. 142. This, as I note in my preface, is an excellent account of Hitler's Germany, and I am indebted to the author for many of my observations.

The Nazi Party promised a special place to the young. The future was theirs. "Make room for us, you old ones," was one of their battlecries.

Propaganda was developed into a fine political art along clear-cut lines suggested by Hitler. Repetition of the same simple slogans and themes; appeal to the emotions; propositions that clearly distinguished the negative from the positive: "this *is* the truth—*they* lie," "*we* can—*they* cannot"; simple answers to complex problems, i.e. "*we* shall solve unemployment by giving jobs to all"; emphasis upon nationalism and national togetherness: "*we* Germans" against the "*they*"—Jews, plutocrats, capitalists, communists, etc. These propaganda themes were to be strengthened by direct action taken against opponents. Truth lay not in demonstration but in belief *and* in action. A Nazi was someone who believed and strengthened his belief by acting. Force became the best vindication of belief.

The use of violence by the various party members and formations among the Hitler Youth, the SA, and the SS, was an integral part of Nazi ideology. Violence as such was attractive to some, who would be recruited for the sheer pleasure of indulging in acts of terrorism and intimidation. But it was not a negative posture limited to destruction. It provided for psychological outlets: it was considered to be a creative form of expression. It gave an opportunity to the followers to test their courage; to realize and clarify their ideas by making them prevail through physical force. Violence was the best medium to sharpen the lance of resolution, as opposed to reasoning and persuasion. Finally there was the ennobling experience of camaraderie in joint combat; of the common sharing in common dangers. It was an integral part of the recruitment and the domination of the biologically strong and virile people over their opponents and victims, and ultimately over all others.

The Nazi pledges were powerful. Party membership in 1930 and 1934 clearly shows that the Nazis had a wide appeal among virtually all groups: see table 9.2. In the 1932 presidential election, the Nazi candidate, none other than Hitler himself, received 36.8 percent of the vote. More than one-third of German voters wanted him as their president!

Who were the German voters? The great majority of farmers voted for the Nazis, as did the majority of the people living in small towns

TABLE 9.2   *Percentage composition of the Nazi Party*
(From K. Bracher *The German Dictatorship*, N.Y.: Praeger, 1970)

	1930	1934	PERCENTAGE OF POPULATION
Working class	28	32	46
White collar	25.6	20.6	12.4
Independent business	20	20	9
Civil service and teachers	8.3	13	5
Farmers	14.7	10.7	9

and in general in rural areas. Protestants tended to vote for them more than Catholics. A great percentage of the middle and low middle classes voted Nazi. But also, so did four out of every ten workers, many among the unemployed. Seymour Martin Lipset wrote that the "ideal type Nazi voter in 1932 was a middle class, self-employed Protestant who lived either on a farm or in a small town and who had previously voted for a centrist or a regionalist political party strongly opposed to the power and influence of big business and big labor."[4] Yet even though the Nazis received a working-class vote that was below the percentage of the workers in the population (about 47 percent), the biggest share of their vote in absolute terms came from the workers. The Nazi Party had become, in 1932, a truly mass party, and its vote approximated the socio-economic configuration of the nation—it came from all groups and professions and classes.

The Nazi Ideology

Nazism as an ideology and a political movement began as a gesture of negation, but there was also the formulation of a number of "positive" themes and propositions on the basis of which the new society would be constructed. Some of them were addressed to the immediate situation; others to long-range social, economic and political problems created by liberalism, and the threat of communism.

NEGATIVE THEMES

These were many:
1. *Against class struggle*   The notion of class, developed by Marx and endorsed by all communist parties, was inconsistent with national unity. As such, it was only an extension of the idea of conflict and competition developed by liberals and Marxists. The Nazis claimed that the notion of class was incompatible with the communitarian values of the German people and the German nation. Germany was "one"!
2. *Against parliamentary government*   According to the Nazis, parliamentary government leads to the fragmentation of the body politic into parties and groups, jockeying for position, compromising their particular interests, forming unstable governmental coalitions. The "real" national interest was neglected. A common purpose could not develop from such a fragmentation of the national will. "There is no principle which . . . is as false as that of parliamentarianism," wrote Hitler in *Mein Kampf.*
3. *Anti–trade-union*   Unions express the sectarian and class interests of the working class. However, the workers were also Germans and citizens. They had to be integrated into the community like all others instead of pitting themselves against other Germans.
4. *Against political parties*   Like representative government, po-

4. Seymour Martin Lipset. *Political Man.* N.Y.: Doubleday, 1963, p. 148.

litical parties expressed special ideological or interest particularisms, splitting the nation. The national purpose called not for parties but for one movement, embodying it. Such a movement, even if it were called a party, should be given monopoly of representation. Hence, all other political parties should be outlawed, and a one-party system instituted.

5. *Against the Treaty of Versailles* The Versailles Treaty, imposing an inferior status upon Germany that deprived it of its army and required it to pay reparations, had to be done away with. But more than that, the existing international system that perpetuated the supremacy of some nations—notably England and France—should be drastically altered to give freedom and space to Germany.

There were a number of other comprehensive negative themes that inevitably blend with some of the "positive" formulations of the Nazis.

6. *Anti-Semitism and racialism* Anti-Semitism had been a common phenomenon in Europe, stemming from religious prejudices, cultural differences and economic rivalries. The Jews were blamed for being responsible for both liberal capitalism *and* for communism. There were extravagant myths attempting to show that the Jews were plotting the domination of the world. This was the case with a document (totally fabricated by nineteenth century anti-Semites) called *The Protocols of the Elders of Zion*, in which the Jews were said to set forth their plans to conquer the world. This was widely used by the Nazis. They added, however, a new twist—that Jews were biologically inferior. Not only, therefore, were they dangerous because of their ideas, their beliefs and their plans to conquer the world (how inferior people could do it was never explained), but because their very presence within Germany endangered the purity of the German "race." There were only half a million Jews in Germany at the time Hitler assumed power over sixty-five million Germans—that is, less than 0.7 percent. More than 200,000 managed to escape the country by 1938. Those who remained were viewed as a germ, just as virulent as botulism. It had to be insulated first and then exterminated.

As soon as the Nazis came to power, they began to reduce the German Jews to the status of non-persons. They could not keep their businesses, could not receive any social benefits. They were assigned special neighborhoods to live, were constantly harassed and intimidated by the members of the Nazi Party, the SA and its various front organizations; they were arbitrarily arrested, could not engage in any gainful occupation, had their belongings confiscated, and were forced to pay special levies to the state authorities that invariably went to the Nazi Party members. Intermarriage was prohibited, and existing inter-faith marriages annulled. The Nazis developed the long-range policy of exterminating all Jews that led actually to the destruction of European Jewry, wherever the Nazi armies gained a foothold.

Given its biological basis, German anti-Semitism left no room for compromise. But the same biological discrimination threatened also other groups and nations which the Nazis found dangerous or "impure"—Slavs, Blacks, etc.

7. *Anti-communism*   If anti-Semitism was based on biological grounds, anti-communism stemmed primarily from political, but also international, considerations. It was aimed not only against communists at home, but against the "fatherland of communism," the Soviet Union. It called not only for the elimination of the German Communist Party, but also the elimination of international communism as spearheaded by the Soviet Union. The ideological crusade against communism would thus serve the secular strategic, economic and geopolitical goals of Germany in its move east.

There were other reasons for anti-communism inherent in the totalitarian ideology of Nazism. The German Communist Party was well-organized and disciplined. It also had an ultimate vision of total control, as did Soviet communism. There was an incompatibility, therefore, between two intensely ideological and inherently totalitarian movements. As soon as they came to power, the Nazis outlawed the Communist party, arrested its leaders, jailed and murdered many of them. The party was dismantled. The same fate awaited the Social Democrats, also a Marxist party which had also opposed the Nazis. But it was not until 1941 that the main clash between the Soviet Union and the Nazi Germany took place, when the German armies invaded Russia.

"POSITIVE" THEMES

Every negation advanced by the Nazis (what they planned to do away with) naturally called for an affirmation (what they planned to do instead). It is only in this sense, therefore, that I am using the term "positive": it does not imply any moral approbation.

Anti-Semitism suggests racialism and the purity of the race; anti-individualism, a communitarian ethic transcending the individual; anti-liberalism, a new political organization; the anti-Versailles posture, the erection of some new kind of international order. It is the combination of the reasoning behind many of the negations that resulted in the new and dynamic synthesis of social and national life. No matter how repugnant morally, it must be analyzed and discussed if we are to understand the full and ominous implications of the Nazi movement and regime.

1. *Nationalism and racialism*   To understand the character of Nazi German nationalism, we must distinguish it from other nationalist movements. There were liberal nationalist movements in the wake of the French Revolution of 1789, identifying with the principle of nationality and demanding that people sharing the same national background—a common history, culture, language, religion—live within a given territory—the nation-state. This is basically the principle of self-determination, allowing peoples to form their own State. There have been also conservative nationalist movements which have extolled national virtues and asserted their superiority over others; they stress

national integration and unity at the expense of particularisms, regionalisms and even individual freedoms. But such nationalist movements are content to see the values they assert cultivated and strengthened within the nation-state. They are not expansionist.

Nazi nationalism was both racialist and expansionist. While naturally insisting on the superiority of Germanic values, it proclaimed also the superiority of the German race and the desirability of imposing its superiority upon others. Aryans were superior not only to Jews but also to Slavs, Turks, Greeks, French, etc. And among the Aryans, the Germans were the superior race because they had managed and, thanks to the Nazis, forever intended, to keep their race "pure." They would not allow for a "mongrelization" similar to what they claimed had occurred in the United States. They were the *master race* destined to dominate all others. This racialist doctrine, coupled with extreme nationalism, led to the inevitability of war and the German domination of lesser nations.

2. *Expansionism* The valor of the race could not be proven by assertion only. It had to be demonstrated on the proving ground of war and conquest. The master race was to be a race of warriors subduing lesser races. Germany was to conquer and Berlin would become the capital of the world. But, in addition to racism, there were of course ideological, economic and strategic reasons to justify an expansionist and war-like policy. A totalitarian system is "total" at home, in that it tries to subordinate everything to its ideology and control. It cannot allow competing units to exist. But the same is true in international terms. The logic of totalitarianism calls for the elimination of competing centers of power everywhere.

Economic reasons were also advanced. One was the notion of "proletarian" nations; another that of "living space." According to the former, World War One had allowed some nations to control the world's wealth—e.g., England, the United States, France—while other nations like Germany, Italy and even Japan were poor, "proletarian," without colonies, raw materials and resources. Similarly, some nations had ample space at their disposal: the French, British and Dutch had their colonial empires. The U.S.S.R. and U.S.A. had immense land at their disposal. Other nations did not, however, and Germany, without colonies, was squeezed into the center of Europe, while its population was growing and its needs increasing. Land, therefore, would have to be reapportioned to meet the German needs. To this argument, yet another one was added—the distinction between "young" and "old" nations, suggesting growth against decay. Germany in historical terms was "young," compared to England or France, and needed "living space" and land into which to grow.

Thus, the conquest of territory and the destruction of neighboring nation-states became an essential element of the Nazi ideology, and a long-range policy goal. It could not be attained overnight. The elimination of Soviet Russia (an old bulwark against German expansion to the east, but also an ideological foe), and of France (the spearhead of the plutocracies, especially England and the United States), would have to come first. The Japanese and the Italians were offered only tactical alliances in the expansionist German ambitions. Their position in the international order that the Nazis would build would have to be settled later.

3. *Communitarianism* The elimination of all freedoms, and their replacement by a single "freedom"—that of obeying the party that represented the German community, and the leader of that party—was the essence of German totalitarianism. It was central to the building of a new political system that would replace liberalism and capitalism. All parties, all organizations, all associations, all religious groups and churches would become subordinated to the communitarian will. After the Nazis came to power, freedom of press, of association, of speech, ceased to exist. All parties were abolished. The individual—alone, free, independent, thinking his or her own thoughts—would give place to the "new individual" imbued with communitarian and nationalist beliefs as dictated by the leader and the party. The individual and the community would become one. Dissenters were, of course, not to be tolerated: they were executed or sent to concentration camps. But individuals who tried to remain aloof and distant from the national community were declared to be "asocial." They had failed to respond to the demands of the party and the community; they were not fully mobilized; they were not one with the nation.

Communitarianism called, therefore, for constant participation; it aimed to inculcate a spirit of individual attachment to the whole and a readiness not only to obey but also to sacrifice everything for the general interest as defined by the Nazis. But communitarianism also suggested the need to subordinate private interest in the economic sphere to general social goals and, therefore, the subordination of the market economy to the party and the leader. The early Nazi ideology was distinctly anti-capitalist, and it advocated the supremacy of national goals over all economic interests.

4. *Leadership ("Führerprinzip") and the party* How do communitarian values manifest themselves? In a number of ways. One is the direct participation of all in decision-making—claimed to be the practice of the early Germanic tribes. A second way is for the community to select its representatives. This notion of representation was given a particular twist by the Nazis. They accepted it but they rejected free elections. The Nazi party "represented" the German people because it was in tune with the people and expressed directly what the nation desired. Within the party, its leader, instinctively and intuitively, acted for the whole. It is the leader, therefore, who best expresses the communitarian values.

Communitarian aspirations gave to Nazism a populist trait. It claimed to embody values and principles that stemmed directly from the people—the *volk*. It was the "people's spirit"—the *volksgeist*—that was tapped by the party and was represented by it. Hence the party, in the name of this unique representative quality, claimed to be the only vehicle of representation, the very essence of direct democracy. But because of this it claimed also to be an entity above the State, to control the State while acting on behalf of the community. The State was nothing, in the last analysis, but an agency, an instrumentality of the party, and all its offices and officials were subordinate to the party.

The leadership principle is the cornerstone of Nazism, and the institution that best combines authority and control with "representation." It is a principle that cannot be easily defined since it can be only "understood" by those who experience it. The leader decides everything and everybody must obey. He can delegate his authority to others but can never give it up. He is the law, and hence above the law. He can legislate and then change that legislation overnight. His will is arbitrary, absolute and superior. He can set procedures and can change them at will. He is free to appoint his successor, just as a Roman emperor could make his horse a consul—and send him to the slaughter-house!

Yet the question remains: from where does the leader derive his representative quality? The answer is very difficult. First it is his capacity to speak on behalf of the national and popular spirit. It is also his special ability to persuade his followers; he has a special charisma that convinces the many to obey. It is also his intuition: his ability to sense what is right and wrong, what must be done and what must not be done, his feeling for what is good for all.

But what about the leader's authority? Why do people obey? The link is the mystical and intuitive link between leader and followers. He speaks for the people, and the people agree with him because he speaks for them! And where his authority does not quite prevail, the leader has at his disposal formidable instruments of coercion, intimidation and downright terror to elicit obedience.

While it is relatively easy to describe the omnipotence and omnicompetence of the Führer, it is far more difficult to explain it. How would a civilized nation, even one in which democratic values and institutions had not gained roots, accept it? And how can one explain the German people's fealty to the Führer until Germany had been reduced to ruins? In the last analysis, there can be no explanation except the very trite one. Hitler, his totalitarian regime and his leadership principle combined with nationalism, racism, and expansionism, must have had, under the particular circumstances already discussed, a strong appeal to some prominent traits of German political culture.

Nazism and the German Political Culture

Much thought has been given to discovering the particular traits of the German political history and culture that made it so receptive to Nazism.[5] Foremost among them is the weakness of liberal democracy. The middle classes had not made a liberal revolution; they did not develop (as in England, the United States and France), a network of associations and interest groups through which they could influence the State and interact with it. In contrast, many authoritarian social and political structures survived—in the army, in the landed aristocracy, in the civil service, and even in industry, which had developed rapidly in the last quarter of the nineteenth century in the form of large-scale monopolistic organizations. Authority and authoritarian structures were valued more than individual freedoms, equality and pluralism.

Respect for the authority of elite groups—the army officer, the top civil servant, the industrialist, the Prussian landowner—inculcated both discipline and deference. There is a well-known story according to which a German mob during an uprising in the early 1920s prepared to storm a post office whose front lawn had a "Keep off" sign. The mob swerved and attacked through the back door! Respect for authority and all symbols of authority accounted for the high prestige of the army— even after defeat. It was a state within a state, and socialist and liberal political leaders trembled before the presence of an army officer in the years of the republic. The army was a socializing force, inculcating authoritarian values and disciplines, determined to preserve them against the intrusions of parliamentarians, liberals and leftists. The universities, too, remained the preserve of the upper classes and there too abject deference to academic authority was the rule. Education from bottom up was centered on passive learning of what was being offered— not on critical examination and creative individual effort.

Germany had remained for a long time a prey to Romanticism, in its letters, art, philosophy and politics. Abstract and general ideas were developed to solve or to answer the most transcendental questions of justice and knowledge through imagination rather than empirical examination and experimentation. Philosophy and theology, the study of God and of fundamental questions, not the study of society and social inter-relationships, was the hallmark of the German intellectual. It inculcated a state of mind that was attracted by what appeared to be absolute and definitive and not by what was problem-solving and pragmatic.

Nationalism as an end in itself remained a powerful force, and when the German nation and the State were considered to be the ultimate vehicle for the realization of justice and goodness on earth there could be no limits to the scope and aspirations of the nationalists. Perhaps because the unification of Germany into a national state came so late, nationalism took the most integrative and absolutist form, bringing all Germans together into one State, and reasserting their superiority and the superiority of what they stood for over all others.

5. See Ralf Dahrendorf. *Society and Democracy in Germany*. N.Y.: Doubleday, 1969.

The vast majority of Germans acquiesced in the Nazi takeover, often with enthusiasm. They showed remarkable loyalty throughout Hitler's stay in power. Many did so out of self-interest; how many submitted out of fear is difficult to tell. Let us see how the various "social groups" reacted to the coming to power of the Nazis and their regime.

THE ARMY

Diminished in status, reduced in numbers, bearing the brunt of defeat, hostile to communism and to left-wing movements, army officers saw in the coming of the Nazis the prospects of their rehabilitation. At no time ever at ease with republican institutions, the army's position was that it either should be a dominant force in the society or a separate and distinct entity for training soldiers, maintaining order, and making war. It would not play a subordinate role. After World War One, many of its officers joined right-wing vigilante organizations against communists and leftists. Throughout Hitler's rise to power, prominent officers cooperated with him or gave him indirect helping hands. He promised the rehabilitation of the nation and saw in war an answer for past failures. As General Blomberg testified at the Nuremburg trials: "Before 1938–39 the German generals were not opposed to Hitler. There was no ground for opposition since he brought them the success they desired."[6] It was only when the fortunes of the war began to turn against Germany that a number of generals became impatient with Hitler, and even conspired to assassinate him.

CIVIL SERVICE

German civil servants, federal and state, responded with satisfaction to Hitler's program and supported his regime. The Nazis seemed to them to represent the basic values of order, centralized authority, and national integrity to which they were accustomed. Once it became clear that party members would not replace them, the support of the bureaucracy was overwhelming. It was strengthened by generous promotions and increases in salaries.

Yet bureaucracies are accustomed to an orderly way of doing things. They accept hierarchical relationships and a careful structuring of inferior-superior lines of command. They are committed to a rational, detached and impartial way of reaching decisions and of implementing them: they are concerned with efficiency. The Prussian, and later on German bureaucracy was always considered to be both well-organized and efficient. As a result the frequent intrusions into it of the Nazi leaders, and the ultimate power they had to intervene and make de-

6. Cited in Pinson, *op. cit.* p. 508.

cisions themselves, alienated some civil servants, forced the resignation of others and often created confusion. However, at no time during the Hitler regime was there an open defiance on the part of the civil service or anything but an occasional outburst of discontent.

THE CHURCH

Religious groups tried to maintain a certain distance from the Nazis but an effort was made to eliminate some and to bring the two major churches, Catholic and Lutheran, under control. Jews were quickly isolated and their synagogues burned; Jehovah's Witnesses were persecuted. A Concordat was signed with the Vatican giving the Catholic Church some autonomy—the right to hold services, raise funds and distribute pastoral letters to the faithful. But the Concordat also legitimized the Nazi State in the eyes of many Catholics. They were particularly receptive to the Nazi anti-communist pledges and during the war they considered it their patriotic duty to support the fatherland, especially when at war against the Soviet Union.

The Lutheran Church maintained, as always, a distance from the State, distinguishing political from spiritual matters. Political obedience was one thing, and the worship of God another. Lutherans too gave their support to the Nazis as citizens, whatever their innermost thoughts might have been. Even to those for whom Hitler was a tyrant, obedience to the State was an obligation, and prayer the only answer.

Individual Catholic prelates and Lutheran pastors raised, occasionally, their voices against the Nazi regime and its atrocities. But they were the exceptions to the general passivity of the churches.

BUSINESS GROUPS

As for business groups, they gave their full support and cooperation once the "socialist" pledges that were in the original platform of the party were abandoned. Neither private property nor business profits were tampered with, and the anti-labor and anti-trade-union measures satisfied them fully. Business elites cooperated closely with the Nazi leaders, trading favors and benefits with them.

THE MIDDLE CLASS, FARMERS AND WORKERS

Germany had never experienced a genuine middle-class liberal movement as had England, France and the United States. Rapid industrialization was grafted upon semi-feudal and authoritarian social structures. Paternalistic and hierarchical relationships were the rule. The middle classes *fitted* themselves into these structures instead of creating their own kind of political and social relationships, egalitarian and participatory. They felt more at home with authoritarian solutions and hierarchical relationships, and hence, they were inclined to accept Nazism and the statist and nationalist philosophy it represented. Furthermore, the Nazi anti-communist ideology and their intention of doing away with trade-unions, reflected the middle-class fear of the working class and their political parties. The overwhelming majority of the middle-class voters voted for the Nazis and supported them throughout their stay in power.

Similarly, the farmers gave the Nazis overwhelming support. The rustic virtues the Nazis extolled were also theirs: protection, in the form of higher tariffs, provided them with added revenue; anti-communism appealed to their traditional nationalism and conservatism. Small towns and rural communities voted overwhelmingly Nazi.

It was only the workers, then, who seemed to demur. But even among them it was only the politically and ideologically organized and committed, those who belonged to trade-unions or were in the communist and socialist parties, who provided the opposition. The unemployed, as we pointed out, tended to join the party in return for promises of employment. With the coming of the war, full employment was attained, and the labor force was by and large materially better off than at any time since before World War One. There was no organized opposition, and no spirit of resistance.

The Economy

The Nazis failed to implement their original economic program. They did not nationalize the monopolies; on the contrary, every effort was made to encourage concentration and cartelization; they did not confiscate war profits or unearned income; they did not undertake land reform and they did not takeover uncultivated lands and transform them into peasant cooperatives. Populist and socialist promises were forgotten when they came to power. The Nazi Party's socialist leaders, many of whom had taken these promises seriously, were massacred in 1934.

Nazi economic policy consisted of a series of improvisations to meet the political objectives of rearmament and war. There is no doubt that the economy was subordinated to political and ideological exigencies, but also to the necessity of planning or waging war. From the very start, controls were put on foreign exchange. Special efforts were made to promote investment and direct it to key areas of economic activity; to secure raw materials and, when it became necessary, to produce them at home (as, for instance, with synthetic gas and rubber). In general, the emphasis was put on reducing imports and promoting self-sufficiency. Priorities were established, wages controlled, and labor scarcities met through the importation of foreign, often slave, labor—especially in the war period. However, cartelization proceeded through the amalgamation of firms or the takeover of smaller ones, and profits remained secure, even during the war. Property—individual and corporate—was respected.

Political imperatives prevailed. But the economy was not absorbed by the State; it was not nationalized. It became subordinate to the State and the party—a subordination that most other countries had experienced in time of war. There was nothing distinct about the Nazi economy—it produced no new blueprint for production, trade, growth, or consumption. It made no effort to establish a new framework for labor-capital relations, other than to disband all trade-unions.

Conclusion

With an ideology that appealed, at least in part, to some of the basic cultural traits of the German people; a militant party to mobilize the people behind it; with a magnetic political leader trying to resurrect the national demons of the Germanic racial and national superiority, but exploiting all the weakness of a deadlocked parliamentary government, the totalitarian state came to Germany with far greater support than anywhere else.

The Nazis were a mass party, far more so than the Russian Bolsheviks in 1917, the Italian fascists in 1922, or the Spanish Falange from 1936 to 1938. They received in free and open elections a greater percentage of votes than any other totalitarian party in Europe, or for that matter than any other party in Germany. They were welcomed by most social groups and classes, including an appreciable part of the workers, and by the important elite groups—including the churches and the military. Nazism was a home-made product. It was "made in Germany."

Italian Fascism

Totalitarian political systems must be judged, like all other political systems, in terms of their ability to fulfill their objectives. Italian fascism did not achieve the degree of control that German Nazism achieved. Its objectives were very similar, but the resources—political, social and economic—were not present. Italy's industrial development could not compare with that of Germany; national integration was still incomplete and civic discipline inadequate; the elites never gave their full support to the new system, or they gave it with many reservations and conditions. The fascist regime was not strong enough to destroy them or to supplant them.

When it came to an expansionist effort, first in Ethiopia (1936) and then in Albania (1938) and Greece (1941) the Italians proved to be woefully inadequate and had to be supported, and later in fact replaced, by German soldiers almost everywhere they fought. Thus while German Nazism showed the terrifying capabilities of a totalitarian system, Italian fascism failed to generate the power without which doctrinal goals and aspirations cannot be realized.

The Fascist Party emerged in Italy at just about the same time as the Nazis did in Germany. But the Fascist State came into being much earlier. The fascists took over power on October 28, 1922— a decade before Hitler. By 1923, when Mussolini was setting the foundations of the new Italian order, Hitler was still a political upstart and in jail for the abortive Munich *putsch.*

The similarities in the way by which the fascists and the Nazis took power are striking:

1. Fascism capitalized on the nationalistic fervor which followed World War One because Italy did not receive the territorial compensation for the war effort that the Italians thought they deserved.
2. The parliamentary institutions could not cope with the problems facing the country. There were many political parties, sharply divided on ideological and policy matters. Governments consisted of short-lived coalitions, and cabinet instability was the rule.
3. Democratic institutions were not valued by major sections of the population and Italy's experience with democracy and representative government had been limited. A small elite consisting of the northern industrialists, landowners, and the Catholic hierarchy ruled the country. The middle classes, the lower middle classes and the peasantry were either weak or unable to exercise political influence and bring about necessary reforms.
4. The workers joined powerful leftist movements, some led by the Socialist Party, some by anarchists and syndicalists, and some by the communists, who, after 1920 began to assume a controlling position in many trade-unions. A strong minority endorsed extremist programs and direct action. They were organized for a revolutionary takeover and used the strike as a vehicle for weakening the State. They occupied factories and led the farmers to the occupation of land. Socialists showed remarkable strength at the polls, gaining 1,834,792 votes and 156 deputies in the legislature in the election of 1919. Again, in the election of 1921, their respective strength was 1,631,435 votes and 138 deputies. This "red menace" threatened not only the conservative forces, the Church, the industrial elites and the monarchy, but also the middle classes, the lower middle classes and the peasants in regions where the Church was particularly influential.
5. In this context, as in Germany, vigilante nationalist groups began to mushroom. They were led by former army officers and veterans. They took the law into their own hands in fighting the leftists, with the complicity of national and local governmental authorities. Gang-wars developed in the cities and the countryside. The newly formed Fascist Party began to play the leading role in combating "the reds."
6. Inflation, and the relative success of trade-unions in maintaining

their real wages through collective action while the middle and low middle classes suffered, accounted for a sharp right-wing reaction on the part of the latter. They were losing income and status and they were increasingly forced down to the economic and social levels of the workers.

7. Mussolini, the founder of the Fascist Party, was not, in contrast to Hitler, a newcomer to politics. But the similarities with Hitler are remarkable. They both came from the lower middle classes; both had read what they found congenial to their activist and romantic dispositions and admired the many writers who had criticized liberalism and extolled will-power and communitarian nationalist values. Mussolini, too, had fought in World War One and had been wounded. He, too, was a great orator. Like Hitler, Mussolini at first propounded ideas that had strong socialist overtones: confiscation of war profits, socialization of industries, workers' participation in the running of firms, the utilization of unused land by those who could work it, and appealed to the poor and the workers with promises of social and economic equity.

8. As with Hitler, Mussolini did not have to shoot his way into power. He was received by the King and was appointed by him.

The Fascist Party

The term fascist comes from the Latin word *fasces*, which was an emblem carried by ancient Roman magistrates as a symbol of their authority. It consisted of many rods tightly banded together, with an axe protruding on top. It conveyed remarkably well the underlying philosophy of the fascists: the combining of individuals together, in order to generate both power and authority.

The Italian Fascist Party was founded in 1919. At that time it was but one of many extremist nationalist groups. Only one hundred persons attended the founding meeting. Its program was both nationalist and socialist. It endorsed workers' revolutionary movements and strikes, and demanded the expropriation of land and the nationalization of industries such as mines and transport. Mussolini tried to straddle right-wing nationalist themes and extreme leftist demands, hoping to gain support from both the left and the right. His early appeal was so similar to Hitler's, that his party could have been easily called the National Socialist Workers' Party of Italy.

At first, the fascists did not fare well. In the election of 1919, in which the socialists gained 156 seats in the Chamber of Deputies, the fascists failed to gain a single seat. Mussolini himself, a candidate in Milan, received less than 5,000 votes out of 346,000 cast. The program of his party contained the socialist slogans to which we have referred: an eight-hour working day, minimum wage policy, participation of workers in the management of industries, welfare measures with comprehensive sickness and old age protection, a capital tax leading to the expropriation of the wealthy, the confiscation of the property of religious organizations and of war profits.

Within two years of the founding of the party, its membership had grown to 300,000. In the 1921 election, the Fascist Party secured thirty-five seats in the legislature and 19.6 percent of the vote (1,289,556). But what strengthened them even more was the private war they began to wage against all leftists. Left-wing clubs, newspapers, trade-unions and party headquarters were sacked. Agricultural cooperative societies were destroyed. The fascists, like the Nazis, appeared the strong men of "law and order" where government failed to provide protection. Their program began also to swing to the right. Mussolini now attacked the "Russian myth" of communism, spoke of rural democracy as opposed to collectivization, rejected class war in favor of national unity and promised to protect the workers but only in accordance "with the interests of production." Subsequently, in a party congress, the concepts of both economic liberalism and a strong State were endorsed. The party declared itself neutral on the question of the monarchy, which it had previously opposed. There was no mention of confiscation of lands held by religious organizations. Thus both the monarchy and the Church were placated.

The decision by the communists and many other leftist organizations and trade unions to organize a general strike late in 1922 gave Mussolini the opportunity for his "March on Rome" and takeover of power there. Actually he did not march; he simply took the train from Milan. His fascist squads, however, had occupied various localities and tens of thousands had moved into Rome and its outskirts. The King received Mussolini and asked him to take office. Thus the Fascist State was born.

Ideology

Fascism, like Nazism, was to be the answer to liberal democracy, doing away with competition, individualism, the quest for profit and material gain, divisions, fragmentations and particularisms. Instead a new regime would be established to create unity and cooperation, discipline and joint effort for the realization of collective purpose under the State. "Believe; Obey; Work; Fight" was one of the mottos of fascism. "Everything within the State; everything for the State; nothing outside the State," was another.

The argument favoring the inclusiveness and the primacy of the State is, as we know, an old one. For the fascists it meant the subordination of all social activities and organizations, of all individual interests, of all cultural manifestations (including religion), and of all rights—material, political and moral—to the State. Without the collectivity of the group, there can be no individual life and freedom and, of course, no common purpose. The State expresses them all. Morality

BENITO MUSSOLINI (1883–1945)

The son of a socialist blacksmith and a Catholic schoolteacher, Mussolini broke with the Italian Socialist Party over his support for World War One, and became editor of the nationalist *Il Popolo d'Italia.* In 1919 he founded the Fascist Party, and on October 22, 1922, King Victor Emmanuel IV asked him to become prime minister. Mussolini began to put into effect his philosophy of a totalitarian one-party state by abolishing republican institutions. He also attempted to realize plans for a "new Roman empire" by embarking on a series of military adventures, including the conquest of Ethiopia (1935–36), support of Franco in Spain (1936–38), and the occupation of Albania (1939). In June 1940 Italy entered into World War Two on the side of the Germans, but its forces were unable to make any genuine contribution to the German war effort. Expelled from office on July 25, 1943, after the invasion of Sicily by allied forces, he was arrested and subsequently executed by partisans on April 28, 1945.

Mussolini provided some good formulations of the fascist ideology, notably in his *The Doctrine of Fascism; Fascism: Doctrine and Institutions;* and in his *Autobiography.*

can no longer be based on individual rational calculations: it exists when we share fully the collective purpose of the State and we obey the State. "Fascism is for liberty," wrote Mussolini, but ". . . for the only liberty that can be taken seriously, the liberty of the State. In this sense fascism is totalitarian and the Fascist State the synthesis and unity of all values . . . [It] interprets, develops and gives power to every aspect of the life of the people."[7] The State, therefore, is a truly moral creative force.

Mussolini went beyond even this by saying that the Fascist State is truly democratic, for democracy in its purest form is "what ought to be." Fascism provides this kind of morality by substituting for the will of the many that of the few, and by subordinating the few to the will of one. The will of the leader becomes their will and in turn the will of all.

At this point, the student should note a subtle but important difference between Nazism and fascism. The first was as we noted a "populist" movement claiming to represent the German *volk* from which the Nazi Party emanated. As a result, the party claimed to be above the State. The fascist doctrine, on the other hand, influenced by the legacy of Roman law, was statist and authoritarian. It presumed a hierarchy of institutions and functions all organized by the State and operating under the State. The Fascist Party, through its national and regional and local organizations, played an important role as an adjunct of the Fascist State. Good fascists obeyed the Fascist State and their loyalty was to the State above all. One of the better exponents of the theory of the Fascist State wrote:

> The idea of the State as a force (which as a result of the general state of ignorance is seen as a German-Prussian idea) is plainly a Latin and Italian one. It is directly linked with the intellectual tradition of Rome . . . It is Italy's duty to reclaim it as a part of our natural heritage, in its genuine form, and translate it into action with the political wisdom that over the centuries has always been part of the genius of our race.[8]

Side by side with the concept of State and often used interchangeably with it, is the nation. In fact, it is the combination of the two, a combination that is "indissolubly" cemented, that the fascists stressed. The nation, and nationalism, provide the ultimate spiritual focus to bind people together within the State that embodies it. Nationalism

7. Cited by Herman Finer. *Mussolini's Italy.* N.Y.: Henry Holt, 1935, p. 201. As I noted in my preface, this book, though written in the 1930s, retains a remarkable freshness. I acknowledge my thanks to the late author.
8. Alfredo Rocco in Adrian Lyttelton (ed.). *Italian Fascism.* N.Y.: Harper and Row, 1973, p. 262.

"is the central inspiration of the human personality living in the civil community; [it] descends into . . . and makes its home in the heart of the man of action as of the thinker, of the artist, as of the scientists." Nationalism "becomes the very soul of the soul" of all of us.[9]

Nationalism and statism, the quest for the absolute ethical ideal, divests fascism, in theory, of material considerations. To live dangerously, to navigate on the high and perilous seas, to be able and prepared to fight at any time at any risk, gives to life a heroic quality which the drudgery of economic man, constantly concerned about his insurance, his wage, his benefits, is incapable of showing. The rational man must give place to the heroic man, and material considerations to dreams of great exploits. The real man must replace the mechanical man produced by liberalism. This rationale in part accounts for the influx of younger people and university students into the fascist movement.

THE LEADER (IL DUCE)

This effort to fashion a new society and a "fascist man" called for leadership and for the right kind of institutions to organize it and lead it. The Fascist Party and the leader (Il Duce) play the key roles. The leader speaks for the party and the State. He combines in his person the highest offices of the State and of the party. The party represents the movement that speaks for the leader and the State and acts on their behalf. Party officials occupy virtually all the important posts in the State. In fact, almost all civil service positions were by law reserved for party members and officials, which assured the party of patronage. The party also organized and structured all social activities and mobilized the rank and file to provide for support and watch out for deviant manifestations. Finally, the leader, with top party officials, controlled the economy, which like everything else was supposed to be subordinate to the State and to its ideology.

Thus the leader is the responsible chief of government. Mussolini allowed the King to stay in office as the formal head of state in order the get the support of monarchists and conservatives. But throughout the fascist regime the King was a mere shadow, and many forgot that he existed. Mussolini was in charge of the Cabinet and often held a number of Cabinet posts at the same time. Parliament continued to meet and to legislate, but all bills came from the leader. The fascists controlled the elections and enjoyed, until the beginning of World War Two, wide popular support. At election time, there was only one slate of candidates, all proposed by the fascists: there was no opposition.

THE DEVELOPMENT OF THE PARTY

The Fascist Party held the monopoly of representation; the virtual monopoly of office-holding; and the monopoly of mobilization and

9. Finer, op. cit., p. 222.

The Ten Commandments of the Fascist Fighter[10]

1. God and Fatherland: all other affections and duties come after these.
2. Whoever is not ready to give himself body and soul for his country and to serve the Duce without discussion, is not worthy of wearing the Black Shirt.
3. Use your intelligence to understand the orders that you receive and all your enthusiasm for obedience.
4. Discipline is not only a virtue of the soldiers in the ranks, it must also be the practice of everyday.
5. A bad child and a negligent student are not Fascists.
6. Organize your time in such a way that work will be a joy and your games, work.
7. Learn to suffer without complaining . . .
8. In actual circumstances, remember that the good lies in audacity.
9. Good actions, like actions in war, must not be done by halves: carry them to their extreme consequence.
10. And thank God every day for having made you Fascist and Italian.

recruitment. But it did not develop a private army as the Nazis did through the SS and SA formations. Throughout the fascist period, the army and the officer-corps maintained their autonomy. The fascist militia remained relatively unimportant.

From the days when it took power, the party grew rapidly. From about 300,000 in 1922–23, it grew to about one million by 1931 and to over two and a half million in the years before World War Two. It controlled the legislature. In the last contested and relatively free election in 1923, the Fascist Party received 4,671,555 votes—65.3 percent of the total. Thereafter it amounted to 100 percent!

The party also controlled a number of "front organizations" among civil servants, retired officers, fascist trade-unions, teachers, students, etc. A total of at least four million people were involved in these organizations. Thus about six to seven million Italians were members of the Fascist Party or of party front organizations. In sheer numbers, the fascists permeated the whole of Italian society.

Of particular significance were the youth organizations, aimed at six to twenty-one year olds, sponsored and controlled by the fascists. Recruitment began at a tender age, and at least one boy or girl out of every two was in some youth organization or another.

But there were many other organizations. For intellectuals, the *Academia d'Italia* was the source of many fascist publications; for

---

10. Adapted from Tannenbaum. *The Fascist Experience*. This is one of the better books on Italian fascism and I am indebted to the author for some of my observations and figures in this section. Also Finer, op. cit., pp. 426–454 contains a survey of fascist youth organizations.

Catholics, the *Centro Nazionale Italiano*; for army leaders, the *Istituto Nazionale di Culture Fasciste* (numbering in 1941 200,000 members). There was also a youth movement for children who had completed school, the *Fasci Giovalini de Combattimente*, while a very active fascist organization recruited many of the university students—the *Gioventi Universitario Fasciste*. A mass front organization was developed to provide various cultural and athletic activities for employees and workers—the Dopolavoro (literally "after work"), which had over two million members by the late 1930s.

The picture of fascist control, then, is fairly clear. The party controlled opinion, the education of the youth, all the media; it outlawed all opposition and through its various agencies intimidated those who were of a different mind. All agencies of the State were in the hands of party members. One is tempted to say that fascism had become the only dominant force in the Italian society. But not quite.

Pockets of Resistance

The aspirations for totalitarian control under the leadership of one person or one group always meet obstacles. There is an inherent diversity and pluralism in all societies made up of individuals, families,

Mussolini leading his fascists on their "March on Rome," 1922. (Photo: Brown Brothers)

groups, associations, regions, interests, professions, political ideologies, cultural differences, and no system can ever reduce all these forces to absolute subordination. Often this is because many of these smaller social entities refuse to be reduced to conformity. They prefer to hear their own drummer instead of marching in step to a dictated tune. But just as often it is because, despite its efforts, a totalitarian state cannot develop enough resources to control and to intimidate *everybody*. This was more true in the case of Italy than of Germany.

THE CHURCH

First and foremost among the various groups that fascism failed to control was the Catholic Church, a powerful spiritual but also social and political force. It had given its support to the conservatives and to Mussolini's coming to power for fear, among other reasons, that the Marxists, materialist and atheist, might come to power first. Mussolini was their bulwark.

It soon became apparent, however, that the totalitarian claims of the Fascist State to encompass and control every social and cultural activity—the very assertion that the State was the highest moral force within society and focus of all loyalties—could not be reconciled with the spiritual claims of the Church. The Church claimed control over education and the spiritual guidance of all members of society, and refused to become subordinate to the State—any State. Yet education was central to the fascist philosophy. It was the means for the development of a new citizen, the mobilization and indoctrination of the young, the inculcation of absolute loyalty. Conflict was inevitable and the fascists had to move very cautiously.

Their first move was to placate the Church. In 1929 a treaty was signed between the Fascist State and the Papacy. It recognized Catholicism as the official religion of Italy, and gave the Pope full sovereignty over the Vatican. The Church also received from the State a lump sum and an annual subsidy. In return, the Papacy recognized the Italian State—i.e., the Fascist State. In a separate agreement, the Concordat, the Church secured freedom to the public exercise of all rites, ceremonies and sacraments. Religious marriages were given civil recognition, religious instruction in Catholicism was made mandatory in all elementary and secondary schools. Hence, the Church was given special and autonomous functions within the State.

Most important of all, Catholic Action, a lay organization for disseminating Catholicism through various social and public undertakings, with more than one million members, was given the freedom to diffuse and encourage religious principles. It was precisely over this role that conflicts emerged. The fascists claimed primacy over education; the Church refused it. It would not allow anybody to interfere with its prerogative to infuse the spiritual teachings of Christ. But nor could the Fascist State allow the Church to become a rival organization, with Catholic Action countering its own efforts to indoctrinate youth in fascist political morality and loyalty. In an encyclical, the Pope refused to let the young and the faithful submit to "the cult of the State," nor to allow the State to monopolize the education of the young in their formative years. Particularly obnoxious to the Church was an oath required by the Fascists to obey the State "without discussion." If that oath was to be required, the Pope instructed Catholics to take it "with mental reservations."

After months of polemic, a compromise was reached. The Catholic Action was allowed to operate, but on condition that it would limit its activities to religious work. "God" was reintroduced in the fascist oath so that citizens would swear allegiance to *both* State and God. In this manner, the Church hoped to maintain some of its spiritual autonomy. It did not outwardly oppose fascism, but it refused to be absorbed into it. It gave its support, especially in the years of war, but the fascists could never take it for granted. Thus, the Church remained throughout the fascist era a powerful and separate organization. It maintained control over the Catholic Action; constantly prodded the fascist leaders, including Mussolini, to take action on certain matters or to refrain from acting on others; maintained parallel youth organizations, schools and universities, and had the monopoly of religious education.

Many have argued that the top Catholic hierarchy, including the Pope, followed a "wait and see" policy. The fascist regime was a positive force in their eyes in eliminating communism and in establishing order. A Catholic intellectual wrote: "Fascism can be proud of the fact that its institutions, its laws and its works are realizing for the first time in history . . . the eternal truth of Catholic and Latin political thought."[11] There was a genuine hope on the part of the Church that its own spiritual dominance would eventually assert itself and that it would be able to harness the Fascist State to the spiritual and political values espoused by Italian Catholicism—humane and social, but paternalistic and authoritarian.

On the other hand, there were many leading Catholics who from the very start opposed fascism, declaring its secular character as well as its political doctrine to be contrary to the spirit of the Church, and asking the believers to resist it. Whatever our appreciation of the policies and the role of the Catholic Church may be—an ally of fascism, a benevolent neutral, a neutral bystander, a spiritual opponent, a political opposition force—what counts most for the purpose of our discussion is that the Church remained a *visible* and *organized* separate force within a regime that claimed to be totalitarian. Fascism was not strong enough to bring the Church within the State. And the Church was strong enough to maintain its aloofness.

11. Tannenbaum, op. cit., p. 200.

Business groups and landowners gave their support to fascism the moment it came out in favor of private property and the profit motive and against agrarian reforms and the redistribution of land. The destruction of the trade-unions and of all political parties, especially the left-wing ones, gave to the northern industrialists what they most wanted. Similarly, the middle classes and the lower middle classes, delivered from the "red peril," saw in fascism opportunities for the maintenance and even the improvement of their material conditions and social status. They became the staunchest supporters of the regime. As in Germany, the only group to maintain its distance was that of the workers, despite efforts by the fascists to entice them into controlled unions. However, it was primarily among the more organized and politically involved workers—those who had belonged to trade-unions and had been politically active in the Socialist and Communist Parties—that this was true. Unemployed, unskilled and migrant workers were easily mobilized into the system. The peasantry remained generally apathetic.

One group that maintained its autonomy was the army. There was no direct interference with the high command and the officer corps from the Fascist Party or the State, which was not the case in Germany. Promotions and higher pay satisfied the army officers. As for the King, he remained, as we have seen, in office but without power. Yet he symbolized for many conservatives an autonomous force that could provide, in time, a rallying point for opposition.

The Corporate State

We have left the discussion of the economic organization of Italy under fascism till last. It took the form of corporatism—used to denote cooperation between capital and labor as opposed to class conflict. Corporatism comes from the word *corpus*, body, and its institutions are designed to bring workers and owners together into "one body," in which there is a cooperation and consultation before decisions are made. It is an old theory, stressing the organic relationships between two groups or classes which according to Marx are inherently antagonistic. It suggests harmony and common interest.

In his famous encyclical, "Rerum Novarum" (1891), the Pope had declared:

> ... Employers and workmen may themselves [establish] ... institutions and organizations which afford opportune assistance to those in need and which may draw the two orders together ... [12]

---

12. Text from *Seven Great Encyclicals*. Glen Rock, N.J.: Paulist Press, 1939, p. 23.

Forty years later, in 1931, in another encyclical, "Quadregissimo Anno," the Pope came out fully for corporatism:

> The Corporations are composed of representatives of the unions ... of workingmen and employers of the same trade and profession and as genuine and exclusive instruments and institutions of the State they direct and coordinate the activities of the syndicates in all matters of common interest. Strikes and lockouts are forbidden ... Little reflection is required to perceive the advantages in the institution thus summarily described: peaceful collaboration of the classes, repression of socialist organization and efforts, the moderating authority of a special ministry.[13]

"We have created the Corporate State," Mussolini proudly announced in 1927. However, constant modifications of the corporate structure, changes in the powers of the "corporations" and in their numbers makes it very difficult to identify exactly what the Corporate State was and whether it existed at all, except on paper.

The regime established twenty-two corporations. Among them the most important were those for cereals, fruit, vegetables and flour, beet and sugar, lumber and wood, chemical trades, textiles and engineering, credit and insurance, building trades, sea and air, inland communications. Every such corporation, corresponding to a broad area of economic activity, included representatives of all interests involved in all the branches of economic activity included in it—employers, employees, managers, owners, and so on. All corporations in turn elected the General Corporate Assembly, consisting of eight hundred members. This was the Corporate Chamber. In each corporation, employers and employees were equally represented, but in each one also there were members of the Fascist Party representing "the public." The trade-unions from which representatives of the employees were selected were of course, fascist trade-unions. A corporation was declared to be an organ of the State, an official body.

What were the functions of the corporations? Mostly to reconcile conflicts among the various branches of activity that were included in it, to better coordinate their respective activities and to regulate employment and the technical training of its members. They were expected also to provide for discipline in production, and, with the approval of the State, to fix prices for goods, services and wages and supervise the working conditions in various firms and services.

The Fascist State had the first and last word. "The corporations were the links in the chain which bound the citizens tightly to the State."[14] They were presided over by a fascist minister, and most de-

13. Ibid., p. 151.
14. Lyttelton, op. cit., p. 31.

cisions could be made only with the approval of the State. The old trade-unions had been destroyed and the fascist unions guaranteed the domination of the fascists. Thus the corporative mechanism turned out to be an instrument to control the workers and provide a link between the Fascist State and the business and industrial elites. This was a far cry from what corporatism was meant to be. It forced the workers underground and did nothing to alleviate class conflict.[15]

Conclusion

There was a great distance between fascist ideology and practice, as there was between the fascist movement and the system of government the fascists built. The original ideology was anti-bourgeois, anti-liberal, anti-establishment, and championed extensive structural reforms of the society in favor of the workers and the poor and against the privileged elite groups and their institutions—landowners, industrialists, the Church, the monarchy.

In practice, and even before the fascists came to power, there was a shift in favor of these powerful groups. The middle classes, the landowners, the Church, the industrial elites, the civil servants, the monarchy, the bourgeoisie, all gave their support and their money. By 1928, the Fascist State had eliminated free trade-unions. By 1931, it normalized fully its relations with the Church. Corporatism never developed into a genuine form of cooperation between capital and labor: at best, it represented a form of state capitalism, in which all business groups, manufacturers and landowners cooperated under the supervision of the State.

In a curious way, the Fascist State that roared upon the scene of Italian history in order to capture and renovate society, became the captive and the instrument of the very power elites that it promised to subordinate. Italian fascism was unable to destroy the existing structural elite of society as the Bolsheviks did, and as the Nazis tried and succeeded in great part in doing. It was unable to dominate all society as the Nazis unquestionably did. The much-vaunted unity of the nation under the Fascist State disintegrated during World War Two. The old political forces and particularisms reasserted themselves when the war was over.

Nazism and Fascism: Interpretations

In discussing Nazism and fascism we alluded to some of the underlying causes of right-wing totalitarian movements. It is time now to restate briefly some of the interpretations that have been advanced, and to

---

15. Finer, op. cit., describes in detail the corporations and the structure of the Corporate State.

raise some questions about the present status of right-wing totalitarian ideologies. Were Nazism and fascism passing phenomena or, on the contrary, can they be considered as ideologies that are likely to endure?

The Abnormality and Uniqueness Theories

A widely held notion a few decades ago was that totalitarianism and its specific manifestations in Germany, Italy, and elsewhere, were deviations from the democratic liberal norm. It was a disease, like measles. It could not affect the normal and inevitable progress of societies in the direction of open and democratic politics, any more than contagious diseases normally affect children's growth.

An equally widely held belief holds that Italian and German fascism were unique phenomena which correspond to the particular histories of these countries (late unification, and defeat or dissatisfaction in World War One) or their particular political cultures (primarily the lack of democratic political tradition and institutions and the corresponding development of powerful left-wing revolutionary movements). In both cases the inference drawn was that the right-wing extremist totalitarian phenomenon was self-contained. It would not spread elsewhere.

The Marxist Theory

A classic interpretation widely used by many authors was the Marxist one, formally endorsed by the Communist Third International. According to it, fascism or Nazism correspond to the "last stage of monopolistic capitalism." It is spearheaded by the most racist and expansionist elements of the capitalist class in an effort to maintain its rule at home and subjugate other peoples and their economies. Expansionism and war are two of the remaining means available to the capitalists, faced with economic depression and the growing contradictions of their system that Marx had anticipated. The evidence was considered clear: both Nazism and fascism geared the economy to war, distracting the people from their economic problems by appealing to their nationalism and by preparing them for war. They maintained private property and profits and destroyed the trade-unions and working class parties.

The Modernization Theory

Another theory views totalitarianism as a movement that corresponds to a stage of economic modernization. As the industrial and, in general, non-agricultural sectors gradually gain, there is a shift of power from the traditional landed and commercial elites to industrial and banking groups. Rapid industrialization accounts for an influx of farmers into the cities and for urbanization, and in general for a rapid growth in the numbers of industrial workers. These shifts bring about a new type of political mobilization and new political parties, attempting to recruit the new workers, the urban masses, but also the disgruntled peasants. Invariably, such a mobilization frightens the middle classes and the industrial elite groups who begin to favor repressive and integrative solutions. One author considers the optimal condition for the development of fascism to be when the non-agricultural occupational groups have increased at the expense of agriculture, to the point where they represent about 40 to 50 percent of the gainfully employed. This is, of course, not an assertion that all such societies will develop fascism, simply that it is one of the many conditions propitious for its emergence.[16]

It is precisely the other and many conditions that account for fascism, that are missing both from the Marxist theory and the modernization theory. For instance, if the highest and last stage of capitalism accounts for fascism, why did it develop in Germany but not in equally or even more advanced economies? Similarly, if we take the theory of modernization to explain Italian fascism, what accounted for its absence in other countries going through roughly a parallel stage?

Psychological Interpretations and the Middle Classes

Totalitarianism has been viewed by many authors as a psychological mass phenomenon. People react to a "threat" or to "alienation," both of which occur during the development of industrialization and the concomitant creation of a "mass society." The first accounts for large-scale, impersonal organizations with a high degree of division of labor and specialization. A mass society corresponds to the breakup of most intermediate social structures—village, family, neighborhoods—and many traditional institutions which structure and shape individual values, attitudes and life. The ultimate result is the "atomization" of society, all the old group disintegrated, the individual now alone and lonely. A reaction sets in, as we saw in discussing Fromm's *Escape from Freedom*, in favor of communal and integrative ideologies.

The perception of threat strengthens totalitarian appeals when the threatened individuals belong to groups that are comfortable, relatively well off, and satisfied with their lot. Such is the case with the middle classes that enjoy a higher income and a better status than farmers or workers or low middle class people. They are, according to some authors, the key to the door to power for right-wing totalitarian movements. They can keep the door closed or open it; the latter when special economic conditions begin to account for a loss of income and when special social conditions make them feel that they are in danger of losing their position in society.

16. A.F.K. Organski. "Fascism and Modernization" in S.J. Woolf (ed.). *The Nature of Fascism*. N.Y.: Random House, 1968.

There is hardly any doubt, as we have seen, that the middle classes, both in Germany and Italy, gave their full support to the Nazis and the fascists in order to protect themselves against threats to their income and status. They sought protection against trade-unions and workers and found it.

Yet, as with the previous theories, this interpretation fails to provide a satisfactory and general explanation. If Germany was a mass society in 1933, so were the U.S.A. and England. Why did right-wing extremism gain the upper hand in one country but not in the others? Similarly, if the middle classes were "threatened" in Germany, so were they in other industrialized systems, including the United States, during the Great Depression. Why did they seek defense in a totalitarian system in Germany but not elsewhere? Why were anti-democratic solutions sought in some countries and not in others? A theory that does not provide us with the explanation of as many occurrences as possible is not satisfactory.

Managerial Revolution?

Totalitarianism and totalitarian regimes have been viewed by some as representing a "managerial revolution" to replace the inept political leadership of democratic regimes. The economic structure of capitalism, they argue, has changed. Property is not in the hands of only a few; it is widely dispersed among stockholders. Property-owners cannot and do not make decisions: their managers do. Decision-making, therefore, is increasingly concentrated in the hands of a managerial elite which enters into close contact with other elites, not only in the economy but also in the army and the civil service; it even enters into close cooperation with labor leaders. It is a coalition, in other words, of persons with technical skills in production, management, administration and group organization.

It is this new managerial elite, then, which makes the major decisions in the economy (often through planning): production levels, the establishment of economic priorities, the utilization of resources, the supply of money, income distribution, wage policy, etc. Gradually the democratic institutions became an obstacle to this *de facto* government of experts and managers who control the heights of the economy and society.[17] Totalitarianism in the form of fascism or Nazism and authoritarian systems in general (even the Gaullist system in France) have been viewed accordingly as the triumph of the technocrat and the expert—of a power elite which finally does away with democracy for the sake of efficiency and organization.

The difficulty with this interpretation is that it assigns to rationality, knowledge and technical expertise a role that neither the fascists

---

17. James Burnham. *The Managerial Revolution*. Bloomington: Indiana U.P., 1973.

nor the Nazis valued. On the contrary, in both systems there was a constant struggle between the political ideological propositions, utopian or downright irrational, and the imperatives of rational management. There were constant conflicts between the economic managers and the party or the state; between the army officers and the State; the economic planners and the party leaders. Fascism and Nazism amounted in fact to the predominance of politics over technical spheres such as competence, organization, management and efficiency. Thus this managerial interpretation cannot be accepted.

Personality Theory

Considerable ingenuity has gone into efforts to show that totalitarianism appeals to and receives widespread support from individuals with a particular type of personality, the "authoritarian" or "potentially authoritarian." A number of attitudinal traits put together constitute a "syndrome" or a "pattern" of the authoritarian personality: anti-Semitism, nationalism, fear of outsiders or aliens, conservative political outlook, strict family upbringing. Persons showing this syndrome are likely to be found among the lower middle classes, the workers, and those without a little education. Similarly, persons suffering from various types of anxiety, even paranoia, unable to make decisions and choices, often afraid of the outside world, divest themselves easily of their freedoms in favor of authoritarian leadership which provides some degree of fixity and stability in their lives.

But there is no adequate evidence to attribute fascism or Nazism and membership in and support for totalitarian movements to personality types. To begin with, both Nazi and fascist movements received strong support from the middle classes, to say nothing of university students—persons, that is, with relatively comfortable backgrounds and higher education. Support was lowest from the working classes, where many of the traits associated with an authoritarian personality would be found. Secondly, even if we concede that there is an authoritarian upbringing in German and Italian families, a random distribution of political attitudes ranging from authoritarian to democratic would show only marginal differences for various countries of Europe and elsewhere. To assume that there was a preponderance of authoritarian personality types and syndromes among the Germans and the Italians, as compared to other nationalities, requires statistical proof that is not available and is unlikely to be found. "Personality" may in some instances be a contributing factor—but a very marginal one.

Conclusion

All the interpretations given of totalitarian movements provide us with only parts of an explanation. In some cases it may well be that levels of modernization provided a setting; in other cases, the lonely uprooted individual may have sought shelter in unity and communitarian effort; in others, totalitarian solutions were sought by business and financial groups to defend the economic system that provided them with profits; in still others, the middle classes and the lower classes, confronted with loss of income and status, revolted against democracy and liberal institutions.

No single interpretation will do; and even if all of them are put together they do not point to the set of conditions that will *inevitably* lead to totalitarianism. They do help us, however, in identifying the conditions under which political systems may be susceptible to totalitarian assault. The study of right-wing totalitarian movements, therefore, becomes not the study of unique manifestations, but the comparative study of a potentially universal phenomenon.

Is Fascism Dead?

As we have noted, ideologies often go through a process of ebb and flow. Right-wing extremism and totalitarianism has deep roots, and it is not at all unlikely that given certain conditions, they may surface again. This does not mean that they will take a form identical to that taken in either Italy or Germany, only that they will follow the same general themes of nationalism, anti-liberalism and anti-individualism in order to impose a national, communitarian and integrative ideology.

Many of the conditions for the rise of totalitarian movements and regimes continue to be present. The mass society has become even more impersonal and atomized thanks to rapid modernization and technological development. Individuals are very much alone, and their discontents and frustrations may lead them to espouse unifying and communitarian themes. The liberal ethic that continues to emphasize individual effort and to promise material well-being has raised high expectations for abundance. But it has also undermined some of the basic control mechanisms of society—the Church, the class, elite groups, the structure of deference and mutuality of respect. Even the modern political party seems unable to hold people together around common programs, and to pattern and regulate their expectations accordingly. The democratic society has been reduced to a myriad of competing and conflicting groups (some refer to them as molecular groups) each one of which tries to maximize its benefits and advantages. It is not unlikely, therefore, that new ideological and totalitarian parties may try to capture the frustrations and discontents of the many that are not satisfied with their position and material well-being.

International tensions may cause a revival of nationalism, defensive or expansionist, which will be used to subordinate individual and group demands, and also a loss of freedoms to absolutist nationalist myths and ends. Lastly, the ruling elites seem to have regrouped into a more coherent "power elite," consisting of the major decision-makers in society—economic, political, labor and military—and the temptation to safeguard their positions through repressive measures cannot be excluded. As for the middle classes, the rate of inflation in many societies may cause the same threat and panic that it caused in pre-Nazi Germany.

All that may be needed for virulent extremist movements to emerge may well be a severe international crisis, or another serious economic crisis. It may account for a resurgence of revolutionary leftist parties, of one denomination or another, which would put the elites and the middle classes on the defensive. It may bring forth a movement or a system that would attempt to control group particularisms, to replace representative institutions, to set aside political competition and to manipulate public opinion around nationalist and communitarian themes. Force will replace consent, even if only to a degree, and propaganda, persuasion. The prospect of totalitarianism, in other words, remains very much alive. So does the the rich ideological background from which it can draw.

Bibliography

Bracher, K. Dietrich. *The German Dictatorship*. New York: Praeger, 1970.

Bullock, Alan. *Hitler: A Study in Tyranny*. New York: Harper and Row, 1971.

Carsten, F.F. *The Rise of Fascism*. Berkeley: University of California Press, 1967.

DeFelice, Renzo. *Interpretations of Fascism*. Cambridge, Ma.: Harvard U.P., 1977.

Gallo, Max. *Mussolini's Italy*. New York: Macmillan, 1973.

Gregor, James A. *Fascism: The Contemporary Interpretations*. Morristown, N.J.: General Learning Press, 1975.

Heiden, Konrad. *Der Fuehrer*. Boston: Beacon, 1969.

Hitler, Adolf. *Mein Kampf*. Boston: Houghton Mifflin, 1962.

Mussolini, Benito. *My Autobiography*. New York: Charles Scribner's Sons, 1928.

Neumann, Franz. *Behemoth: The Structure and Practice of National Socialism* 2nd ed. New York: Oxford U.P., 1944.

Shirer, William L. *The Rise and Fall of the Third Reich*. New York: Fawcett-World, 1978.

Smith, Dennis Mack. *Mussolini's Roman Empire*. New York: Viking, 1976.

Tannenbaum, Edward R. *The Fascist Experience*. New York: Basic Books, 1972.

10

The Authoritarian Right

*And in him consisteth the Essence of the Commonwealth;
which (to define it) is One Person of whose Acts a great
Multitude . . . have made . . . the Author, to the end he may
use the strength and means of them all, as he shall think
expedient, for their Peace and Common Defense*
THOMAS HOBBES Leviathan

Authoritarianism is much more a form of governance than a political
ideology, and it must be sharply distinguished both from conservative
ideology and from totalitarianism. A conservative ideology, as we have
noted, is basically consistent with the tenets of democracy: constitutionalism and the rule of law, representative government and individual freedoms. Authoritarian regimes are not. They are forms of government which rely upon force, eliminate oppositions and freedoms
and often stress nationalism at the risk of becoming expansionist.

Similarly, despite some superficial resemblances, a sharp distinction should be made between authoritarian and totalitarian regimes.
Totalitarian systems stress the mobilization and the participation of
the citizenry; authoritarian systems try to keep the citizen in a state of
passive obedience. Authoritarian rulers are satisfied when the citizenry
remains apathetic and does not oppose the government. The official
political ideology in totalitarian systems is "total"—it affects every
aspect of social life, economic, political, religious, family, etc. The aim

is to create "new" men and women. Authoritarian systems on the other hand have no such all-embracing ideology; they are satisfied to leave social groupings alone—whether Church, family, economic groups, sports, or individual and cultural activities.

In totalitaritan systems the single party is the most dynamic vehicle of change and control; in authoritarian systems that have a single party, it has far less power and is not important as a vehicle of control and governance. The party yields to the government and to powerful socio-economic groups. These distinctions must be kept in mind. The reach and grasp of totalitarian systems is longer and firmer; that of authoritarian ones shorter and relatively weak. The goals of totalitarian regimes are comprehensive; those of authoritarian ones specific. Totalitarian systems try to dig deep roots in the society and manage to endure against many adversities—even military defeat; authoritarian systems have no strong supports and are very fragile—adversity easily topples them. Finally, though personal rule is common to both systems, the party plays a far more important role in institutionalizing and organizing power in totalitarian systems. The death of the leader is almost always fatal in authoritarian systems; totalitarian ones have managed to survive it.

Particular forms of authoritarian systems are many. They may be *traditional, bureaucratic, charismatic* or *military*. In traditional systems, authority stems from historical rules and customs: rulership is hereditary; in charismatic systems leadership stems from the popularity of the leader and the support he or she manages to elicit; bureaucratic authoritarian systems rely upon respect for the authority of the State and its agents, the bureaucracy, and authority is neither personal nor hereditary but statist. Military authoritarian regimes, finally, are based on either the coercive power of the army or the respect and deference the citizens develop for it, or on both. Its cornerstone is the army's discipline and organization, but leadership generally is personal—it comes from one of the army's officers. "Collegial" military dictatorships do not last long if they do not acknowledge the predominant position of one officer or another.

Bonapartism is a term that represents, historically, a good approximation of authoritarianism. We find in it the charisma of the leader, bureaucratic organization (what we called statism), and a strong military basis. Napoleon Bonaparte was a young French general before he became First Consul in 1801. Even elements of traditionalism were injected when Napoleon was crowned Emperor in 1804 by the Pope in the Cathedral of Reims, where the French kings had been crowned. His nephew Louis Bonaparte established the Second Empire, using by and large the legacy that Napoleon had bequeathed from the First, and ruled from 1851 to 1879, also as Emperor.

We find in Bonapartism four basic traits: (a) personal government; (b) centralized bureaucratic authority and organization—i.e., statism; (c) nationalism; and (d) the bypassing of the representative assemblies

and institutions in favor of direct popular consultations in the form of
plebiscites. There was no mass party to mobilize the people, and although the police used coercive practices, and there was widespread
intimidation, opposition was never eliminated.

Franquismo

In a similar way, Spanish fascism became intimately interwoven with
one man—General Francisco Franco (1892–1975), otherwise called the
Caudillo (the leader). The governance he established lasted only as
long as he himself lived. Franco never called himself or his regime
fascist, even if he admitted to admiring many aspects of the Italian
fascist regime. He combined through his personal rule, forces that were
outright fascist, others that were ultra-conservative and monarchist,
some that came from the various conservative political parties, but also
the military, the Church, the landowners and the economic and industrial elites, the middle classes and many of the peasants, especially
in the areas where the Church was a dominant force.

Authoritarianism in one form or another was hardly new for Spain,
which did not have a genuine republican tradition. Moreover, the

*Franco inspects the
battlefront prior to his
insurgent army's as-
sault on Valencia in
1938. (Wide World
Photos)*

economic and social profile of the country made it particularly receptive to authoritarianism. The majority of the people were illiterate; modernization and economic growth had lagged way behind Western Europe; the Church had opposed republican institutions and governments and the economic and landed oligarchy favored repression rather than reform. The lower classes—workers, but many farmers too—were in a state of constant defiance and revolt. Many workers joined anarchist syndicalist organizations committed to direct action rather than political participation and party politics. The Communist Party, weak at first, managed to gain strength during the Spanish Civil War (1936–39). At the same time, powerful separatist movements in Catalonia and the Basque region often joined forces with the left-wing against the centralization that the right-wing forces and the army tried to impose. The middle classes, which might have been able to exert a moderating influence, were weak and when faced with the danger from the left went, as middle classes almost always do, to the side of the right-wing forces, and eventually Franco.

In the 1930s all the elements of a civil war were present. As in Italy and Germany there were strikes, occupations of factories, takeovers by farmers of land belonging to absentee landowners and the Church. Again as in Italy and Germany, "nationalist" bands and organizations began to take the law into their own hands and to indulge in direct action and intimidation. Fascist organizations developed, notably among them the Falange, which claimed to be a genuine totalitarian party. Yet unlike Italy and Germany, the Spanish "revolution" began as a classic military uprising among the officers and special troops in Spanish Morocco. Franco marched into Spain and into political power behind his troops. There was no equivalent of the March on Rome and no formal invitation by anybody to Franco to form a government. It was a military, not a political, uprising, designed to crush the communists and their republican allies. It was a pragmatic and on the spot solution. Franquismo never became a genuine political doctrine with a comprehensive political ideology.

The same pragmatic and opportunistic stance was followed by Franco from his takeover of power in 1936 and until his death in 1975. He followed a policy of compromise and adjustment both at home and abroad, changing policies as the fortunes of World War Two changed and reconciling and neutralizing conflicting forces at home so as to keep his hand free. With most of the communist and left-wing leaders eliminated during, and immediately after, the civil war, he had little to fear from the left. To the right he had to contend with and try to balance a number of forces: there were the loyalists who considered Franco only a temporary interlude before the restoration of the monarchy; the Catholic Church that maintained control over education and insisted on imposing its ultra-conservative doctrine upon the State; there were the genuine fascists, the falangists, highly ideological, pushing for revolutionary changes, for a Corporatist State and social justice. The Falange was also anti-clerical. There were of course the military, the pillar of Franco's regime, interested particularly in order and in their own autonomy and privileges. There were, finally, the economic elites, wary of both the Falange but also of the Church. The one ·was an obstacle to their own privileges and profits, the other to economic modernization.

At no time did Franco allow any of these forces to become dominant over the others. But at no time did he envisage the subordination of any one of them or some of them to a combination of others. He played a balancing act that could well be called controlled pluralism— which of course is another way of saying that the system never assumed an encompassing and dominant role by subordinating all forces under it. At best it played a mediating role. A historian of Spain writes that the regime, by 1950, had adopted the posture of "a pragmatic, middle of the road authoritarian state, not fascist but resolutely anti-Communist, with stress on domestic development and survival."[1]

The Falange

Franco's Spain had a Fascist Party but in contrast to Germany and Italy it never became a mass party and never played an influential role in the regime.[2] Founded in 1934 by a number of young intellectuals, some of whom were deeply influenced by the social doctrine of the Catholic Church, and others, even more, by the secular aspirations of the Nazis, the Falange became the only political party in Franco's Spain. Its name (literally "phalanx," after the first phalanx, the ancient Macedonian army, which deployed its soldiers in close ranks in depth, providing both for strength and quick movement) was chosen to symbolize mass, organization and power. As with other right-wing totalitarian parties, its aim was to assume control of the State, to create a comprehensive ideology and to mobilize the masses and bring under it even the Church and the army. It was anti-capitalist, corporatist, stressed egalitarianism and popular participation and mobilization; it was nationalist and of course intensely anti-communist. Among the twenty-five points of its original program the following are of particular significance:

1. Political unity for Spain and elimination of regional separatism.
2. Abolition of political parties.
3. Establishment of a national dictatorship led by one party.
4. Use of violence in the regeneration of Spain.
5. Development of Spanish imperial power.
6. Expansion and strengthening of the armed forces.
7. Recognition and support of Catholicism as the official religion of Spain, but rejection of any clerical influence in government.

1. Payne. *Franco's Spain.* pp. 38–39.
2. Parts of my account of the Spanish Falange comes from Stanley Payne's excellent monograph *Falange* (Stanford U.P., 1961) and I owe thanks to the author.

In economic and social matters the Falange promised an economic revolution to include:

8. Establishment of national syndicates embracing employers and employees.
9. Sweeping agrarian reforms to reclaim wasteland, to improve techniques, concentrate scattered holdings and reorganize the large landed estates *(latifundia)*.
10. Industrial expansion.
11. Respect of private property but nationalization of credit facilities.

Personal Government

In its aspirations the Falange soon began to clash with the Church hierarchy, the army and the bureaucracy and to frighten the economic elites. The party was kept carefully under control by Franco. Its memership remained small. By the end of 1945 party officials began to reconsider their doctrine, asserting now that totalitarianism was incompatible with moral values (i.e., religion). It dropped all corporatist ideas, especially pronouncements favoring joint decision-making by workers and owners. Eventually it ceased to be an important force.

The fundamental reason for the failure of the Falange was Franco and his authoritarian regime. The party had an ideology and wanted to politicize and mobilize the masses. Franco was opposed to both. Franco would have preferred to depoliticize his regime as much as possible and to let the mass of the people acquiesce to its control out of ignorance, rather than having them involved in political crusades. When the Falange was useful Franco used it in his balancing act against other political forces; otherwise he gave it no support nor did he allow it to become a dominant political force.

Franquismo continued in the direction of statism and personal government, concerned after the 1950s with economic development and modernization, but maintaining the same hard repressive and exclusive policies with regard to leftist parties. The trade-unions remained under the control of the State thanks to the device of the Corporate State, the establishment of vertically organized corporations consisting of managers and workers in the same industry, as had been the case with Italy and neighboring Portugal.

Limited efforts in the direction of liberalization were made—the abolition of prior censorship of press and books, the election of some of the members of the legislature (many of whom continued to be appointed); a broadening of educational opportunities; economic reforms; but above all industrialization and urbanization, which began to move forward at an accelerated pace. The active population engaged in agriculture declined between 1950 and 1970 from over 50 percent to not more than 30 percent. What is more, new political elites emerged. As Richard Herr points out, they were "made up of high government officials, bankers, technocrats, and corporation managers, as in Germany and France and other industrial nations."[3] They began to influence the regime. But this was not incompatible with Franquismo since it had never developed a strong ideological position and had never allowed a mass party to develop and overshadow all other groups.

Franco's Spain tells us something about the flexibility and the pragmatism of authoritarian regimes. Franco adjusted both at home and abroad to changing circumstances; he allowed representative assemblies to operate as long as he could manipulate them; he framed constitutional documents; provided for laws of succession—but Franco himself remained the highest law. When international circumstances changed, he, like the second Bonaparte, Louis, began to liberalize the regime, without ever abandoning the political control he held. Like Louis Bonaparte, he began to make room for new elites and to press for economic development and modernization. But the flexibility of the regime and its pragmatism also indicate its inherent fragility. Without an ideology and a strong mass political party, it had to rely on an intensely personal element of leadership. So that when the leader died, there were no institutions to carry on the governance that had been established.

The Authoritarian Right in the U.S.A.

"Extremism," writes Seymour Martin Lipset, with particular reference to American political history, "describes the violation, through action or advocacy, of the democratic political process."[4] Despite sporadic flare-ups from what has come to be called the American "extreme" or "radical" right, the democratic process in the U.S.A. has held remarkably well. Extremist movements hardly ever succeeded in synthesizing their various negations into a program or an ideology, or in transforming them into some kind of positive political formula in order to seek, let alone gain, broad national support and political power.

The strains and stresses of American society have, inevitably, spawned extremist movements. Most, but not all, of these have come from the right. They have been movements of disaffection, appearing in "periods of incipient change"; they are addressed to groups that "feel deprived" or feel "that they have been deprived of something they consider important" but also to particular groups whose "rising aspirations lead them to realize that they have always been deprived of something they now want."[5] Under such circumstances, and unless there is a deep commitment to democracy, the success of authoritarian movements becomes a distinct possibility.

---

3. Richard Herr. *An Historical Essay on Modern Spain.* Berkeley: University of California Press, p. 260.
4. Seymour Martin Lipset and Earl Raab. *The Politics of Unreason.* p. 428.
5. Ibid.

Underlying economic factors have always played a crucial role in the rise of extremist movements. But in the American experience ethnic, racial and religious factors have been more important. Only after World War Two have economic as well as international and genuinely ideological political factors begun to gain prominence.

The Know-Nothings

One of the earliest extremist movements was the Know-Nothing Party that developed in New England, with particular strength in Massachusetts, in the 1820s. It was primarily composed of workers and artisans who feared that the influx of immigrants would depress their wages and drive them out of work. They advocated the exclusion of immigrants and wanted to prevent their participation in politics. Direct action was often taken against foreigners: members were supposed to "know nothing" about such action. Even if wages appeared to be the central issue, psychological factors played an important role. In an expanding economy, there could be work both for immigrant workers and also for the indigenous Anglo-Saxons. But the very fact that "foreigners" would attain the income of the native workers appeared to the latter an affront to their position and status within the community.

The Ku Klux Klan

The Klan emerged in the South right after the Civil War, to intimidate blacks and thwart the federal measures taken to give them citizenship and extend consitutional rights after they had been freed. It was a regional movement based on community and vigilante organizations and gangs, designed to keep blacks out of politics and the economy, to deprive them of access to property, and keep them at the level of farm hands and unskilled workers. It kept a tight control also upon all whites suspected of showing tolerance and sympathy to blacks. In the years following World War One the Klan had a particularly strong revival, emerging not only as the advocate of white supremacy but also as the champion of "Protestant" and native superiority over all immigrant and non-Protestant religious groups. It became the proponent of the purity of Americans—against Italians, Jews, Mexicans, Japanese, etc. At one point in the 1920s, it numbered more than four million members and extended beyond the South into the Southwest and California. It exerted a strong influence over the Southern state legislatures.

The Klan did not directly challenge the Constitution. It gave it, however, a special interpretation, favoring state rights and state autonomy. It was unwilling to see individual protection and civil rights extended to the groups and to the minorities it had singled out. It favored restrictive and repressive legislation, and when it was not forthcoming resorted to direct violence with burnings, intimidation, evictions and not infrequently, lynchings.

Like the Know-Nothings, the Ku Klux Klan's membership consisted of low-income and low-status groups: artisans, shopkeepers, unskilled workers, farmers who had moved from the farm to small towns.
Leadership came from petty officials—policemen, for example, small-
town businessmen, realtors and an assortment of veterans. Local ministers of various Protestant denominations played an important role
and added biblical zest and justification to the movement, especially
in the campaign against Catholics and Jews. In general, the movement
preached religious orthodoxy and conformity, the simple values of
rural life and of the small town against the big city, and against American entanglements abroad. It was fearful of industrialization and modernization because they were changing American society and shifting
the weight of population and of economic and political power into the
cities and away from the countryside. The movement against the immigrant was a desperate effort to vindicate the position of white, small-
town, low and middle-class Protestant America, and to maintain their
economic, social and political status in a changing world.

Father Coughlin

The first genuine ideological and national extremist right-wing movement was developed by Father Coughlin, a Catholic priest, between
1928 and 1940—the years of the Great Depression. Unemployment
peaked at a level of about eight to nine million until 1939, despite the
New Deal measures. Not only did blue-collar and white-collar workers
suffer, but also the farmers, the middle-classes and many of the industrial and managerial groups. Fascism had triumphed in Italy, and
the Hitler movement had begun the upward climb in Germany. Democracy, as we have seen, was on the defensive, and socio-economic
conditions in the U.S.A. were ripe for a strong movement against it.
Father Coughlin tried to exploit all this.

His movement had many of the characteristics of a totalitarian
right-wing movement, similar to those of Italy and Germany. First, it
purported to be a mass movement. According to surveys conducted at
the time almost one-third of the American people "approved" of what
Father Coughlin said. What he said was not addressed to native Americans. It did not pit them against immigrants: it almost did the reverse.
It struck at the major American institutions and the elites.

A second important feature of the movement was its anti-Semitism.
It endorsed the racist doctrines of the Nazis and described Jews in the
same racist terms. But there were other special reasons, one of them
manifestly religious, exploiting the Catholic bias against the Jewish
faith. It viewed the Jews as an "internationalist element," distinct from
the American melting pot. The infamous and malicious *Protocols of
the Elders of Zion*, which, as we have seen, Hitler had publicized, were
frequently broadcast and printed by spokesmen and in the various
pamphlets of the movement.

Its third feature was anti-communism. Communism was a threat both because of its anti-religious appeal, and also because of its emphasis upon class, as opposed to the national and communitarian philosophy Father Coughlin wished to impart.

Finally, while a staunch nationalist and an isolationist, Father Coughlin began to lean increasingly in the direction of the Nazi and the Italian models, favoring the support of both countries. Just before the demise of his movement in 1940, (by this time its popularity had waned, and at the beginning of the war it was outlawed) he identified fully with the cause of the Nazis to the point of declaring himself to be a "fascist."

His program had all the familiar "antis": it was anti-elite, anti-Semitic, anti-internationalist (but with a growing sympathy for Hitler and Mussolini that in the last years of movement became outright support), anti-democratic, anti-liberal, anti-capitalist and anti-Constitution. It was one of the first movements to directly advocate the overhaul of the Constitution of the U.S.A. It also suggested a new social order against *both* big capital and big labor. The name of the movement, characteristically enough, was The Union Party for Social Justice, and it merged with other extremist factors to form the National Union. It preached unifying and communitarian themes.

The social configuration of its support was not dissimilar from the one found in the early stages of Nazism and fascism. It came from low middle-class groups, from rural areas and small towns; there was considerable support among the middle-classes, higher support among Catholics and from among the unemployed.

Joseph McCarthy

It was a convergence of many factors that both sharpened and deepened the content and the thrust of the American extreme right in the 1950s. The major ones were similar to those which accounted for the emergence of fascism in Italy after World War One: profound discontent with the settlement that followed World War Two. Many in the United States felt that the Russians had strengthened their position, and began to search for scapegoats. Senator Joseph McCarthy found one in "international communism" and its agents in the U.S.A. Single-handed, he began to mount a campaign against not only communists, but also their sympathizers—left-wingers and liberals—the so-called "fellow-travelers." The term included intellectuals, university professors, members of the "Northeastern establishment," bankers and supporters of the United Nations. Not only Democrats, but also Republican leaders—even including President Eisenhower—were accused. McCarthy, in many highly publicized appearances and through investigations conducted by his Senate Committee, discovered "hundreds" of card-carrying communists in the State Department. He claimed that agreements at Yalta and Potsdam during and after World War Two, were engineered by the fellow-travelers to give undue benefits and advantages to the Soviet Union. The United States had been cheated by them from its victory.

While McCarthy never managed to organize a national movement, national response was widespread and positive. This was the period of "The Great Fear,"[6] when wholesale purges of "crypto-communists" occurred in the federal government, in universities, the army, the trade-unions. It was also a movement which began to show clearly the impact that the media of communication, especially TV, can have in creating a "national" state of mind. McCarthy and his activities were widely publicized.

Conspiracy theories are common in extremist movements. With Hitler it was the conspiracy of the Jews and the failure of the civilians to support their soldiers in war that played an important role. The conspiracy of the communists against the United States was a notion

6. David Caute. *The Great Fear: The Anti-Communist Purge Under Truman and Eisenhower.*

Senator McCarthy, whipping up an anti-communist terror in New York, 1954. (UPI)

that satisfied many conservatives and appealed to others who felt that the international position of the United States was slipping. In a peculiar way the McCarthy crusade appealed also to the forces of nativism that we found in the Know-Nothings and the Klan. There were the "ins," the good Americans, and the "outs," the communists, fellow-travelers, crypto-communists, left-wing liberals, etc.

The 1960s

With the demise of McCarthyism in the middle 1950s, a number of new extremist right-wing organizations and "third parties" mushroomed. They all followed the same basic themes—anti-communism, a bellicose attitude towards the Soviet Union, and a blanket endorsement of nationalist ideals. But right-wing extremism assumed also a blatantly conservative posture with regard to domestic issues—social and economic ones. It began also to broaden its attack against the major American political and economic elites, and to criticize the American system of constitutional democracy. Many organizations assumed the posture of the minuscule nationalist organizations that had developed in Germany before the Nazis managed to bring them together. They urged direct action and formed vigilante groups.

The John Birch Society, founded in 1958, became in a sense the intellectual inspiration for these movements. It kept a check of "communist penetration" and "communist control" of the U.S.A. This ranged from as low as 30 percent to as high as 60 percent! President Eisenhower and John Foster Dulles, the Secretary of State, were considered to be "communist agents." Its membership in the late 1960s was almost 100,000, but it appears that it has declined since. It has about four thousand local chapters some of which are now inactive. It publishes the *American Opinion*, a monthly review, and its official ideology can be found in the John Birch Society *Blue Book*. It owns a publishing company and several bookstores through which it disseminates its material.

The Minutemen

"Minutemen" was an extremist vigilante organization founded in 1960 by Robert DePugh, a Missouri businessman, with the purpose of training Americans in guerilla warfare. This would be used to fight the communists once they had conquered the United States, an event which the Minutemen saw as highly probable, either through internal subversion or invasion. Membership estimates ranged from DePugh's claim of a high of 25,000 to a low of 500. In the late 1960s, the Patriotic Party was established as the political branch of the Minutemen. Both groups have had links to various neo-Nazi and rightist paramilitary groups, as well as the KKK.

Several groups of Minutemen have been seized with illegal arms caches which have included rifles, submachine guns, explosives, mortars, and anti-tank weapons. In August 1968, members were arrested after a gun battle with state police resulting from an armed attack on a farm run by the New England Committee of Nonviolent Action at Volunstown, Conn., in which several people were wounded. DePugh himself was implicated in a plot to rob a Seattle bank. He was arrested in July 1969 and subsequently sentenced to a ten-year prison term.

The Prospects of American Extremism

American right-wingers can be identified in terms of their "antis." Against the United Nations and all its international organizations; against NATO; against diplomatic relations with the Soviet Union; against the social legislation of the New Deal; against capital gains taxes; against income tax; against the Rural Electrification Administration; against the National Relations Labor Board; against federal wage and price controls; against the Federal Reserve System; against urban renewal; against all forms of federal regulatory controls and federal intervention in the economy. What they favor is a free enterprise system. They represent the extreme right of the neo-conservatives. What distinguishes them sharply from all those who call themselves conservative is that they have raised questions about the democratic process itself, urging constitutional revision, direct action and repression. Extremists show little respect for constitutional individual guarantees. Yet aside from the commitment to economic liberalism, they have developed no positive ideology other than an exclusive form of nationalism in which communists, "collectivists," "liberals," and New Dealers can have no place.

At least two particular circumstances have strengthened the extreme right and have provided it with considerable popular support. The first, and perhaps most important, was the "black movement." In the beginning this took the form of urban riots, and later, with desegregation, decided by the Supreme Court in 1954, and implemented by various federal district courts enforcing equal opportunities and integration. Non-discriminatory provisions for blacks in buying houses, in employment and in education, caused a backlash among many workers, low income groups and white immigrants. A new "Know-Nothing" mentality developed. A militant and "preservative" (to use Lipset's term) posture emerged. Deep-set psychological forces came together in the late 1960s to enhance this posture. According to David Riesman, one generation had already gone by since the New Deal legislation had been in force, and its impact was now causing a feeling of threat and frustration among many in the middle classes and many other groups. What was the threat?

The "old middle class" of the 1930s—the independent physician, the homebuilder, farm-owner, small-town lawyer, realtor, automobile dealer, gasoline station owner, small businessman and the like—were being definitely shoved aside. The small town and its ways of life were perishing as urbanization gained momentum. The coming of the immigrant groups to full political power and even to social status intensified the feeling of threat on the part of "middle America."

But the new elites found themselves in danger too, and on the defensive. The managerial elites that replaced the family-owned enterprise or a small corporation were without roots and property. They were self-made men or women. Success alternated with failure in the fast-moving and highly impersonal large organizations, firms and corporations. The military themselves found their traditional claims to authority challenged by the experts—from universities, various think-tanks, business and technical schools. A new intelligentsia, well-versed in military, technical and international problems, began to supersede the military establishment. It was Secretary McNamara, a President of the Ford Motor Corporation, who under President Kennedy and Johnson, directed the Pentagon, with the help of civilian experts.

So, while the "old middle classes" were in a state of frustration, the "new middle classes"—technicians, engineers, teachers and professors, white-collar workers, middle managerial groups, the bureaucracy—which had been steadily growing in numbers, income and social status and position, began, too, to experience the same predicament. New groups, notably the blacks, began to make their bid for power and income. At the same time, inflation began to endanger all middle-class groups, old and new. Finally, an intractable international situation and what amounted to defeat in the war in Vietnam shook the myth of American supremacy. In a fast-changing world at home and abroad, the traditional landmarks that spelled security and confidence for the American public were being washed away.

A feeling of frustration, resentment and impotence has always provided the best climate for the growth of extremist movements—with simple answers to complex problems and nationalist solutions to deep-set social and economic difficulties. More than forty years after the New Deal, and a generation after victory in World War Two, this is the spirit that may be prevalent in the 1980s. The foundations of American democracy and constitutional government may be tested as never before.

Bibliography

Bell, Daniel (ed.). *The Radical Right*. New York: Doubleday, 1964.
Caute, David. *The Great Fear*. New York: Simon and Schuster, 1978.
Epstein, Benjamin, and Forster, Arnold. *The Radical Right*. New York: Vintage, 1967.

Hobbes, Thomas. *Leviathan*. Baltimore: Penguin, 1968.
Lipset, Seymour Martin, and Raab, Earl. *The Politics of Unreason:Right Wing Extremism in America 1790–1970*. New York: Harper and Row, 1970. Second Edition. University of Chicago Press, 1978.
Payne, Stanley. *Falange: A History of Spanish Fascism*. Stanford, Ca.: Stanford U.P., 1961.
———. *Franco's Spain*. New York: Crowell, 1967.
Rogger, Hans, and Weber, Eugen (eds.). *The European Right: A Historical Profile*. Berkeley: University of California Press, 1965.

part four

IDEOLOGIES IN FLUX: OLD AND NEW

A new heaven and a new earth.

In this last part of the book I have tried to group together some ideological movements which *appear* to be new and, at least in some cases,
quite explosive, though in fact they hail from the past. The virulent
nationalist movements in the countries of the so-called Third World
trace their ideological origins to nineteenth century European nationalism, which I shall also discuss briefly. Similarly, powerful separatist
and autonomist movements within nation-states project an ideological
profile which combine elements of nineteenth century nationalism
with democratic theories of participation and communitarian control,
while others borrow from Marxist theories of imperialism to adapt it
to conditions prevailing within nation-states.

Powerful movements of protest—the New Left—which I discuss
at some length, stem from a strand of moral individualism, with religious overtones, which can be found among many anarchists and advocates of civil disobedience. They also borrow from Marx's early works
precisely those parts relating to Marx's indignation with the existing
social conditions and his moral condemnation of the system that gave
birth to them. It is in essence a neo-Romantic movement that wants to
do away with industrialization, technology and science in order to
liberate human emotions and intuitions—again a recurring theme of
nineteenth century protest movements, including those that came from
the extreme right.

The fact that old wines are being poured into new bottles does not
mean that the vintage remains the same. As any expert wine-taster can
tell, the "body", the "aroma" and the "taste" differ. But whatever the
various brews, they all account for a serious crisis of political authority,
and they are an expression of a profound upheaval in the values of
advanced industrialized nations.

The New Left:
Revolution
of the Imagination

I am nothing and I should be everything
KARL MARX Critique of Hegel's Philosophy

The term New Left is used to describe the general movement of agitation, protest and revolt organized and led in great part by young people and university students in the 1960s. The system under attack was, and continues to be, that of the modern industrialized societies—democratic or not. Seen by its opponents, its major characteristics are repressiveness and comprehensiveness: bureaucratic, impersonal, authoritarian. Everything is subordinated to management, thanks to the advances of technology; production is geared to material gain and profit; standards of measurement and evaluation become exclusively quantitative. The State, hand in hand with the huge industrial organizations, socializes people to accept the values the system manufactures—the ideology of consumerism, production for waste, and the inculcation of work discipline. The individual becomes an empty shell, losing all capacity for pleasure, joy and fulfillment. He or she becomes "dehumanized." This is "the system" the New Left paints, in order to call for its destruction.

Different manifestations of the New Left movement appeared at approximately the same time, throughout the 1960s[1] in democratic

---

1. For an overall account of the various left-wing student movements, see Lipset and Altbach. *Students in Revolt.*

industrialized countries such as Japan, England, France, Germany, Italy, Holland and the U.S.A. While varying in intensity from country to country, there were a number of common characteristics: it occurred in rich countries where the standard of living was high; it rejected the whole scheme of values, organization and structure of authority in these societies; it was not and is not communist (indeed it sharply criticized the Soviet political, social and economic system and ridiculed the various national communist parties). "Please leave the Communist Party as clean on leaving as you find it on entering" was one of the slogans of leftist French students.

Even in its best days the New Left had little organization and no clear program, nor a blueprint of the kind of society it wanted. It seemed to be a spontaneous movement, and it was in the spontaneity that brought it into being that its leaders and followers hoped to find the secret of its strength and continuation. But few workers participated, and the trade-unions rejected it (as did the leadership of the various communist parties). The bulk of the movement was made up of the sons and daughters of the middle classes. The young revolutionaries had breakfast at home with their fathers and mothers before going out on to the streets to try and destroy the way of life in which they had been brought up. They were organized into small Action Committees.

The revolt of the students was naturally addressed at first against university and university life—the dry knowledge it imparted, the overcrowding of classes, the impersonality of instruction, the lack of adequate financial supports, the emphasis upon natural sciences and rational discourse, tests and examinations. "When examined answer with questions" was another motto of the French students. But the university reflected the values of society, and was meant to educate and prepare the young people to live in the society: it was society's major socializing force. By attacking the university, the whole society came also under attack. Criticism of the university was, essentially, social and political criticism, and the revolt spilled out of the campuses to appeal to everybody who was dissatisfied and unhappy.

One of the highest points of the New Left movement was the uprising of May and June 1968 in Paris and many other French cities. The students led the way by striking, occupying the universities, throwing out their professors, deriding the meaning and validity of what they were being taught and asking for a new university—the "anti-university." The revolt spread to workers, public servants, salaried personnel. Public buildings were occupied, TV and radio stations taken over, barricades built, battles with the "forces of order" fought, and the students seemed on the verge of taking power. In an unprecedented show of spontaneity, and against the instructions of their trade-union and political leaders, the French workers began to join. They went on strike, occupied factories, and brought the whole economy to a standstill. One firm after another, one organization after another, one administration after another, one service after another, were "taken over" by those who worked in them. Theaters, newspapers, the opera, the ballet, even soccer teams were taken over by actors, reporters, singers, dancers and players. The only organization that was not taken over seemed to be the Paris Stock Exchange—it was set on fire!

Another high point in the political and revolutionary activity of the New Left took place in the U.S.A. at the Democratic Party convention held in Chicago at the end of August 1968. Demonstrations against the war in Vietnam had already reached a peak, forcing Lyndon Johnson to announce that he would not seek renomination. A number of students and other leftist organizations decided to demonstrate at the Chicago convention and to force upon the Democratic Party a peace candidate. But their demands were broader, and the participants ranged from those who favored peace and were against the military draft to genuine revolutionaries, driven by the vision of a new society. The National Mobilization Committee to End the War in Vietnam (a loose organization which appealed to all liberals and leftists who were against the war) played an important role. In addition there were the Committee for an Open Convention, seeking the nomination of Eugene McCarthy; the Students for Democratic Action; and the Youth International Party (Yippies), advocates of the "counterculture."

All these groups assembled in Chicago, coming into confrontation not only with the police but also the National Guard. What followed

"Under the cobblestones, the beach!" A street scene from the 1968 student uprising in Paris. (Photo: Wide World Photos)

was almost a week of violence often amounting to pitched battles: one thousand persons were injured, including almost two hundred policemen. The demonstration failed, with the nomination to candidacy of Hubert Humphrey, but it injected a renewed militancy into the antiwar movement; it led to the March on Washington in May 1969 in which over ten thousand marchers were arrested.

Four years later some of the same groups pressed for the end of the war with the new Democratic candidate, George McGovern, asking among other things for a guaranteed income, and legalization of marijuana and of abortion. They also organized a massive demonstration at the time of the Republican Party's convention in an effort to prevent Richard Nixon from delivering his acceptance speech. But by 1972 the nature of the war in Vietnam was changing with the withdrawal of the American forces, and the strength and militancy of the New Left began to decline. For over four years it had challenged some of the most powerful myths and institutions of American society.

The Ideological Foundations

The New Left and the student uprisings should be put in their proper ideological and historical context. They represented, and still represent, long-standing grievances against industrialization since it made its appearance at the end of the eighteenth century.

Criticisms of industrialization, and in general against the principles and practices of economic liberalism, as we have already seen in discussing fascism and Nazism, took three major forms.

At first there was a utopian romantic reaction, best represented by the utopian socialists who we discussed earlier, and more particularly two French thinkers, Charles Fourier (1772–1837) and Pierre-Joseph Proudhon (1809–1865). Theirs was almost a gut reaction against rational and scientific organization and industrial production and the discipline it entailed. Fourier proposed a social system in which "emotions" would be given precedence, so that social and economic cooperation and production would be based upon emotional affinities and compatibilities and companionship. To achieve this, Fourier suggested that work and living be organized in small units—*phalanstères* (of about 1500 persons each) to provide for intimacy and belongingness, and to make work pleasurable.

Proudhon, after attacking private property, capitalism and the dangers of bureaucratic and centralized organizations, including the State, began to espouse anarchism. Like Fourier, he believed in the formation of small groups (he called them *associations*) which would collectively own property, and produce and organize work. Such associations would provide the feeling of belongingness needed and also put an end to the exploitation of workers by the property-owners. Above all, they would replace the State—its centralization, bureaucracy and repressive authority, which stunted individual life and growth.

The second type of reaction against industrialization is represented, as we know, by Marx and the Marxists. But it was almost the
opposite, in form if not substance, from that of the utopian socialists.
For Marx, capitalism and industrialization were necessary steps for the
coming of socialism. Marx acknowledged the misery, deprivation and
dehumanization that a capitalist society brings, and deplored the exploitation to which the worker was subjected. He was among the first
to discuss the alienation of the worker who is separated from what he
or she produces. Yet all these miseries were necessary, according to
Marx, so that the working class would become conscious of its predicament and change it. By taking away property and socializing the
means of production, the workers would regain their freedom and
decide what and how and for what purpose to produce. But Marx
continued to think in terms of a highly centralized and bureaucratic
means of controlling the economy. It would become such an instrument
only in the hands of the newly liberated working class. He had no
patience with Fourier's phalanstères or Proudhon's associations.

The third reaction to industrialization and capitalism came from
the anarchists. According to some of their spokesmen, industrialization, technology, scientific management are welcome but only if they
come under the direct control of those who produce. Large authoritarian structures must be done away with and production must be
lodged in smaller units that will use technology, division of labor and
scientific principles of production—it should be based upon rational
and not emotional considerations. This leads to the institutions of
"workers' control" and "workers' councils" such as we discussed with
regard to Yugoslavia, and to "guild socialism," "self-management" and
many other cooperative arrangements.

Thus some, like Fourier, have rejected both bigness and scientific
management. Marx accepted both but only if they were lodged in the
hands of an administrative mechanism which had collectivized the
means of production and was run *by* the working class *for* the working
class and the collectivity. Many of the anarchists accepted scientific
management and rational organization for work, but were against bigness, centralized direction and State authority.

Where did the New Left stand? Before we answer this question,
we must turn to two concepts that play a crucial role in the ideology
of the New Left—the concept of alienation and the role of ideology in
modern industrialized societies.

Alienation

The term "alienation" to describe the state of mind of the people living in an industrialized society appears more often in the literature of the
New Left than the word "spirit" in the Bible. To be alienated is to be a stranger (alien); in French the word means insane (*aliené*). In Roman law the
term applied to those who could not legally make decisions:

the *alieni juris* (women, slaves, minors) were under the jurisdiction of somebody else who made decisions for them and about them. Another word for alienation is "estrangement"—being or feeling like a stranger. Its opposite is "integration" or "participation," when an individual feels like part of a whole—whether family, neighborhood, university, factory, city, State, etc. How to make individuals feel part of the whole, how to make them into social beings without, however, depriving them of their freedoms, individuality and spontaneity—how to reconcile the "natural" person with the "social" being—has been one of the major and most difficult problems in political philosophy.

No matter how you look at it, alienation, with its consequences, is very serious. To be a stranger in your own home, village, town, factory, is not only to be alone but also to be without means to reach out into the world and the people surrounding you, and to communicate with them. Even worse, it is a state of mind that makes it difficult for the alienated individual to receive messages and communications from others. He or she shuts them off: the individual is literally "spaced out." And the more the society develops new and rapid mechanisms of communication, the more individual loneliness becomes unbearable. There is boredom at first, then frustration and then sheer anger. The individual searches for an outlet to find togetherness, love and fellowship, but in vain. Most other individuals are in the same state of mind and whatever communication there is among them, it is superficial—skin deep. All share the same feeling of estrangement. The mass society is a state of "collective loneliness"—a lonely crowd[2]—as anybody who walks the streets of a big city or drives his car during the rush hour can tell. The social man has devoured the individual. Spontaneity, creativity, desire, pleasure are gone. What has brought this situation about?

Types of Alienation

There are at least three basic types (and explanations) of alienation. All of them relate directly to the rapid growth of industrialization and technology.

Firstly there is the phenomenon of uprootedness—the severance of the individual from a primary group—family, village and the simple values of rural traditional life to which the individual was attached. Such a phenomenon occurs at first in the early stages of industrialization but recurs in waves, as industrialization develops. Individuals move from the country to the city in search for jobs in new surroundings that are alien. Emigration is essentially the same phenomenon and is characterized by the same feeling of alienation. It was clearly the sit-

---

2. The term is the title of David Reisman's path-breaking book, *The Lonely Crowd*. New Haven, Conn.: Yale U.P., 1950.

uation of many immigrant groups which came to the United States, as some of the books of the noted historian Oscar Handlin portray so well.[3]

Alienation is also present when an individual severs ties with his or her natural environment: the soil, the simple uncomplicated life over which one has some control and can understand, the freedom to dispose of one's time and leisure, the satisfaction of simple needs through the performance of simple tasks—fishing, hunting and farming. With industrialization, division of labor, specialization and interdependence, the individual's ability to control the environment and to understand it diminishes. New economic and social relations are built, upon which we become increasingly dependent for our livelihood and way of life. We are no longer our own masters: impersonal forces and relationships are at work that shape us and our lives.

A second type of alienation appears when technology, and more particularly rational and scientific thought, advance. It all started, New Left thinkers claim, with the famous saying of Descartes, "I think, therefore I am," equating rational thought with existence. It led to all the "evils" of the Enlightenment, the search for "objectivity" and our inclination to try to understand the world in terms of laws and regularities.

The New Left considers "objectivity,"—science, the search for laws—to be a major cause of alienation. The scientific method claims to be limited only in what can be shown to be valid and what can be proven through measurement and empirical verification. This scientific outlook, however, misses the very essence of the individual—emotions, feelings and intuition—and subordinates truth to demonstrable correlations. Scientists commit themselves to explaining how things work in order to control the environment better and make it work even better, i.e., more efficiently. They gradually lose the ability to think in terms of moral values. They never ask the crucial question as to whether things that work efficiently should be allowed to work at all.

Scientific inquiry provides only a partial, if at all valid, explanation of existence. It never attains what Bergson called "the ultimate reality" (les réalités profondes), which can be grasped only intuitively. It deals with the external manifestations of reality, never with its essence. Even worse, the scientific mind ultimately associates the individual with "things," to be correlated, aggregated, classified, and "explained." It leads, therefore, to the manipulation of the individual in the same way in which various chemical elements can be manipulated to manufacture a product.

Finally, a third, perhaps the classic type of alienation, as suggested by Adam Smith and fully developed by Karl Marx, is the separation of the workers from what they produce. In industrial society, the workers have no control, no physical hold of what they produce, and nat-

3. Oscar Handlin. *The Uprooted.* Boston: Little Brown, 1951.

urally, no freedom to decide what to produce and to dispose of what they produce. Part of their produce is taken away from them in the form of surplus value that is translated into profit for the capitalists; the rest becomes merchandise, a commodity to be sold at the market. The worker does not recognize it as his or her own. Furthermore, a product is produced not because the workers need it or want it or will be able to buy and enjoy it. It is something that others want and can buy. Finally, the workers find no fulfillment in the performance of routine tasks that the specialization of labor requires; work is no longer creative.

For the Marxists this type of alienation will end when the means of production are socialized so that the working class as a whole will be free to decide what and how to produce and how to allocate the product. They will become masters of themselves again by mastering production. Their alienation will end. From nothing, they will become "everything."

It is characteristic of their indictment of our industrialized society that the New Left not only emphasizes all three types of alienation as outlined above but that they propose to reintegrate the individuals back into the three ways of life that they have been deprived of. Their purpose is to bring them back into some of the primary associations they had to abandon; to replace science and rationality with feeling, imagination and intuition, and to give back to the workers their produce and with it their freedom to decide upon *what* to produce.

The Invasion of the Individual

It was the assertion of the individual conscience—of the "inner man"— as distinguished from the outside world and the social group which represented the early awakening of freedom. The tribal individual mentally broke away from the tribe to develop his ways and to liberate himself from the repressive conformity it imposed. The "we"—the group or the tribe—gradually became "I," the individual. Stoics and Christians asserted the claims of individual conscience against the awesome power of the Roman emperors. The liberals, much later, confronted the power of monarchs. Whether in moral or economic terms, the ultimate goal of their philosophies was to build a wall between the individual on the one hand, and the State but also the society on the other. The tyranny of a conformist society over the individual might be just as repressive as that of Caesars, emperors or dictators.

Liberalism, therefore, was originally a great liberating force. Social and economic development throughout the nineteenth century and into the twentieth, produced, however, some unanticipated changes. The individual entrepreneur was replaced by the big corporation; concentration led to the increase of power and decision-making for some while producing a vast mass of salaried that followed. Big firms began to dominate the economy. At the same time, advanced technology spread not only to production but to all forms of social life. Big organizations and new organizational techniques of management created new forms of control that subordinated the individual. Mechanization became the rule. Mario Savio, one of the leaders of the New Left in the United States, wrote:

> There is a time when the operation of the machine becomes so odious, makes you so sick at heart that you can't take part; you can't even tacitly take part, and you've got to put your bodies upon the levers, upon all the apparatus and you've got to make it stop. And you've got to indicate to the people who run it, to the people who own it, that unless you're free the machine will be prevented from working at all.[4]

The demand for efficiency and profit develops its own logic, which leads to the production of goods as an end in itself without reference to social goals. Herbert Marcuse, philosopher of the New Left, claims that in advanced industrialized societies:

> the technical apparatus of production and distribution (with an increased sector of automation) functions not as the sum-total of mere instruments which can be isolated from their social and political effects, but rather as a system that determines . . . the product of the apparatus as well as the operations of servicing and extending it. . . . The productive apparatus, tends to *become totalitarian to the extent to which it determines not only the socially needed occupations and skills and attitudes but also individual needs and aspirations.*[5]

Thus the productive forces obliterate the line that separates the society from the individual, between private and public existence, between the "I" and the "we," between the inner self and the social whole. This is the crux of the problem. The individual is invaded by the outside forces and values of organization and production.

To put this idea quite simply: society as a whole is supposed to be run by a managerial and technologic elite which in the name of efficiency and profit develops methods of organization and coordination that propagate a conformist ideology to its methods and goals. All individuals are required to "march in step." Production is geared to those needs which will keep the industrial apparatus working, even

---

4. Massimo Teodori (ed.). *The New Left: A Documentary History.* N.Y.: Bobbs-Merrill. 1969, p. 156.
5. Marcuse. *One Dimensional Man.* p. xv.

if production is not geared to real needs. Ideology, however, will be used to make the objects produced *seem* desirable and "real." The individual is being made to conform to the needs of management, organization, technology. Thus the social man leaves behind him the inner man, and his own freedom to choose and decide. The technological rationality of the industrialized society:

> reveals its political character as it becomes the great vehicle of better domination, creating a truly totalitarian universe in which society and nature, mind and body, are kept in a permanent state of mobilization for the defense of their universe.[6]

There can be no better definition of the Nazi principle of "synchronization" which we mentioned earlier.

The Role of Ideology

The absorption of the individual into the system of the advanced industrialized societies is a gradual process, and ideology plays the crucial role. It rationalizes and legitimizes production and efficiency; socializes the young people in the school and the university to accept them; sets the tone for their preparation to play special roles within the system. It is primarily the ideology of production in which consumerism and material satisfactions predominate. Modernization and growth are viewed exclusively in quantitative terms. It is a materialist ethic which gradually invades our lives until we can no longer refute or avoid it. It affects our moral judgements, our tastes, our pleasures, our leisure time. Political and ethical considerations are subordinated to it. Education, performance, lifestyles are reduced to pure material considerations which can be checked, double-checked and tabulated.

It is an ideology that becomes totalitarian. People are free—but only to accept it and live by it; they are equal—but only to participate in it; they can compete with each other—but only on its terms; there is pluralism and group life—but only among the associations and groups that conform to it. The crucial point, then, according to the advocates of the New Left, is that individuals are free within the framework of this ideology but cannot declare their freedom *against it* or *against* the political system that sustains it. Industrialized advanced societies have created a consensus through the wholesale inculcation of the values of technology, material abundance, and efficiency and consumption. Democracies manage without repressive tactics precisely because the ideology they have fashioned has permeated all of us. Soviet totalitarianism still relies on repression, according to Marcuse, simply because the values of its industrial society have not as yet been thoroughly assimilated and internalized.

6. Ibid., p. xv.

The student will notice here the sharp departure of the New Left from the classic Marxist critique. The argument against capitalism is not that it fails to produce enough but that it produces a great deal! The indictment made by the New Left is that capitalism has created abundance and continues to be capable of producing an ever growing variety of material goods. It has become dangerous to all of us precisely because of its efficiency and its ability to give to all of us a relative degree of well-being. It is because of this efficiency that democratic capitalism has managed to integrate everybody or virtually everybody within its own logic and ideology. Its tentacles have spread into every home, and into every social, economic, political or religious group. It is a threat to all of us because it has proven so successful.

The industrial and technological society of today has managed to bring together hitherto antagonistic forces. Business and organized labor; Democrats and Republicans in the U.S.A.; Labourites and Conservatives in England; Christian Democrats and Social Democrats in Germany; Communists and Christian Democrats in Italy; Gaullists and Communists in France: all accept it. They compete within an economic and industrial system which they all want to maintain. Genuine revolutionary movements aimed at transcending the system and replacing it with a different one, exist virtually nowhere in any of the advanced industrialized societies. In fact, it is difficult to envisage revolution in societies where the vast majority of men and women fully accept the prevalent values. The only possibility is that there are still forces in society which may, as Marcuse puts it, "explode the society."

From where, then, will the explosion come? Only from a realization by the citizens, or some of them, that the ideology they have accepted, and the consciousness of the social world that it has imparted to them, is false. Explosion will then result from the outright rejection of what is false; it will be the assertion of the real consciousness of individuals; of real interests against fabricated interests. Ultimately it will be the explosion of the individual's inner or moral self against the ideology of the industrial society.

But what is the nature of the threat? I believe the answer lies primarily in the distinction between "false" and "true" consciousness that Marx elaborated from a somewhat different perspective.

False and True Consciousness

The terms "false" and "true," "real" and "fabricated" are not new. Rousseau had argued that it is possible for all the people to be fooled and to lose sight of their real interests. Marx and Lenin feared that the workers would accept reformist policies dealing with their material conditions and thus lose sight of their real interest, which was to make a revolution and socialize the means of production. Even alienated individuals can be made to think that their alienated status is normal, and in accord with their individuality. "Alienation" may, in other words, through advertising propaganda and socialization, be so rationalized as to become acceptable. In a frightening passage, Marcuse identifies the situation and the predicament: "the subject which is alienated ... is swallowed by his alienated existence."[7] This simply means that we have all been made to accept the values that account for our alienation, *which are false and contrary to our real interests*, and take them to be true. We have been made to believe that we are free when in fact we are slaves. Our "false" and "fabricated" consciousness has swallowed up our "true" and "innermost" self. We think we are "I" when in fact we all have become "they." The "manufactured" social individual has destroyed the true and moral self.

Nothing could be more frightening than the notion that alienation has become socialized and accepted and that what we all believe is false. It amounts to saying that we take shadows to be real things, and that our false consciousness has replaced truth. It almost is as if in the name of rationality, to which we all pay lip service, we have established a society that is collectively insane. Yet we do not know it, we have no means at our disposal to show it, and there is no doctor to diagnose our case!

The Disappearance of the Proletariat

The distinction between true and false consciousness is essential to Marxism. Yet Marx assumed that the proletariat would maintain a hold on its true consciousness and reject the false consciousness that capitalism was attempting to impose. Thus the revolution as a revolution would be the outburst of what was true against what was false and fabricated. However, it appears that Bernstein's thesis, and some of the fears Marx himself expressed, were just. Industrial capitalism has created a society in which the working class has lost its solidarity and consciousness and increasingly accepts the ideology of industrial capitalism. Advanced industrialization has created an ever-growing number of technical and high-paying jobs; specialization has diversified the working class; the introduction of technology has made the worker at the assembly line almost obsolete; so that the proletariat as a solid and self-conscious class no longer exists. Thus not only has the traditional notion of the working class lost its validity, but the consciousness of the workers has also changed. It is no longer a class with a consciousness that is antagonistic to the ruling class and the ideology or consciousness that the latter tries to impose. Politically it has accepted the principles and policies of reformism and welfarism. Morally it accepts material standards of production, industrial organization and abundance. It has accepted the philosophy of consumerism. The workers have become an integral part of technological society.

"The proletariat and wealth are opposite," wrote Marx in 1845.

7. Ibid., p. 11.

"Private property as private property, as wealth, is compelled to preserve its existence . . . The proletariat on the other hand is compelled
to abolish it."[8] This is no longer so. Many of the workers have wealth
to protect, too, and many more seem satisfied with what they have and
with the prospects that it is likely to increase under the system. From
where, then, will revolution or the explosion come?

The Explosion

The explosion can come only in the form of a moral outburst—a moral
rejection of the existing society. It will stem from moral indignation,
and its objective will be moral rehabilitation. It will not spring from
deprivation. Nor will it come from the workers. It will come from all
those who have maintained their inner self intact from the ideological
contamination the advanced industrial societies spread. It will come
from all those who have not been swallowed up by their alienated self:
men and women who have somehow managed to maintain their true
consciousness and who will defy the society that tries to mold and
shape them.

But defiance is not an explosion. An explosion suggests destruction, not simply a change in the management or leadership of society,
nor just the replacement of one class by another as in Marxism. An
explosion is the destruction of the dominant ideology, the fundamental
values of society and of the social relations and working practices that
its ideology legitimizes.

What are they to be replaced with? Although the New Left makes
a number of suggestions, there is no blueprint: many among its supporters would argue that none is needed. A prisoner, they would say,
must escape from the jail first before he begins to think of where he
will go.

Revolutions follow careful guidelines, which revolutionaries provide. They spell out organization, discipline, leadership and specific
procedures. Lenin used to write instructions on the specifics of *where,
when* and *how,* and, similarly, guerrilla warfare and guerrilla revolutions have today been raised to the level of science. The New Left has
produced virtually no such guidelines. By appealing directly to the
individual conscience they neglect the requirements of common organized effort. In fact, they seem to rely to a great degree upon anarchy
as the only creative response to organization and totalitarian control.
But even so, an explosion requires, as any student of physics or chem-
istry knows, the bringing together of some ingredients, substances or
chemicals. The explosion of society also requires some such social and
human ingredients. What are they?

The three essential elements are imagination, action, and rejection.

8. Cited in Robert C. Tucker. *The Marx-Engels Reader.* N.Y.: Norton, 1978, p. 133.

All three are linked together in terms of a deeply moral disavowal, almost religious in its fervor, of the ways of life of our contemporary industrialized societies.

Imagination The French sociologist Alain Touraine points out that the revolution of the students and the New Left in general was "the revolution of the imagination," and that, perhaps because of it, it turned out to be "an imaginary revolution."[9] "Be realistic; think of the impossible"; "Under the cobblestones, the beach"—these were two recurring slogans of the French students during their uprising in 1968. Imagination is clearly seen as the outlet for the enslaved self. It is the vision of a new world, without policemen, coercion, rules, roles and duties; where time will not be measured by minutes and hours; material needs will no longer weigh on our minds; desires will be fulfilled almost instantly; where intuition will provide for truth that can be "understood" and not measured and verified; where there will be no masters, no bosses, no hierarchies; where struggle, domestic and international, will give place to peace; where, finally, everything that separates us from each other—walls, rooms, offices, blocks and national boundaries—will be erased. There will be no "No Trespass" signs anywhere: this will be the world of the "real self," of the natural self, spontaneous, creative, intuitive and almost instinctual. It is the exact opposite of the alienated self: the real "I," not the fabricated and collective "they."

Action Imagination must be coupled with action. To be "engaged" is essential not only to promoting one's ends but to understanding them better. "Being" should not be, and cannot be, separated from "doing." Theory must lead to action and action will refine theory. For it is only in action, and only by acting, that an individual can "enter into the essence of things" and understand them fully. The New Left discards objectivity, the separation between the actor and the object. The actor must "enter into" the object. To think of something in a detached way is meaningless; but to think of something and to do it is the essence of comprehension. The New Left is, therefore, activist, but action is not an instrument to attain predetermined objectives. It is, rather, essential to the understanding and the refining of objectives. We learn while we act, and we act in order to learn!

The same is true with the revolution: it is not an instrument for bringing about a new preconceived order of things; it is rather an action that will help the revolutionary develop the revolution. "The revolution in the revolution" was another slogan: goals will become more complete and more definitive as the revolution develops, they will be elaborated as the revolution unfolds itself. The important thing is to begin with action, and to learn from it.

Rejection Imagination and action, however, must both be in-

9. Touraine. *The May Movement.*

spired by a powerful personal and moral rejection of the existing order of things. In the philosophy of the New Left there are many powerful negations—as many as in the totalitarian movements we discussed earlier. The New Left however, is distinctly anti-State, anti-nationalist, anti-authoritarian.

Anti-Liberalism

Liberalism is the major target of scorn. There are four reasons for this. First, the liberal emphasis upon a consumer economy and materialistic achievements. The *homo economicus* is the opposite of the spiritual man (almost the evangelic man) they wish to resurrect. An economy committed to the mere production of goods for the mere satisfaction of wants, creates "a society of pigs," in which quantitative considerations take precedence over qualitative ones. Secondly, liberals generally defend private property, an institution considered by the New Left to be divisive. Thirdly, the individualistic philosophy of liberalism atomizes society, pits individuals against individuals, and becomes an obstacle to companionship and togetherness. Lastly, by atomizing the society, liberalism makes the individual more vulnerable to controls and more susceptible to manipulation and control.

But the New Left's greatest scorn is for what they consider liberals' double-talk. Liberals are supposed to be committed to pluralism, moral, political, and economic. Yet all they allow in practice is pluralism and competition *for those who accept the principles of liberalism,* with its private property, market economy, industrial organization, material considerations, etc. Political competition—real competition with regard to basic values—does not exist. Political battles present a choice between Tweedledee and Tweedledum, between spending a little more or a little less on, say, defense; taxing corporations a little more or a little less, and so on. The basic issues of whether there should be a military establishment, private property, or a State at all, are not discussed. There is no competition regarding them: they are taken for granted—which is another word for saying they are imposed.

The New Left has no patience with the democratic process, elections, the theory that governments and regimes depend upon the consent of the people and the concept that in democracies the people participate in decisions. To the extent to which the people participate through elections they do so to choose among candidates who are very much alike. As for consent, it is only part of a manufactured ideology. The people give it because they have been socialized and indoctrinated in the values of the liberal industrial society.

Anti-Intellectualism

Scientific objectivity and rationality are responsible for alienation. Rationality ignores the non-rational elements of our consciousness: our

intuition and imagination and instincts. Industrial technology subordinates work and life in general to the logic of organization, specialization and efficiency. Scientists who claim to be objective are in fact
responsible for the expansion of the Industrial State. Their discoveries
have been allowed to be used to subordinate the individual in the name
of objectivity, and to produce techniques of control and destruction—
nuclear energy, for instance. But social scientists are to be blamed also.
Their studies of organizations, labor-relations, and scientific management have led to conditions requiring maximum efficiency which enslave the worker and the individual. In so doing, scientists have by-
passed moral judgement in their concern for functionality and with
what makes things work. Yet, despite their alleged objectivity they
propagate the value of the capitalist industrial order.

According to the New Left, the modern scientific thinking becomes
an instrumentality which leads to repressive practices. It forces individuals into certain roles, which are only partial and deprive them of
the opportunity to understand the environment and their place in it.
In any discipline, the trend is toward the kind of specialization that
prepares the individual and the student for specialized roles. It is the
organization that controls specialization and the specialist. The latter
fits into it, just as spare parts fit into the motor of a car. The "organizational whole" becomes bigger than its parts—the individuals. Students complained that their universities were training specialists and
fitting them into the organizational structures that the industrial society
had created: they rejected such an "education" in favor of experience,
learning-by-doing and intuition. Learning, they claimed, should be a
source of pleasure and fulfillment, not preparation for specialized tasks
and jobs. In some universities laboratories were destroyed while poetry,
literature, theater, music and other creative arts received a new
emphasis.

Against Organization and Bureaucracy

All organizations and bureaucracies have essentially two characteristics: hierarchy and role-allocation. A hierarchy institutionalizes su-
perior/inferior relations: some people make decisions, others obey and
execute them. There is a chain of command from top downwards, and
a chain of compliance from bottom upwards. At the same time, in all
organizations there is a role structure, with each role corresponding to
specific operations and tasks. Some people do research, some decide
on policy (what to do or what to produce), some sell the product, while
others produce it. The State, the corporations, the universities are large
bureaucratic organizations in which specialization is the rule. Each
person does his or her thing and few, if any, know what the whole is
about. In all such organizations, superior/inferior relationships and
specialization of roles become fixed and highly impersonal. They become institutionalized. Rules, rather than common sharing and com-

mon perception of goals, is what keeps them going. The individuals become faceless and detachable parts: "Nobody is indispensable."

Hierarchy, specialization and the impersonality they engender make bureaucratic organizations the targets of the New Left. Individuals have no power of decision in them; they have no feeling of purpose, belonging or achievement. Rules stifle initiative and creativity, and the organization becomes a coercive entity. The way to avoid these pitfalls as far as the New Left is concerned, is simply to destroy all large bureaucratic structures and replace them with small associations where people know each other, are equal with each other, work for the pleasure of it, and together make the major decisions. Organizations must shed their hierarchical structure to establish equality and the full participation of all; they must become simple instrumentalities for common effort, based upon common fellowship.

The Counter-Culture

What will the world be like after the explosion? The revolution of the imagination will result in a Utopia, which is of interest not only to see what the New Left believes, but also to find out how people will live in it. Even if there is no comprehensive blueprint, and even if the New Left assumes that once the revolution is started it will gain momentum and shape as the people gain knowledge from the revolutionary experience, there are enough bits and pieces that we can put together. What emerges from them, as Theodore Roszak points out, is a "vision."[10]

It is a vision of a communal society divided into small neighborhoods and groups; of a simple, almost pastoral life, where the complexities and ugliness of city life are done away with; of a free and egalitarian society without hierarchies, authorities and coercive agencies; of an intensely individualistic society cultivating individual freedom and spontaneity. It is also a participatory society: people within different groups take charge of their own affairs. Finally, it is a worldwide society—or rather a world-wide community—without national boundaries, armies and states, and without customs officials.

The New Left contends that each of the three forms of alienation we discussed earlier must be taken into account and eliminated. Small groups and a simple life will give to individuals a sense of belongingness, and bring them back closer to nature and to their primary organizations—the family and the village. The control and ownership of production by the producers will do away with the workers' alienation; the full participation in decision-making of all those affected by the work done or the decisions to be made will do away with the imper-

10. Roszak. *The Making of a Counter-Culture.*

sonality of bureaucratic organizations and their coercive character. Finally, the establishment of working and living conditions based upon individual inclinations will make work again pleasurable and life joyful.

Some of the principles of the New Left were spelled out during the 1968 uprisings in France, and were elaborated by the spontaneously-formed Action Committees:

1. Take collective responsibility for one's own affairs, that is, self-government.
2. Destroy all hierarchies which merely serve to paralyze the initiative of all groups and individuals.
3. Make all those in whom authority is vested permanently responsible to the people.
4. Spread information and ideas throughout the movement.
5. Put an end to the division of labor and of knowledge which only serves to isolate people one from another.
6. Open the university to all who are at present excluded.
7. Defend maximum political and intellectual freedom as a basic democratic right.[11]

One American leader has put the goals of the New Left very succinctly:

> I think it has to do with two types of goals. One which we might call "existential humanism" is expressed by the desire to change the way we, as individuals, actually live and deal with other people. We speak of the attempt to achieve "community," to reach levels of intimacy and directiveness with others unencumbered by the conventional barriers of race, status, class, etc. . . . Second, we say that we seek a radical transformation of the social order. In short, that we act politically because our values cannot be realized in any durable sense without a reconstruction of the political and social system. Thus we say that we want a redistribution of wealth and power in the society; that we want to develop new centers of power as a basis for such a redistribution; that we look forward toward the emergence of new political and social institutions which can authentically provide the conditions for freedom.[12]

In the vision of the future new society three elements predominate: anarchism, participation, and the quality of life.

---

11. Cohn-Bendit. *Obsolete Communism: The Left-Wing Alternative*, p. 90.
12. David Flack "Some Problems, Issues and Proposals," in Jacobs and Landau. *The New Radicals*, p. 163.

Anarchism literally means "without government," or "without officials and leaders." It can also mean "without rules." As a political ideology and movement throughout the nineteenth century, it advocated the abolition and the outright destruction of the State and all its repressive agencies—police, army, the courts, the bureaucracy, etc. Some anarchists championed the use of direct violence against persons and property, including political assassinations. Others considered anarchism to be a system towards which society was inevitably moving, thanks to the growth of mutual aid and of free associations. As with the New Left, a hundred and more years later, anarchism envisaged a utopia, a formulation of objectives in terms of which society would be reshaped. What were they?

The society envisaged by most anarchists was one that would correspond to, and do justice to, the natural drives of men and women. Without authority and hierarchies, without government of "man by man," it was to be a free society giving free rein to all individuals to live in it and express themselves. It would provide "free play" for the individuals and for the full development of their gifts. In one word, it should make for "individualization."

Two institutions were basic to the new order: mutual aid and associations. Mutual aid was the answer to the Social Darwinists who saw society in terms of competition and struggle for survival. Human beings, some anarchists countered, survive thanks to mutual help and cooperation. Cooperation and reciprocity of aid is the reality of life in society and in nature. Wherever the State does not exist, people find their own ways, spontaneously, to help each other. A common solidarity among them is established. Free association is an extension of the principle of mutual aid: it is the result of the common decision of people to work together in order to meet some of their needs. Such associations should be not only voluntary but small, so that people work together, play together, and create a spirit of fellowship and cooperation. Such association will spell out on the basis of common agreement the conditions and the hours of work needed, while allowing the individuals to live and do as they please in their spare time. Thus, the anarchists wished to avoid bigness, impersonality and the coerciveness that all large organizations entail.

ANARCHISM AND THE NEW LEFT

The proponents of the New Left echo some of the same anarchist themes: rejection of bigness; destruction of authority and of political and economic organizational hierarchies and, of course, of the State. They emphasize work and living in small groups—communes and associations through which the individuals control their environment, organize their work and take charge of their own affairs. The New Left shares with the anarchists the same quest for individualization, for spontaneity and creativity and for free play. They, too, reject private property in favor of communal or associational collectivism. The New Left, finally, like the anarchists, believes in the use of force and direct action and shares the anarchists' outright moral rejections of existing society. A small number of activists among the New Left have joined conspiratorial and terroristic organizations bent upon destruction and political assassination.

Participation

Participation of all in the management of common affairs is for the New Left one of the most potent instruments for putting an end to alienation. Limited forms of participation, especially of the workers in industrial firms, have been practiced in many countries. They involve consultations, profit-sharing and the autonomy of the workers to determine their working conditions. They do not question, however, the basic rules of the capitalistic economy with regard to property ownership and the managerial and hierarchical organization of the firms.

The demands of the New Left are far more comprehensive. First they apply not only to industrial firms and to economic activities, but to all others, political, social, cultural: all those involved in a given activity and in any organization that makes decisions which affect them should participate in making them. Secondly, the New Left has specific notions about organizational structures, advocating their reduction in size and complexity. Finally, it proposes the socialization of all economic units that are privately owned. Participation is in effect equivalent to socialism plus internal democracy.

In the Port Huron statement of the SDS (Students for a Democratic Society) Tom Hayden, one of its leaders, set the following goals:

> We would replace power rooted in possession, privilege, or circumstance by power and uniqueness rooted in love, reflectiveness, reason, and creativity. As a *social system* we seek the establishment of a democracy of individual participation, governed by two central aims: that the individual share in those social decisions determining the quality and direction of his life; that society be organized to encourage independence in men and provide the media for their common participation.[13]

The closest approximation to participation advocated by the New Left is similar to the workers' councils we discussed in connection

13. In Teodori, op. cit., p. 167.

*The New Left in America. Confrontation with the National
Guard, Chicago, 1968. (Photo: UPI)*

with Titoism. It is a method of creating grass-root socialism; of decen-
tralizing as much as possible as a way to avoid the Stalinist model, in
which socialism took the form of centralized and bureaucratic planning
that became authoritarian. But there is a difference between what the
New Left advocates and the Yugoslav experiments. For the former,
large organizations must be cut down to size; competition among firms
is not encouraged and industrial management techniques and technology are suspect. There is a definite emphasis for it in the direction
of making our needs simpler and in directing production to immediate
qualitative considerations. The Yugoslav experiment, on the contrary,
emphasizes competition, industrialization, and scientific management
techniques. The Yugoslavs advance their model as the best way to
industrialize; the New Left model leads to de-industrialization.

There is no specification about the size of a self-governing unit. It
should, however, be small: communes or small towns which can be
governed directly by those who live in them. Big cities should be broken
down into self-governing neighborhoods where people will decide
about their affairs: libraries, sports centers, artistic centers, garbage
collection, sanitation, clinics, etc. Hospitals should be governed by all
those working in them and those receiving medical help should have
their say. Universities should be run by the "university community":
teachers, students, administrators and staff. The same should be the
case for libraries, museums, public transportation, orchestras. Consumers in all cases should become an integral part in the decision-

process of all firms providing goods or services, such as electricity, gas, television, etc. In this manner, production and service can be better evaluated and geared to real demand and need. In industrial production, the workers in various firms and associations play the dominant role and should have ultimate control over all decisions. Emphasis is put on equality, in rewards and pay, to avoid the growth of hierarchies, and to eliminate as far as possible role specialization and distinction.

All organizations should be managed in this manner. Direct participatory democracy should spread to all forms of social activity. Through this system individuals will become real citizens, in charge of their own destinies. The inner self of humanity will reassert itself, and work will again become a medium for self-realization.

The Quality of Life

One of the recurrent themes of the New Left is the degradation past, present, and future, of the quality of our lives in the industrially advanced societies. Everybody seems to agree that our industrialized societies have come close to solving the problem of material well-being and of creating the conditions for a better life. But somehow industrial society has been victim of its own success: efficient production of goods has become an end in itself, not a means to a better existence. From conspicuous consumption, where people buy and consume to impress others, we have moved to a stage of "wasteful consumption." Artificial needs are created through advertising, in order to produce more and to diversify products. The consumer society proudly displays its success with elaborate statistics of per capita wealth, measured in cars, calories consumed per day, radios and TV sets, houses, clinics, hospitals, etc. But what about quality? According to the New Left no attention is being paid to it. Our environment is in danger and our style of live impoverished when defined simply in terms of *how much* and not *of what*.

Our environment has been used and abused for the sake of immediate benefits and profits. Our forests have been spoiled, lakes and rivers polluted, neighborhoods uprooted in the name of urban renewal, ugly scars have deformed our mountains, and millions of Americans (and even larger numbers of Europeans) live in areas where the air is fast becoming unbreathable. Cities themselves grow, as population growth continues unchecked, without any consideration to health and beauty, and without the realization that cities are for people to live together. High structures have replaced neighborhoods and neighborly amenities have given place to supermarkets, super-hospitals, and multi-universities. Life in the city has become as impersonal as life is in the big organizations where people work. The private motor vehicle, given its appetite for roads and fuel, begins to dominate our lives and our economy.

Styles of life have been affected adversely. The monotony and impersonality of life where people work and live has deprived men and women of personal creative entertainment. Many cities are without theaters, art centers, music, recreation centers or even sports and athletic facilities. Individuals are deprived, therefore, of opportunities for self-expression. They fall back on "canned" entertainment, on what is offered through TV or various other mass activities.

The New Left stands resolutely for quality. It advocates, in effect, a totally new way of life. In substance it wishes to extirpate the evils of materialism and replace them with the purity of spirituality. Its world will assert the kingdom of the spirit (but not of reason) over material concerns: imagination and feeling, intuition and insights will take the precedence they had before the Enlightenment and the Industrial Revolution. To accomplish this, a vast change in attitudes, beliefs, methods of learning and consumption habits is needed.

Foremost among the qualitative demands of the New Left is the rehabilitation of the environment and with it our return to nature. Agricultural communes will provide the joys of farming and for the simple necessities of life and companionship. Industrial production will be geared to essentials and carried out in small associations. Population will have to be controlled and the environment cleaned up simply by prohibiting the use of all noxious chemicals and substances. Nuclear energy will be scrapped, together with everything that may endanger humans and also all species and birds and bees. The simplicity of life will return, so to speak, to our natural selves and will release the suppressed energies and creativity bottled up for so long inside us because of the oppressive conditions under which we live and work. The words "joy" and "pleasure" recur constantly in the literature of the New Left. It is feeling against reasoning: play rather than work, enjoy immediate satisfaction rather than a deferred one. It is a new kind of hedonism, with self-gratification as its cornerstone.

This is then the new world of the New Left. It is the exact reverse of what the New Left sees in our contemporary industrial societies. For collectivity, read individualism; for bigness, smallness; for complexity, simplicity; for imposition, self-government; for coercion, freedom; for hierarchy, equality; for private property, socialism; for profit, social need; for materialism, spirituality; for war, peace; for competition, cooperation; for science and technology, intuition and spontaneity; for knowledge, experience; for reason, feeling. It is a different, new and shiny world.

Two representative authors of the New Left in the United States give the best summation of their vision of the new society. It is:

> . . . the vision of a society in which human needs take priority over the imperatives of capital. . . . These needs are almost self-evident. First, the minimum biological conditions for human life must be met: adequate food and shelter, clean air, free and easily accessible medical care, freedom from the threat

of an arbitrary death in war. Just above the bare minimum for human survival are the needs for recreation, leisure, basic possessions and enough education to guarantee employment. But there are other sorts of needs, felt faintly or acutely, depending on the pressures of biological needs: we need friendship, affection, love. We need work—not jobs but work, work which is both personally satisfying and socially meaningful. Finally . . . we must have freedom. Freedom for a man to work out what he has to do, and to do it.[14]

The New Left: An Evaluation

Even if we consider the New Left movement and ideology only as a "confrontation," it was one that shook many assumptions that were being taken for granted. First, it showed that many young men and women (and some of their elders, too) were not after all absorbed into "the system." The system had not become "totalitarian"; it had failed to create the "one-dimensional man." The outright rejection of its values and of its technology indicated clearly that many had remained immune to it. The uprisings in most of the industrial democracies showed that men and women can still see the angels and the stars, even while they claim that our society has only neon lights to offer and has reduced all of us to the impersonality of computer cards!

The New Left reasserted the importance of politics, and reminded us that priorities and problems about basic issues, the style of life, the powerful qualitative imperatives from which to choose, continued to be the very stuff of politics and, with politics, of ideology.

Finally, by rejecting centralization, the New Left heightened our awareness of the need to give more power to smaller political units—localities and towns and neighborhoods. In countries like France, where centralization had been the rule, it contributed to the movement favoring decentralization. In other countries where there are powerful ethnic and linguistic minorities the demand for self-government and autonomy is increasingly being heard. The power of the State, in other words—allegedly impersonal, omnipotent, and uncontrollable—continues to be contested.

Thus there were some important contributions. But the movement also had many negative aspects to it—indeed some ominous ones, potentially destructive of the very individual freedoms they proclaimed. The first thing that strikes us is the New Left's emphasis on feeling and will. Individuals should express what they feel and should act the way they feel. No constraints, no "repressive mechanisms" should come between feeling and fulfillment. The ego in its full richness should

---

14. John and Barbara Ehrenreich. "From Resistance to Revolution," in Teodori, op. cit., p. 460.

reign supreme. One simply wonders how this position can be reconciled with social life. Society does involve rules, and every rule amounts to some degree of repressiveness. If all constraints are to be done away with, what forms of social interaction can crystallize into predictable patterns of behavior? To answer by saying that the innate goodness of the individual will prevail and will become the basis of sociability is to beg the question: what if some people's innate goodness fails to manifest itself? Social life and rules are based on the assumption that some of us *may* be "bad."

The second source of deep concern with the ideology of the New Left is its downright anti-rationalist and anti-intellectual approach. Understanding should take precedence over knowledge; scientific thought is only partial, for full understanding must be intuitive and must bring the "subject" and the "object" together into some kind of mystical union. Even if we agree, and acknowledge the validity and the need for intuition, it does not follow that we should discard rationality and science. A good doctor must "understand" his patients but without knowledge of medicine, understanding may be of small help. All the compassion and intuitive insights of a doctor cannot replace a measured diagnosis based on physical examination. Scientific knowledge is a storehouse of verified theories and hypotheses about the universe, the planet, ourselves—down to our appendix when it hurts. It gives all of us, as social beings, a degree of control over our environment and lives that is essential to our freedom.

Next there is the New Left's insistence on joy and pleasure: "unrestricted" gratification. Nobody can object to demands for more joy and more pleasure in a world that some find increasingly gray. But again, the question arises: whose joy, and what kind of joy? In some World War Two documentaries, Nazi aviators are shown flying to bomb England. They are full of joy, singing, in a state of bliss. It was the Nazis who coined the slogan "strength through joy." Joy, pleasure, adventure may mean different things to different people. For some it may be the science of discovery and (much despised by the New Left) the laboratory; for others it may be canoeing down the river. Are *all* forms of joy to be tolerated, or is someone to decree which joys are harmful to society and which are not? There are clear indications that many proponents of the New Left were anxious to make the decision for all of us.

Again the manner in which New Left advocates the improvement of the "quality of life" is a source for concern. All of us are, of course, in favor of improving it. But who will decide, and how is it to prevail? The New Left turns its back to material considerations to the point, as we have seen, of advocating a pastoral existence. By simplifying life, they want to purify it and spiritualize it. There is for some a mystical urge insisting on the things of the spirit, but the very simplification of life and the dismantling of the large industrialized machinery of the modern society raises the fundamental question of how people will meet their needs. One answer that is given is that the population should be reduced, which of course is likely to need coercive controls. The prospects of totalitarian control and ideological orthodoxy, stating what the quality of life *ought to be* and attempting to impose it, are clear. In order to save us from the alienation of the industrial society, the New Left may enslave us in its own values and norms.

The political program of the New Left raises some other and more difficult problems. While a greater degree of participation may be needed in the making of decisions, the problems of who will participate and how participation will be organized remain unresolved. Participation may be geared to functional considerations (one's job); to immediate matters regarding living conditions (neighborhood or town); or to national problems—defense, taxes, foreign policy. It is physically impossible to cope with all decisions that affect an individual. The New Left's response is to eliminate all central and national units of decision-making and limit participation only to those areas and units (one's job, one's neighborhood) where it can be made operational. Presumably, associations of workers, consumers, producers, teachers, and other groups will be established in which the people involved participate. But who will coordinate the various associations and the various local or neighborhood units? Who will coordinate environmental measures? Sanitation? Communications? The cleaning of the air we breathe? And who will decide what to produce? About the exchange of goods? Investment? Defense? These questions are not answered in the literature of the New Left.

Some of the same problems are to be found with the New Left's economic program—if they have one. The unit of production becomes the association of producers: the workers. Are they to decide what to produce? On the basis of what incentives? For what purpose? Is the association to be a self-sufficient unit consuming what it produces? If not, where does the consumer fit into the picture? Participatory democracy or self-government in the economy are very appealing slogans, but it is very hard to translate them into practice.

The New Left has made a contribution by pointing out some of the shortcomings of our industrial society, but has not succeeded in developing a coherent and convincing program in order to replace it. It brought forth utopian slogans for a new culture: the appeal to the moral man, the emphasis on spirituality, the reaffirmation of qualitative standards, the glorification of the free and spontaneous individual, the need for pleasures and joy, the advocacy of new social forms of interaction that strengthen solidarity and fellowship, the destruction of the State and all its agencies, a return to a simple, almost pastoral, kind of existence.

One of the most eloquent advocates of the new culture that would replace the old, states that its first step will be "to proclaim a new heaven and a new earth so vast, so marvelous that the inordinate claims of technical expertise must of necessity withdraw in the presence of such a splendor to a subordinate and marginal status in the lives of men."[15] This is a call for religious and moral reawakening rather than for political action.

15. Roszak, op. cit., p. 240.

Bibliography

Aron, Raymond. *The Elusive Revolution*. London: Pall Mall, 1969.

Carr, E.H. *Michael Bakunin*. New York: Vintage, 1937.

Carter, A. *The Political Theory of Anarchism*. New York: Harper and Row, 1971.

Cohn-Bendit, Daniel and Gabriel. *Obsolete Communism: The Left-Wing Alternative*. London: André Deutsch, 1968.

Draper, Hal. *Berkeley: The New Student Revolt*. New York: Grove Press, 1965.

Erikson, Erik H. (ed.). *The Challenge of Youth*. New York: Anchor, 1965.

Goodman, Paul. *Growing Up Absurd*. New York: Vintage, 1956.

Jacobs, Paul, and Landau, Saul. *The New Radicals*. New York: Vintage, 1966.

Lamb, Robert, et al. *Political Alienation*. New York: St. Martin, 1975.

Lipset, Seymour Martin, and Altbach, Philip G. (eds.). *Students in Revolt*. Boston: Houghton-Mifflin, 1969.

Long, Priscilla (ed.). *The New Left: A Collection of Essays*. Boston: Porter Sargent, 1970.

Marcuse, Herbert. *One-Dimensional Man*. Boston: Beacon Press, 1968.

Murchland, Bernard. *The Age of Alienation*. New York: Random House, 1971.

Olman, B. *Alienation*. New York: Cambridge U.P., 1977.

Reich, Charles. *The Greening of America*. New York: Bantam, 1971.

Roszak, Theodore. *The Making of a Counter-Culture*. New York: Doubleday, 1969.

Sale, Kirkpatrick. *SDS*. New York: Vintage, 1973.

Teodori, Massimo (ed.). *The New Left: A Documentary History*. New York: Bobbs-Merrill, 1969.

Tolstoy, Leo. *The Law of Love and the Law of Violence*. New York: Holt, Rinehart and Winston, 1970.

Touraine, Alain. *The May Movement*. New York: Random House, 1971.

Woodcock, George, and Avakumovic, Ivan. *The Anarchist Prince*. New York: Kraus Reprint, 1970.

12

Nationalisms
Old and New

Without a country. . . . You are the bastards of humanity.
Soldiers without a banner . . . you will find neither faith nor
protection.   GIUSEPPE MAZZINI The Duties of Man

Ours is a world of nation-states. Nationalism has become one of the
most tenacious ideological bonds binding human beings together into
separate political communities. Its values may vary, its particular content may change, but fundamentally the nationalist feeling is described
in terms of a common feeling of togetherness that identifies the "we"
against the "they." Nations are invariably defined in terms of a *community* and in terms of the *loyalty* of the individual to the community.
It is a community of values, a common heritage, a common history, a
common character, a common race, a corporate will, a common soul.
Loyalty is invariably described in terms of dedication, sacrifice, subordination, love, and affection. Nations are either a motherland or a
fatherland, evoking the obedience and affection that children owe to
their parents.

Even if taken as natural, nationalism is a relatively recent ideology.
What is more, it is primarily a political ideology that developed in
Europe in the latter part of the eighteenth century and throughout the
nineteenth, to spread after the end of World War Two into the Third
World (the then colonies in Africa and Asia and the Middle-East).

Like all political ideologies, nationalism is an instrument for the acquisition of political power by certain groups, and the organization of political power on the basis of new principles—notably popular participation. Hugh Seton-Watson in a recent book, *Nations and States,* quite properly defines nationalism to be an ideology "of creating national consciousness within a politically unconscious population"[1] and he notes that its purpose was precisely the mobilization of a population behind new leaders and new leadership groups.

Nationalism was, and remains, a unifying and an integrative ideology aiming at manufacturing consent on the basis of strong common symbols and identification. It generates emotional supports, creates a state of exaltation and sacrifice and provides for loyalty to new political elites. Nationalism solidifies a community, creates allegiance, establishes uniformities and attempts to absorb the citizen into the purpose and the life of the nation-state. In the last analysis nationalism tends to be a totalitarian ideology.

Nationality, Nation-States, and Nationalism

Some clarifications are needed in order to better understand the dynamics of nationalism—old and new.

Nationality denotes an ethnic and cultural identity. A *state*, on the other hand, is a political organization holding supreme power and exercising it through its various agencies over a given people within a given territory. A state may include a number of "nationalities" and the most outstanding example of such a state was the Austro-Hungarian Empire which until 1918 was a political and administrative organization governing Slavs, Slovenes, Croatians, Italians, Montenegrins, Hungarians, Poles, Austrians, Czechs, and quite a few others. A state, in other words, may be "multinational" and the best examples today are the Soviet Union and Yugoslavia.

A *nation-state* exists when we have both a state and a nationality. Political power stems from and applies to a given national group within a given territory. So there may be nationalities without their own state and there may be also states that do not derive their legitimacy and identity from a nationality. Catalonia is an example of the first and the Soviet Union an example of the latter.

Nationalism is the ideology that asserts the right of a given nationality to form a state and becomes a movement to attain it. Nationalism is an ideology that rationalizes such a demand; it becomes a powerful political movement mobilizing all nationals to form their state. It was the case with the Greeks throughout the centuries of occupation by Turkey; with Poland as it attempted to reaffirm its nationhood by creating a Polish State; it has notably been the case with most

1. Seton-Watson. *Nations and States.* p. 449.

of the erstwhile colonies after World War Two. Nationalism then, is the ideology that has led to the mushrooming of nation-states, and continues to be an ideological force which propels every single nationality—no matter how small—to become a nation-state.

Objective Criteria of Nationality

The most common characteristics of nationality remain (a) language; (b) religion; (c) a consciousness of common traditions and history and a will to maintain them; and (d) a common territory. But sometimes, as has been the case with the Jews and, occasionally, the Greeks, it is the *memory* of a territory occupied sometime in the past, and a desire to recover it, which has been the motivating influence. Different authors of nationalist movements have stressed at different times one or another of the various factors.

Religion was particularly important in the period of the formation of national consciousness and the assertion of political independence of nation-states in the sixteenth and seventeenth centuries. Religious wars were fought both to emancipate the State from the Papacy and also to create internal unity that was endangered both by Papal control from outside or by the existence of religious minorities inside. People were expected to hold, or were coerced into holding, the religion of their King.

Language is an important criterion for a number of authors, especially German. It was a common and distinct vehicle that bound people together creating a special bond among its users.

Race was used primarily, as we have seen, in the twentieth century by the Nazis to "prove" the unique character of the German nation. It is supposed to refer to specific biological traits which are not always clearly perceived or agreed upon. *Ethnicity* is a broader term which may or may not include race but usually refers to a number of the common cultural attributes that we find in the term nationality.

The *common past* has been constantly invoked and when one could not easily be found, every effort was made to manufacture it by rewriting history.

Geography—a common territorial basis—is invariably invoked. Nations, like individuals, had to have a "home," a space under the sun.

Subjective Factors: Nationalism and Self-Determination

All the objective traits we have outlined—religion, language, common history, etc.—may exist, and they may be commonly shared by a given "nationality." Nationalism becomes an ideology and a movement when it translates this self-consciousness into a demand to form a state, when it becomes a political movement. The subjective element is an element of will and of purpose. It asserts the validity of the objective factors of nationality for *certain* political purposes; it affirms their uniqueness and often their exclusiveness. It is not only the will to live together but to have a government. It is the assertion that such a purpose has an inherent claim to be heard and to realize itself.

The nation-state may be viewed, therefore, as the creature of the individuals who make it up; it exists and derives its existence from the support and consent the individuals give to it. As Ernest Renan put it, it is the result of a contract or of "a daily referendum."[2]

Nothing exemplifies better the differences between those who stress objective factors and those who rely upon subjective ones in defining a nation—the first relying upon history and tradition and the second upon individual will and consent—than the conflict between Germany and France over the provinces of Alsace and Lorraine. Renan, the French publicist, in his famous essay *What is a Nation?* (1882) was willing to accept the verdict of the peoples of the area given through a referendum. German writers, on the other hand, asserted their claims in terms of historical right: "These provinces are ours by the right of the sword," wrote a German nationalist, "and we shall rule them by virtue of a higher right. . . . *We desire even against their will to restore them to themselves.*"[3]

Self-determination is the right of those who constitute a nationality with common religious, linguistic and ethnic characteristics to form their own state. It became a doctrine when it was expressly stipulated in the famous 14 Points that President Woodrow Wilson issued to serve as the guidelines for building a new political order in Europe after World War One.

"Self-determination," Woodrow Wilson declared "is an imperative principle of action, which statesmen will . . . ignore at their peril." He claimed that World War One "had its roots in the disregard of the rights of small nations and of nationalities which lacked the union and the force to make good their claim to determine their own allegiance and their own form of political life." He suggested among other things, in the form of guidelines for the Peace Conference that was to follow the end of the hostilities, "a readjustment of the frontiers of Italy . . . along clearly recognizable lines"; "the freest opportunity of autonomous development" for the peoples of Austria-Hungary; the redrawing of some of the frontiers in the Balkans "along historically established lines of allegiance and nationality"; "an absolutely unmolested opportunity of autonomous development" for the national minorities within Turkey; "an independent Polish state . . . inhabited by indisputably Polish populations."[4]

2. Ernest Renan. "What is a Nation?" in Hans Kohn (ed.). *Nationalism: Its Meaning and History.* Rev. ed., N.Y.: Van Nostrand, 1965, pp. 135–40.

3. Cited by Karl W. Deutsch. *Nationalism and Social Communication.* N.Y.: Wiley, 1953, p. 11.

4. Cited by Alan P. Grimes and Robert H. Horwitz. *Modern Political Ideologies.* N.Y.: Oxford U.P., 1959, pp. 501–3.

The French Revolution
and the Nineteenth Century

It was the French Revolution of 1789 that in line with some of Rousseau's theories of popular sovereignty asserted the sovereignty of the people *and* the nation. But it was also the French Revolution in its various stages that highlighted the integrative and totalitarian dimensions of nationalism. The revolution began as an assertion of individual freedoms and popular sovereignty. It finished with an absolutist ruler and an expansionist nationalism that changed the map of Europe.

With the destruction of feudal privileges and the overthrow of the monarchy in 1792, the French Revolution quickly established patriotism as the highest ideal and as the most intimate bond among the people. Rituals, national festivals, symbolisms, national songs, all were used to create solidarity among the French. A system of national education was instituted to propagate patriotic values. Every attempt was made to wipe out regional and linguistic particularisms in favor of cultural unity, territorial integration and centralization. The republic was to be "one and indivisible." Compliance with the revolution and its policies was promoted everywhere, requiring coercive measures which gradually were transformed into an outright tyranny. A revolutionary leader spoke of "the tyranny of liberty against despotism."

The last phase of the revolution produced an expansionist nationalism and a desire to conquer and subdue other peoples in the name of liberty *and* France. French men and women were made to conform to the nationalist ideology: "The citizen is born, lives and dies for the fatherland," was the inscription in every French municipality. "Oh sublime people! Accept the sacrifices of my whole being. Happy is the man who is born in your midst; happier is he who can die for your happiness," exclaimed the revolutionary leader, Robespierre. The citizen-patriot gradually became transformed into the citizen-soldier, ready to die for his country.

Throughout nineteenth century Europe, nationalism played the same important role in forging tightly integrated communities. It was strongly related to the rise of the middle classes and the destruction of feudal structures. Politically speaking it was a vehicle for the acquisition of power by the middle classes by mobilizing the masses as they had never been mobilized before. Controlling "their minds and souls" was a source of far greater power than any ruler or class appealing to status, tradition, authority or divine will had ever claimed or possessed before. No cosmopolitan idea, no internationalist efforts of any significance appeared to mitigate nationalisms. What is more, movements developed in the name of liberalism and socialism and in the form of various international organizations were ineffective in curbing nationalisms.

Nation-states mushroomed in Europe throughout the nineteenth century and after World War One. But the rest of the world remained relatively immune to nationalism. Colonial empires—British, French, Dutch, Belgian, Portuguese—covered virtually the whole of Asia (except for China and Japan), the Middle East, and Africa. In Africa, on the eve of World War Two there were no independent states other than South Africa and Liberia. Today there are some thirty-five independent states in Africa; some sixteen in Asia and nine in the Middle East, including Cyprus—at least seventy new states in Africa, Asia, and the Middle East alone!

A number of factors that had been at work converged after World War Two to bring forth the nationalist independence movements. One of the most important was the weakening of the European colonial powers and the emergence of two non-European powers, the United States and the Soviet Union, both favoring, for different reasons, colonial emancipation and independence. Other major factors, however, can be traced into the past. The impact of Leninism was more recent; and still others related to special circumstances as they developed during and after World War Two. Underlying all these independence movements was a political phenomenon: the growth of native elites aspiring to political power. As with European nationalisms, colonial nationalism became an ideology for mobilizing and organizing the quiescent masses. It proved to be a potent force, just as it had been in Europe ever since the French Revolution.

Long-range Factors: Assimilation to Rejection

In discussing long-range factors we must always keep in mind that nationalism is a mobilizing ideology. It incites people to action, calls for conformity and discipline, and is totalitarian in scope. The strength of its appeal will depend, therefore, on the state of mind, the psychology and the level of awareness and of consciousness of the people involved. The catalyst that welds various factors together is a sense of moral indignation stemming from direct personal threat and humiliation: the history of the colonial independence movements shows that this was present after World War Two.

The intrusion of the colonizers during the nineteenth century into Africa and Indochina, and much earlier in India and other Asiatic countries, undermined the organization, lifestyles, authority structures and the economy of native societies. Traditional societies were opened up; the village life was disrupted; new forms of economic organization and production were introduced, and there was a massive exposure to new types of goods for consumption purposes. The traditional values of authority and deference and the group life that many tribal societies had practiced from time immemorial were seriously weakened. The child of European liberalism and capitalism, the individual, was fostered also in the colonial world.

For some the exposure to western influence was welcome. It was a chance to learn new ways. Indigenous elites sent their children abroad—to London and Paris and elsewhere to better learn the new ways. Some, as was the case with French colonial natives, became assimilated, even marrying French women. Assimilation of European ways and learning of European culture might have been one way to overcome colonial status. However, it was limited, as might be expected, to only a handful.

Whatever this minority sought to accomplish, however, in alliance with the colonial powers and their leaders, was thwarted for two reasons. First, the European elites—army, financiers, businessmen, investors, administrators—were not willing to relinquish their roles, positions and profits. The indigenous elites could play only a subordinate role. Secondly, there was the inevitable phenomenon of discrimination and inequality. The Europeans lived in their own world, with their own clubs, servants, schools and hospitals, eating their own food and drinking their own water and liquor. They lived in a separate world that was equated with status. Natives could not penetrate it, even if they had studied at Oxford or the Sorbonne.

Together with the impenetrability of status went the difference in color, making the separation even more blatant. Gradually, therefore, it became clear that assimilation was not possible. "We could assimilate mathematics or the French language," wrote Leopold Senghor, a Senegalese leader and intellectual who had received his doctorate at the Sorbonne, "but we could never strip off our black skins or root out our black souls."[5]

The alternative to the unattainable goal of assimilation was rejection. The feeling of being discriminated against bred deep resentment against the colonial master and created the moral indignation which brings out the prophet and the saint. The destruction of the traditional patterns of existence produced a large population which had lost its attachments to authority and traditional life styles; one that began to discern even in a confused way the discrimination to which it was subjected, but even more the deprivation to which it was condemned. Without structured and patterned relationships, moving from the countryside into the urban slums, isolated from each other, the indigenous populations became the *Wretched of the Earth*.[6] Their color symbolized their lowly status, and sealed their fate. But they were easy to mobilize

---

5. In Sigmund. *The Ideologies of Developing Nations*. p. 248.
6. The phrase is taken from the title of Franz Fanon's book.

and organize, and became the base of subsequent nationalist liberation movements.

It was at this juncture that two of the most powerful European ideologies we have studied joined forces. Nationalism and Leninism met, to fashion the national independence movements in the colonial world. The ideological aspirations of these movements went even beyond what communism and nationalism could promise. There was, Kedourie claims,[7] a powerful millenialist spirit in the colonial world, something like the religious vision of the Second Coming. It promised a new heaven and a new earth. For the poor and the downtrodden a new vision of paradise became also a call for action.

It was a call for action that knew no limits. Nationalist guerrillas in Kenya, the Mau-Mau, took the following chilling oath:

I speak the truth and vow before our God
That if I am called to go to fight the enemy
Or to kill the enemy—I shall go
Even if the enemy is my father and my mother, my brother or
  sister[8]

Nationalism

Colonial assertion of national independence borrowed directly from European nationalism: the same assertion of a natural right to be a nation; the same search in the past for tradition and culture in terms of which the claims could be justified; the same emphasis upon the basic factors of religion or language or ethnicity, as the occasion suited; and, finally, the same liberal vocabulary about equality, individual rights, and self-determination.

WHERE IS THE "PAST"?

The Germans found their past in the Germanic tribes. The modern Greeks similarly had no difficulty: in their solemn declaration of independence on January 27, 1821, they asserted their glorious past to be the cornerstone of their future as a nation. "We, descendants of the wise and noble people of Hellas . . . believing it to be unlawful for us . . . to live henceforth in a state of slavery suitable to unreasoning animals than to rational beings . . ."[9]

In Africa, however, the search took many nations to a mythical past. Only in some countries, such as Burma, was there a genuine heritage to which the leaders could look for the vindication of their

---

7. Kedourie's *Nationalism in Asia and Africa* is an excellent anthology with a penetrating introduction by the author to whom I am indebted for both.
8. Cited in Kedourie, op. cit., pp. 466–68.
9. Cited in Kohn. *The Idea of Nationalism.*, pp. 116–17.

efforts for independence. Ethiopians found it in the Bible: "Ethiopia shall soon stretch out her hands unto God." Why not unto Eritrea and Somaliland as well? The Israelis, as Jews, have valid historical credentials to most of the land they now have, including Jerusalem. African nations looked for past African empires such as existed in Mali and Ghana, and Arab nationalisms invariably found past glories in the days when Islam controlled most of North Africa and had moved deep into Spain. Pakistan also sought its own past in its Moslem heritage, as opposed to India's Hinduism, claiming to be the historically "oldest" of the ten nations that had existed in the Indian sub-continent.

WHAT LANGUAGE?

The search for the past often meant the search for a language. Again, the example of the modern Greeks trying to resurrect the ancient Greek language illuminated the way for the new nations. "Every word in our language, with the exception of scientific terms must be in Turkish, if possible, and if not possible at least Turkified. . . ."[10] But language proved to be a serious problem for India and many of the African nations, where tribal dialects could in no way coincide with national boundaries. English or French continue to be widely used.

RACE

Race began to play a prominent role, and became a powerful motive in the rejection of the European colonialists. No other than Marcus Garvey, president general of the Universal Negro Improvement Association in the United States, had proclaimed the purity of the Negro race and the purity of the white race: he was against intermarriage. In his search for "ethnicity" for the blacks in Africa—what he called "negritude"—Leopold Senghor spoke of an "anti-racial racialism." Negritude was the "whole complex of . . . values—cultural, economic, social and political—that characterize . . . the Negro African world."[11] God was declared by many black nationalists to be black. He was the "glorious Father of the blacks." One of the leaders of the Congo declared himself to be "the banner of the dominion of the black race." Race leads to the exaltation of its characteristics and suggests that every effort should be made to maintain its purity. Algerian and African leaders fell into disgrace because they had married European women.

Sometimes the search for identity in the past, in religion, in language took on absurd manifestations. For instance, European-trained African doctors began to use magic and witchcraft for cures; and there were desperate efforts made to find and imitate primitive African art. But emphasis upon race was not exclusively anti-European and anti-white. In East Africa and Southeast Asia race was used against diverse minorities, especially Chinese and Indians.

---

10. Cited in Kedourie, op. cit., pp. 207–15.
11. Cited in Sigmund, op. cit., pp. 248–50.

Irrespective of the many extreme manifestations, the independence movements had a genuine claim which could not be denied: self-determination and self-government. Its logic, since it had been advanced and practiced by the Europeans, was irresistible. Even pan-African movements failed to gain momentum in the face of claims for the national independence of specific populations in given areas. Thus, colonial nationalisms followed the footsteps of European nationalisms.

LENINISM

Marxism appealed to many of the colonial elites seeking independence. It rejected liberal capitalism, which was taken to be synonomous with the capitalist exploitation of the colonial world, and it provided a vision of a new world of equality and prosperity. But it was Leninism that had a far more profound impact, both because of its analysis and explicit condemnation of imperialism, and because it provided a theory and an organizational tool for revolution.

From a tactical point of view, as we saw earlier, Lenin considered colonies to be the "weakest link" in the capitalistic chain and pledged Soviet support to colonial national revolutionary movements. The second congress of the Third International in 1920 provided a number of "theses" on "national" and "colonial" questions.

With regard to those states and nationalities where a backward, mainly feudal, patriarchal, or patriarchal-agrarian regime prevails, the following must be borne in mind: (1) All Communist Parties must give active support to the revolutionary movements of liberation. . . . (4) It is of special importance to support the peasant movements in backward countries against the landowners and all feudal survivals; above all, we must strive as far as possible to give the peasant movement a revolutionary character, to organize the peasants and all the exploited classes into the Soviets, and thus bring about the closest possible union between the Communist proletariat of Western Europe and the revolutionary peasant movement of the East and of the colonial and subject countries; . . . (5) It is the duty of the Communist International to support the revolutionary movement in the colonies and in the backward countries. . . .[12]

The Third International under the leadership of the Soviet Communist Party stressed, therefore, three basic elements in the struggle for colonial emancipation and independence: first, nationalism; second, an outright appeal to the peasantry (since both the middle classes and the proletariat were virtually non-existent); and third, the role of a well-organized party to provide for leadership and direction, and to

12. Cited in Kedourie, op. cit., "Theses of the Second Congress of the Communist International on the National and Colonial Questions," pp. 540–51.

bring the people to the appropriate level of mobilization and militancy. It was to consist of trained revolutionaries.

National Independence Movements

The double impact of Leninism and nationalism, and particularly the adoption of a party organization that was inspired by Lenin, accounted for the authoritarian and paramilitary characteristics of the national independence movements in many colonies. They purported to be "mass movements," including everybody who favored independence from the colonial power. But the leadership was carefully selected, trained and disciplined. Thus the base was as broadly popular as possible, but the leadership was exclusive. All liberation movements developed their own special armies to wage war against the colonial power—a war that could range from acts of sabotage and terrorism to full-fledged military encounters. The party was the political arm, acting on behalf of and organizing the people; the guerrillas were the military arm operating under the direction of the party but with the support of the people. Gradually, national liberation movements became like states with their own army, tax collectors, tribunals, and political leaders and warriors.

As in Europe more than a century before, nationalism proved to be a very powerful ideological force in the colonial world. For the first time apathetic and indifferent populations became genuinely mobilized; they were gradually given a political consciousness and a cause. The national movements became vehicles for the acquisition of power by native elites while the native populations found in the independence wars an identity and a sublimation of anonymity and past miseries. Above all, they were given hope about their future. Thus nationalism, skillfully manipulated by a small group of leaders, gradually asserted itself to lead virtually all colonies to independence and statehood.

The Nation-State and Ethnonationalisms: Current Trends

Nation-states, it appears, are beginning to get an unpleasant taste of the heady medicine of nationalism which first brought them into being. It is what has been referred to as *ethnonationalism*—the search for and expression *within* the nation-state of particular ethnic, cultural, regional, religious or linguistic autonomy. These separatist movements range from demands for outright independence and the assumption of statehood to requests for "self-government."

Such manifestations sometimes have a clear-cut territorial base—linguistic, ethnic, religious, racial or cultural groupings are easily identifiable within a given region of the nation-state. For instance, the French-speaking minority in Canada, which is also predominantly

Catholic, lives in Quebec—one province of the Canadian State. So do the Georgians or Uzbecks or Ukranians in the Soviet Union; the Corsicans or the Bretons in France; the Scots and the Welsh in the United Kingdom; Sicilians in Italy; some Native American tribes in the United States; the Ibos in Nigeria—all these ethnic groups are located in certain regions of the respective states in which they live.

But not infrequently a territorial identification of an ethnic minority is difficult. The particular people which shares the specific ethnic attributes may be spread throughout the nation-state. This is the case, for instance, with the blacks in the U.S.A., with the Protestants in France, Catholics in England, Armenians in the U.S.S.R. It is not easy to draw a clear territorial line to separate the Walloons from the Flemings in Belgium.

In addition to ethnonationalism and at times paralleling it there are manifestations which for lack of a better term may be called *loconationalisms*. The assertion of local autonomy in these cases is based explicitly and uniquely on *political considerations*, that is, on the demands made by peoples in regions, localities and at times even neighborhoods to govern themselves and take care of their own affairs.

Ethnonationalist and Loconationalist Ideologies

Ethnonationalist movements have become so widespread that it is just as difficult to generalize about them as it is to undertake a detailed study of all of them. There is virtually no modern nation-state where the phenomenon is not present. In each and every case they have generated ideological movements of varying degrees of intensity which assume the following patterns: (a) they are downright *nationalist*, borrowing from the nineteenth century ideology of nationalism; (b) they are *reformist*, calling for administration reforms of the nation-state in the direction of increased federalism and decentralization; (c) despite their professed attachment to local, communal, and regional values they project at the same time a vision than is *transnational*. These are revolutionary ethnonationalist movements; (d) some attempt to reformulate a theory of democracy by stressing *direct participation*, *loyalty and control* by the citizens within local or small units, very much along the lines suggested by the advocates of the New Left.

Many explanations have been advanced for the phenomenon of ethnonationalism and loconationalism. They range from self-determination to assertions of individual spontaneity and freedom. Economic theories have also stressed the discrepancies in wealth between regions and localities within one and the same state stemming from the exploitation of the poorer areas by the wealthier ones. Arguments about efficiency have also been advanced, claiming that the centralized bureaucracy of the nation-state tends to be wasteful, while small local services could handle more efficiently and less expensively the unique local problems.

Some see in the phenomenon the beginning of the decline of the national state. There has been growth on a world-wide scale of communications and of regional international organizations, like the Warsaw Pact, the Common Market, or NATO. Such organizations supersede the nation-state and undermine its importance for those living within it. Individuals in localities and regions feel freer than before to turn elsewhere to find the feeling of belongingness and communality that nationalism originally provided. There is, in other words, more leeway for smaller units within the nation-state to claim their identity. They look both *inward*, within their own community and locality, race, religion, culture, etc., and *outward*, to a political, legal, economic or military organization beyond the nation-state.

What we have suggested here are indications and manifestations of some powerful new forces within the nation-states. These influences seem to be subverting the power nation-states once claimed over the citizens, suggesting new loyalties and moral imperatives that the nation-state may no longer be able to satisfy. The children and grandchildren of the nationalist ideology of the nineteenth century are beginning to challenge its parenthood; but in terms of many of the slogans and ideas under which they were brought up.

Bibliography

Betts, Raymond F. *Assimilation and Association in French Colonial Theory 1890–1914*. New York: TMS Press, 1970.

Fanon, Franz. *The Wretched of the Earth*. New York: Grove Press, 1968.

Gerassi, John. *The Coming of the New International*. New York: World Publishing, 1971.

Hinsley, F.H. *Nationalism and the International System*. London: Hodder and Stoughton, 1973.

Hobson, John A. *Imperialism*. Ann Arbor: University of Michigan Press, 1965.

Kedourie, Elie. *Nationalism*. Rev. ed., London: Hutchinson, 1961.

———. *Nationalism in Asia and Africa*. London: World Publishing, 1970.

Kilson, Martin (ed.). *New States in the Modern World*. Cambridge, Ma.: Harvard U.P., 1975.

Kohn, Hans. *Nationalism: Its Meaning and History*. Rev. ed., N.Y.: Van Nostrand, 1965.

———. *The Idea of Nationalism*. New York: Collier, 1967.

Schuster, Derek. *Bad Blood Among Brothers: An Inside View Behind Today's Separatist Movement*. New York: Vantage, 1962.

Seton-Watson, H. *Nations and States*. Boulder, Co.: Westview, 1977.

Sigmund, Paul E. (ed.). *The Ideologies of the Developing Nations*. 2nd rev. ed. New York: Praeger, 1972.

Smith, Anthony. *Theories of Nationalism.* London: Duckworth, 1971.

Von Der Mehden, Fred R. *Politics of the Developing Nations.* 2nd ed. Englewood Cliffs, N.J.: Prentice-Hall, 1969.

Waltz, Kenneth W. *Man, The State at War: A Theoretical Analysis.* New York: Columbia U.P., 1954.

Index